Algorithms for Solving Financial Portfolio Design Problems:

Emerging Research and Opportunities

Fatima Zohra Lebbah
Ecole Supérieure en Génie Electrique et Energétique (ESG2E), Oran, Algeria & Laboratoire de Recherche en Informatique de Sidi Bel-Abbès (LabRI-SBA), Equipe de Computational Intelligence and Soft Computing (CISCO), Ecole Supérieure en Informatique de Sidi Bel-Abbès, Algeria

A volume in the Advances in Finance, Accounting, and Economics (AFAE) Book Series

IGI Global
DISSEMINATOR OF KNOWLEDGE

Published in the United States of America by
IGI Global
Business Science Reference (an imprint of IGI Global)
701 E. Chocolate Avenue
Hershey PA, USA 17033
Tel: 717-533-8845
Fax: 717-533-8661
E-mail: cust@igi-global.com
Web site: http://www.igi-global.com

Library of Congress Cataloging-in-Publication Data

Names: Lebbah, Fatima Zohra, 1976- author.
Title: Algorithms for solving financial portfolio design problems : emerging research and opportunities / by Fatima Zohra Lebbah.
Description: Hershey, PA : Business Science Reference, [2020] | Includes bibliographical references and index. | Summary: ""This book provides algorithms for solving financial portfolio design problems"--Provided by publisher"-- Provided by publisher.
Identifiers: LCCN 2019035499 (print) | LCCN 2019035500 (ebook) | ISBN 9781799818823 (hardcover) | ISBN 9781799818854 (paperback) | ISBN 9781799818830 (ebook)
Subjects: LCSH: Portfolio management--Mathematical models.
Classification: LCC HG4529.5 .L426 2020 (print) | LCC HG4529.5 (ebook) | DDC 332.601/5181--dc23
LC record available at https://lccn.loc.gov/2019035499
LC ebook record available at https://lccn.loc.gov/2019035500

This book is published in the IGI Global book series Advances in Finance, Accounting, and Economics (AFAE) (ISSN: 2327-5677; eISSN: 2327-5685)

British Cataloguing in Publication Data
A Cataloguing in Publication record for this book is available from the British Library.

All work contributed to this book is new, previously-unpublished material.
The views expressed in this book are those of the authors, but not necessarily of the publisher.

For electronic access to this publication, please contact: eresources@igi-global.com.

Advances in Finance, Accounting, and Economics (AFAE) Book Series

ISSN:2327-5677
EISSN:2327-5685

Editor-in-Chief: Ahmed Driouchi Al Akhawayn University, Morocco

MISSION

In our changing economic and business environment, it is important to consider the financial changes occurring internationally as well as within individual organizations and business environments. Understanding these changes as well as the factors that influence them is crucial in preparing for our financial future and ensuring economic sustainability and growth.

The **Advances in Finance, Accounting, and Economics (AFAE)** book series aims to publish comprehensive and informative titles in all areas of economics and economic theory, finance, and accounting to assist in advancing the available knowledge and providing for further research development in these dynamic fields.

COVERAGE

- Economic Indices and Quantitative Economic Methods
- E-finance
- Finance and Accounting in SMEs
- Applied Finance
- International Economics
- Economics of Risks, Uncertainty, Ambiguity, and Insurance
- Theoretical Issues in Economics, Finance, and Accounting
- Managerial Accounting
- Ethics in Accounting and Finance
- Economic Downturn

IGI Global is currently accepting manuscripts for publication within this series. To submit a proposal for a volume in this series, please contact our Acquisition Editors at Acquisitions@igi-global.com or visit: http://www.igi-global.com/publish/.

The Advances in Finance, Accounting, and Economics (AFAE) Book Series (ISSN 2327-5677) is published by IGI Global, 701 E. Chocolate Avenue, Hershey, PA 17033-1240, USA, www.igi-global.com. This series is composed of titles available for purchase individually; each title is edited to be contextually exclusive from any other title within the series. For pricing and ordering information please visit http://www.igi-global.com/book-series/advances-finance-accounting-economics/73685. Postmaster: Send all address changes to above address.

Titles in this Series

For a list of additional titles in this series, please visit:
https://www.igi-global.com/book-series/advances-finance-accounting-economics/73685

Recent Advances and Applications in Alternative Investments
Constantin Zopounidis (Technical University of Crete, Greece & Audencia Business School, France) Dimitris Kenourgios (National and Kapodistrian University of Athens, Greece) and George Dotsis (National and Kapodistrian University of Athens, Greece)
Business Science Reference • © 2020 • 315pp • H/C (ISBN: 9781799824367) • US $205.00

Mapping, Managing, and Crafting Sustainable Business Strategies for the Circular Economy
Susana Serrano Rodrigues (Polytechnic Institute of Leiria, Portugal) Paulo Jorge Almeida (Polytechnic Institute of Leiria, Portugal) and Nuno Miguel Castaheira Almeida (Polytechnic Institute of Leiria, Portugal)
Business Science Reference • © 2020 • 280pp • H/C (ISBN: 9781522598855) • US $195.00

Growth and Emerging Prospects of International Islamic Banking
Abdul Rafay (University of Management and Technology, Pakistan)
Business Science Reference • © 2020 • 500pp • H/C (ISBN: 9781799816119) • US $215.00

Economics, Business, and Islamic Finance in ASEAN Economics Community
Patricia Ordoñez de Pablos (The University of Oviedo, Spain) Mohammad Nabil Almunawar (Universiti Brunei Darussalam, Brunei) and Muhamad Abduh (Universiti Brunei Darussalam, Brunei)
Business Science Reference • © 2020 • 374pp • H/C (ISBN: 9781799822578) • US $215.00

Handbook of Research on Theory and Practice of Global Islamic Finance
Abdul Rafay (University of Management and Technology, Pakistan)
Business Science Reference • © 2020 • 888pp • H/C (ISBN: 9781799802181) • US $445.00

For an entire list of titles in this series, please visit:
https://www.igi-global.com/book-series/advances-finance-accounting-economics/73685

IGI Global
DISSEMINATOR OF KNOWLEDGE

701 East Chocolate Avenue, Hershey, PA 17033, USA
Tel: 717-533-8845 x100 • Fax: 717-533-8661
E-Mail: cust@igi-global.com • www.igi-global.com

To my mother

Table of Contents

Preface

This book is the result of a long scientific research project in proposing a constraint system to the problem of CDO Squared portfolio optimization, and implementing reliable and effective algorithms which provide optimized portfolios.

Writing this book, I had a twofold purpose: defining the critical and complex financial problem of optimizing portfolios in a distinctive and simple manner, to be understood by financial and non-financial communities; and introducing a mathematical model representing appropriately the features and the behavior of the financial Portfolio Design (PD) problem, to be tackled by a panoply of algorithms and techniques coming from exact and approximate methods.

Handling a financial portfolio problem is a big, even a huge challenge, which should be tackled by a large team of financiers, economists, socioeconomists, statisticians, lawyers and mathematicians. As a non-financier, when I started my reading stage in the finance field, more precisely in the stock exchange branch, I found it as an infinite space where various aspects coming from different disciplines are strongly interconnected. We cannot study the portfolio problem without starting with a deep analysis of the financial disaster which occurred in 2007-2008. Reading each specialized financial document leads us to the critical criterion of the optimized portfolio building, and how the least lack of rigor could be very costly. The first point that I personally have raised is the credit risk and the interest management which were the origin of the well-known financial disaster. The process of the optimized portfolio building is largely based on complicated statistical and probabilistic calculus, which reflects the risk of uncertainty.

In this book we tackle the problem of the CDO Squared portfolio, a financial instrument which has proved its effectiveness in the field. The CDO Squared portfolio is structured in a double-layer to guarantee better diversification of the selected assets, depending upon their classification in tranches and in portfolios. This should minimize the risk rate of the constructed portfolio.

The problem consists in constructing a reliable and optimized portfolio of assets to clients or investors; a portfolio which maximizes gains and minimizes risks. Unfortunately, the risky assets are the most profitable, and as long as the client is exposed to the risky asset, the risk of the failure of the portfolio is greater.

In the other words, the safe assets and the risky assets should be selected in an optimized way.

At first glance, maximizing gains and minimizing risks seem like two contradictory aspects, which highlights the multicriterial feature of the problem. Consequently, many scientific works have been produced on the problem of portfolio optimization. Markovitz was the first to set out the foundations of modern portfolio theory (MPT) in 1952. His dynamic approach was based on the analysis of the historical behavior of assets within companies. Fabozzi introduced in 2002 a stochastic portfolio theory (SPT). Sharpe proposed in 1991, an efficient approach which provides a partitioning of the assets in classes/tranches. Nowadays, Information Technology techniques are more attractive for the financial world, and the algorithmic aspect is included in handling of the MPT and SPT theories. Kom Samo and Vervuurt integrated in 2016 machine learning techniques to improve the SPT results. Grothey proposed in 2009 a parallelization approach to improve the time resolution. Ray, Mukherjee, Dey and Klepac proposed in their book in 2019 a variety of approximate methods to tackle the portfolio optimization problem.

While these approaches are based on the historical behavior of the assets to build an optimized portfolio or to classify the assets, we describe in this book another side of the financial Portfolio Design (PD) problem, based on selecting assets from previously classified assets in tranches. At first, it was introduced, modeled and tackled by Flener, Pearson, Reyna and Sivertsson in 2007. The problem was characterized as strongly combinatorial, which reflects the complexity of handling the problem with exact approaches.

For the purpose of a deep analysis of the problem and the behavior of different approaches over non-trivial instances of CDO Squared portfolios, we introduce in this book different modeling and solving techniques coming from different branches of the Operations Research field.

The mathematical model adopted in this book is the 0-1 matricial model, which verifies thoroughly the features of the studied financial portfolio. The model is quadratic and strongly symmetric, which requires more precision in choosing, applying and analyzing the different approaches. The approaches introduced in this book to handle the problem of the CDO Squared optimized portfolio come from exact and approximate algorithms, as given below.

Integer Programming (IP): Due to the 0-1 domain of the handled variables in the problem, the problem is tackled as an Integer Program (IP). Thus, thinking in terms of implementing appropriate exact methods on the corresponding IP proved unavoidable. At first, the linearization step of the quadratic constraints is successfully realized, and the model is translated in Integer Linear Program (ILP). Thus we apply linear programming techniques.

Constraint Programming (CP): Furthermore, we investigate in an exact approach exploiting the Constraint Programming (CP) notions, where symmetry-breaking techniques have a real success on actual complex problems. Translating the model Constraint Problem should be taken into consideration. Through proposed CP models, we applied efficient algorithms coming from the CP paradigm.

Simple Local Search (SLS) methods: Namely Simulated Annealing, Tabu Search and IDWalk (Intensification Diversification Walk) algorithms. These algorithms were adapted to be applicable to the problem studied in this book. Accordingly, implementing an evaluation and neighborhood function, and a greedy algorithm to generate a good initial solution, were necessary to improve the provided portfolio's quality.

Variable Neighborhood Search (VNS): This type of methods appeared after a long analysis of the first success of SLS methods in solving the problem. We applied two variants of VNS, namely based VNS and Skewed VNS approaches combined with Simulated Annealing and IDWalk.

Population Method GWW (Go With the Winners): It consists of launching a local search from various and different solution particles, which should offer a good neighborhood diversification and improve the given results. Nevertheless, GWW was very slow and rarely converged to the optimal solution.

This book includes eight chapters, which can be divided into five parts: (1) introduction to the financial portfolio design problem, (2) description of the useful models and solving techniques, (3) applying exact approaches and analyzing their behavior on the problem, (4) applying approximate approaches and analyzing their behavior on the problem, and (5) giving a general analysis and synthesis of all the applied techniques. More precisely, the book is organized as follows:

Chapter 1 presents the elementary and basic definitions of the financial Portfolio Design (PD) problem. The useful financial terminology is also given in details through illustrative figures. The great significance of financial risks and their types are provided, as well as the classification of the financial assets according to the risk type. We focus on the CDO Squared financial instrument, the structure chosen to be studied and solved. We highlight the most important aspect affecting the quality of the financial portfolio, which is the degree of diversification. Having a high level of diversification leads to a balanced and adequate portfolio.

Chapter 2 introduces the exploited solving techniques in the book. Firstly, we describe the basic techniques' notions, coming from exact techniques, namely Constraint Programming, breaking symmetry and Integer Linear Programming. Secondly, we introduce the SLS (Simple Local Search) exploited algorithms (Simulated Annealing, IDWalk, Tabu search), a PLS (Population based Local Search) method (GWW) and Variable Neighborhood Search (VNS and Skewed VNS). At the end of the chapter, we give an overview of landscape types and an efficient approach of performance evaluation. This evaluation should allow a high quality of synthesis of the achieved results.

Chapter 3 provides a state of the art of the existing mathematical models of the (PD) problem. We look at the set model, matricial model and MiniZinc model, which represent the Portfolio Design problem and the building of a balanced financial portfolio.

Chapter 4 analyzes the application of the Integer Linear Programming on the problem. We introduce the mathematical model in Linear Programming language. We propose a linearization of the model in order to tackle the problem via a linear solver. Since the problem is considered strongly symmetric, we propose including a new constraint to the corresponding LP, to break statically the row and column symmetries.

Chapter 5 aims to introduce the CP models corresponding to the matricial model. Static and dynamic techniques of symmetry breaking are also considered in this chapter. Solving the problem is given in four ways, namely without symmetry breaking, with static symmetry breaking, with dynamic symmetry breaking and finally with hybrid (static and dynamic techniques) symmetry breaking. All the experiments are launched under the GECODE solver.

Chapter 6 presents all the SLS proposed approaches with adapted algorithms, and analyzes their behavior on the instances tackled. We implement neighborhood and evaluation functions by considering the particular semantic of (PD) constraints. A greedy algorithm is also included in this chapter to compute an optimized initial solution. An efficient implementation is realized under the INCOP environment. We analyze the obtained results through the performance evaluations of all the implemented methods, depending on the number of successes and the CPU time.

Chapter 7 proposes VNS based approaches. In addition to a new neighborhood function that we give in this chapter, we exploit the proposed evaluation and neighborhood functions given in Chapter 6. The experiments performed which are realized under the INCOP solver show the efficiency of VNS with simulated annealing on non-trivial instances of the problem. Finally, a performance evaluation of the experimental results is given according to the number of successes and the CPU time.

Chapter 8 assesses the results realized over the exact and approximate methods. Curves are drawn on the best results provided by CP and ILP techniques, according to the realized CPU time. A performance evaluation is applied to the implemented approximate methods. This evaluation technique is applied to the best obtained results with the SLS and VNS based approaches, depending on the number of successes and the CPU time. A global synthesis of exact and approximate approaches is given for each separately, due to the substantial difference between the two.

Acknowledgment

First of all, I would like to acknowledge all those who made this work possible, especially the editors of IGI Global who have offered me the opportunity to make available to the scientific community this research work, which presents relevant Combinatorial Optimization algorithms to solve financial Portfolio Design problems.

I would like also to thank the Computer Science Department of University of Oran 1 Ahmed Ben Bella in Algeria for giving me access to its Intensive Computing Unit to launch my scripts, which have often taken more than a day, so as to provide the final results of the implemented algorithms.

I am also thankful to Mark Alexander who honored me to do the proofreading of this book, as well as all the teachers of the British Study Centres of Oran in Algeria.

My warm and earnest acknowledgment goes to my mother who is my source of inspiration and the strong pillar of my life, my father, Hocine, Tassadit, Fadéla and Meriem who have encouraged and supported me to write this work.

Chapter 1
Financial Engineering and Portfolio Design Problem:
State of the Art

ABSTRACT

Any financial institution is in charge of assigning to a client's portfolio a set of assets in a reliable way by minimizing the risk of loss and maximizing gain. All portfolios should share in an equitable way risky assets and safe assets with respect to a financial structured product such as CDO^2 (collateralized debt obligation squared). Realizing a balanced portfolio requires a good level of diversification on the chosen assets. Many works have made proposals for modeling and solving the (OPD) problem, but each one has taken into account specific types of risks and cases. However, in this chapter, the authors introduce the problem in a general way by using the CDO^2 structure. The authors focus in this chapter on the basic and useful notions of financial engineering, followed by a description of the financial portfolio structure CDO^2, the most used and structured financial product. The chapter introduces the financial portfolio optimization problem through the CDO^2 structure, the effect of the diversification on the efficiency of the financial portfolio.

DOI: 10.4018/978-1-7998-1882-3.ch001

INTRODUCTION

Financial engineering is a discipline of finance, which creates and implements complex financial instruments. Through the financial disaster which occurred between 2007 and 2008, we highlight basic causes and the main role of the financial institutions of a famous financial crisis. Good management of risks and creating a balanced financial structure should guarantee a good level of profit to investors.

The main role of financial engineering is to help financial heads or banking establishments to manage the related risks to market fluctuation. It is a complex task which should provide at the end of the route an efficient optimized portfolio, satisfying clients and investors. Any financial institution should comprise a skilled and talented team of financiers, economists, statisticians, mathematicians, etc. to be able to follow, analyze and control the evolution of markets, and evaluate the measures of the risk exposure of financial products.

The financial operations have two major issues: profitability and risk. Each financial operation focuses on maximizing its profitability and so its net profit, while minimizing its failure risks. Those aspects of profitability/risk are actually opposite and characterize the core difficulty of any financial structure and its management. In practice, increasing profitability is achieved by taking important risks. On the other hand, modest profitability is often realized with little risks. Thereby, for example, a company which is marketing a new product can generate very large profits, if the product is well received by consumers, because of the monopoly of the company. Furthermore, the company may experience big losses if the product is badly perceived. However, if the company manufactures an appreciated product, which is already commercialized by other companies, it should obtain reduced profits due to competition.

There are various types of financial structure in the finance world, but among the most complex and the most used structures we have CDO Squared architecture and its combinatorial optimization mathematical aspect.

The chapter is organized as follows. In section 2, we introduce the background of the chapter, which frames the financial portfolio problem, through a detailed analysis of the well-known financial disaster. In section 3, a basic and useful financial terminology is given. Additionally, we define the financial risk and its common types. The complexity of risk management is also exposed. In section 4, we describe the Collateralized Debt Obligation (CDO) structure. In section 4, we concentrate on the CDO squared, the structure adopted in many financial institutions. We address the diversification concept through its two-layer architecture. In section 5, we describe in details the diversification concept and its impact on the computing of a financial portfolio. A soft example is adopted in this section to allow a good understanding of the reader. In section 6, we introduce different techniques, realized to solve the financial portfolio optimization. In this section, we highlight the side of the portfolio optimization problem tackled in this book. In section 7, we summarize the problem of financial institutions in managing risks and increasing diversification. We address future research directions, to increase the diversification level and to compute an efficient financial portfolio. In section 8, we conclude the chapter.

BACKGROUND

Financial structures such as CDO (**Collateralized Debt Obligation**), CPDO (Constant Proportion Debt Obligations), CDO squared, CDO cubed, etc. were developed to address the issues resulted from human decisions.

We deduce through different finance documents (Clauss, Roncalli & Weisang, 2009; Black & Myron, 1973; Papst, 2011; Black & Scholes, 1973; Dufour & Orhangazi, 2014; Robinson, 2014; Wong, 2012; Numora, 2006; Graham & Dodd,1951; Barnett-Hart, 2009), that analysts' opinions on the origins of the economic disaster which appeared in 2007-2008, are divided into three classes:

Class 1

The crisis is a result of series of laws and regulations given by Community Reinvestment Act (CRA) of 1977, and the FED in 1990, which have forced American financial institutions to relax the credit criteria of mortgage credit (Ashwani, 2007; Cochran, 2012).

Since the Community Reinvestment Act (CRA) of 1977, a series of enactments pushed American financial institutions to ease mortgage credit criteria under the pretext of fighting against discrimination. During the 1990s, American banks were threatened with sanctions, indeed pursued by the Federal Government, if they did not maintain a good rating with CRA.

Therefore, subprime were granted to borrowers characterized by insufficient income, bad credit rate and low or no personal contributions. Countrywide Financial, the biggest lender in the American market, was close to bankruptcy before being acquired by Bank of America in early 2008.

From the beginning of the years 1990 to 2004, these housing politics had the effect in increasing the number of property-owning households from 64% to 69%. The housing bubble, which had begun at the end of the1990s,grew.

The decreasing of the interest rate from 2000 to 2004 swelled the bubble more and more. After reaching a peak in 2006, property values fell. Clients who bought their houses with low personal contributions found that the loan mortgage was bigger than the value of the house. Consequently, most of them decided to simply give up the loan, which is generally made easy by some American states. Thus, the loan mortgage and the related other loans fell with repercussions on the remainder of the financial system.

The most important and complex financial structures were basically created to overcome the economic recession and the apprehended financial crisis.

The financial disaster appeared in 2008, and pushed the financial analysts to speak and write about the chronic instability of capitalism, economic recession and the apprehended financial crisis. The majority of them opted for strengthening the market regulation, which is called *financial market regulation*, whereas the analysts were thinking about giving the best regulation which allows a free running of market, knowing that the basic cause of the crisis stems from the extraordinary variability of U.S. monetary policy in recent years. Thus, this variability was decided by the government authorities instead the financial market. Therefore, the FED (*Federal Reserve System*) moved from 6.5% interest rate in 2000 to 1.75% at the end of 2001, and 1% in 2003. Afterwards, a slight increase in rates appeared from 2004,reaching 4.5% in 2006 (Ksantini & Boujelbène, 2014).

During the period of low rate interest and easy credit, liquidity was awash in the system and profitable opportunities appeared in the economic world. The financial institutions granted loans to the unreliable debtors, instead of investing in good projects. Thus, as soon as interest rates had reverted to the correct values, the financial bubble burst.

Class 2

As given in Investopedia website (Kenton, 2019), Bernard Lawrence Bernie Madoff is an American financier and also a pioneer in electronic trading and chairman of the Nasdaq in the early 1990s. He executed a very complex mathematical structure, which was the largest Ponzi scheme in history. This pyramid structure promised high rates of return with little risk to investors. Thus, the American financier was defrauding thousands of investors out of tens of billions of dollars over the course of at least 17 years, and possibly longer. He simply deposited client funds into a single bank account that he used to pay existing clients who wanted to cash out. He funded redemptions by attracting new investors and their capital, but was unable to maintain the fraud when the market turned sharply lower in late 2008. He surrendered to the authorities on December 11, 2008, and the fund's last statements indicated that it had $64.8 billion in clients' assets.

Many economists and financiers have analyzed the Madoff impact on the 2008 financial crisis:

- The Madoff scandal is an actual case of operational risks, since it illustrates the close connection between financial and operational risks, especially for the investors. Moreover, the past performance which could be indicative of past misdoings is one point demonstrated by the Madoff affair and quantitative analysis (Clauss, Roncalli &Weisang, 2009).
- As given above, the failure of the operational risks management is the first observed problem through Madoff fraud. But, more precisely, the failure of the quantitative measures used in the management of this kind of risks by the asset management industry should be considered the origin of the problem. The risk is perhaps underestimated since the Basel Committee considered the asset management firms as low risk activities (Clauss, Roncalli &Weisang, 2009).
- The major role of Madoff Ponzi scheme in the financial scandal represents the new era of economic catastrophe, but it is not really connected to the financial crisis of 2008. The collapsing housing market is the origin of a domino effect which trigged this crisis, in addition to the solvency problems of large financial institutions, illiquidity and distortions in the credit market and severe subsequent global recession. On the other hand, the scandal and financial crisis developed in a climate of recklessness and malfeasance over the entire financial industry, and the inability or unwillingness to regulate bad behavior (Robert, 2009).

Finally, we deduce that the origin of the financial disaster was the failure of regulation, which was not based on strong foundations. In the other words, the problem lies in the regulators, who are generally lawyers. The resolution process of the problem should start from the root and we should think about academic training of qualified regulators. It's a logical reasoning that is also given by different specialists:

- In our world which is obviously becoming more complex, the financial crisis conveys innumerable lessons for lawyers, bankers, regulators and society. Clauss et al. suppose that the biggest lesson is just to realize how complex our financial system and economic organization are(Clauss, Roncalli &Weisang, 2009).
- Since the crisis was the failure of regulation and the regulators are lawyers, the lawyers in our complex world must be aware and basically knowledgeable of the nature of this complexity. In the other words, it is illogical that a lawyer regulator, from the most senior to the most junior rank and file, can be able to regulate complex financial legal definitions, qualitative institutions and regulate half-guesses. Professional experience and natural curiosity are the origin of much of the understanding of a lawyer regulator, but acquiring knowledge with a foundation based on education and training should be easier. The suggestions given to lawyers is that instead of having advanced degrees in the technical fields they regulate; they should have a level of knowledge and the capability to analyze the technical details of the transactions in question. A lawyer regulator should at least be aware enough to know what they do not know and to ask the relevant questions (Robert, 2009).
- By analyzing the different results of the financial crisis, Anastasiu et al. conclude that there is a major problem located in the higher school education system, which should provide the best candidates for the competitive labor market. There is a real divergency between the students and the employers regarding employability. Therefore, the universities should be more efficient if they find ways to provide qualified and professional people, more than training providers in different specialties (Anastasiu, Anastasiu, Dumitran, Crizboi, Holmaghi & Nicoleta, 2017).

Class 3

This class should be seen as a generalization of the previous given two classes. Some financial analysts and researchers characterized the origin of the financial disaster by the utilization of the very complex and huge financial structures, whereas the technology development level at this time was not very helpful to manage such structured finance. Moreover, the financiers were trying all the time to create more complicated financial instruments, when the current one did not work. They moved, for instance, from CDO (one-level structure), to CDO Squared (two-level structure), then to CDO Cubed (three-level structure).

This kind of issue is discussed by different specialists:

- As given in Barnett-Hart, 2009, once a money-making machine on Wall Street, Collateralized debt obligations (CDO) structure was responsible for $542 billion of the nearly trillion dollars in losses suffered by financial institutions since 2007.
- The problem is due to unfinished research area. The CDO structure should be theoretically efficient, but until now there is no fully-tested operationally satisfying and single name consistent dynamic model capable of a consistent calibration of indices and CDO tranches across capital structure and maturity. Even though the structure was not operationally tested, it was exploited by many financial institutions. Although the quant community was aware of the limitations of copula models before the crisis, the CDO structure has been widely used (Brigo, Pallavicini & Torresetti, 2010).

Bringo et al. highlighted the importance of developing and using new techniques to build and manage efficient and promising financial instruments. They consider that the creativity in the range of derivative (financial instrument) contracts is limited only by the imagination of man (Brigo, Pallavicini &Torresetti, 2010). Obviously, the financiers have developed complex and thought-out financial instruments such as Constant Proportion Debt Obligations (CPDOs) or CDO squared, but the actual issue is how to develop new techniques to compute a balanced financial portfolio and to manage all financial data concerning the financial institution. We should utilize Information Technology techniques in modeling and computing an efficient portfolio. The automation of the operational test process turns out to be essential. Thus, we present in this book:

1. Mathematical models to CDO Squared structure, which is characterized theoretically as an efficient financial portfolio according to the diversification concept.
2. Exact and approximate approaches to building the portfolio.

BASIC TERMINOLOGY IN FINANCE ENGINEERING

At the beginning, we start by giving basic financial definitions, which belong to banks and companies jargon.

- **Credit:** A provision of loan between creditor and debtor.
- **Claim:** The creditor's right to require remittance of the sum of money to debtor.
- **Debtor:** An entity or a person beholden to another part of an amount of money or another form of claim.
- **Debt:** An amount of money that needs to be repaid by the debtor to the creditor.
- **Liquidity:** The degree that measures the debtor's ability to repay his debt in the case of pursuing his activities. In contrast, solvency is setup considered in the case of his activities' cessation. Liquidity describes the degree to which an asset or security can be quickly bought or sold in the market without affecting the asset's price.
- **Issuer:** A legal entity that develops registers and sells securities to finance its operations. Issuers may be corporations, investment trusts, or domestic or foreign governments. Issuers are legally responsible for the obligations of the issue and for reporting financial conditions, material developments and any other operational activities as required by the regulations of their jurisdictions.
- **Security:** A financial instrument issued by companies, financial institutions and the government as a means of borrowing money and raising new capital. The most commonly used financial securities are shares, stocks, debentures, bills of exchange, treasury bills and bonds.
- **Securization:** The procedure whereby an issuer designs a financial instrument by merging various financial assets and then markets tiers of the repackaged instruments to investors. This process can encompass any type of financial asset and promotes liquidity in the marketplace.
- **Asset:** Anything of value or a resource of value that can be converted into cash. Individuals, companies, and governments own assets. For a company, an asset might generate revenue or the company might benefit in some way from owning or using the asset.
- **Financial Portfolio:** A grouping of financial assets, which are owned by an institution or an individual. A portfolio is characterized by its diversification level that allows a good compromise between the risk

and the profitability, by taking into consideration the expected duration of the holding of the assets.

- **CDO (Collateralized Debt Obligation):** A financial product that pools together cash flow-generating assets and repackages this asset pool into discrete tranches that can be sold to investors. It is named for the pooled assets that are essentially debt obligations that serve as collateral for the CDO.

In the financial field, there are many types of risks, which should be measured by specialized people and establishments. Each financial institution is considered unique according to the adopted types of risks and the realized measurements of these risks. Globally, financial institutions are faced with different risks falling under major categories (Duffie & Singleton, 2012) which are summarized as follows (Investopedia n.d, & U.S Department of Treasury, 2020):

- **Market Risk:** A risk linked to the unexpected changes of values and exchange rate. It is the probable risk of loss resulting from a borrower's failure to repay a loan or to meet contractual obligations.
- Traditionally, it refers to the risk that a lender does not receive the owed principal and interest, which results in an interruption of cash flows and increased costs for collation. Although it is impossible to know exactly who will default on obligations, properly assessing and managing credit risk can lessen the severity of loss. Interest payments from the borrower or issuer of a debt obligation are a lender's or investor's rewards for assuming credit risk.
- **Credit Risk:** A risk of loss resulting from a borrower's failure to repay a loan or meet contractual obligations.
- **Liquidity Risk:** A risk that the costs of adjusting financial positions will increase substantially or that a firm will lose access to financing. It involves the possibility that bid-ask spreads will widen dramatically in a short period or that the quantities that counterparties are willing to trade at given bid-ask spreads will decline substantially, thereby reducing the ability of a portfolio to be quickly restructured in times of financial stress. This includes the risk that severe cash flow stress forces dramatic balance-sheet reductions, selling at bid prices and/or buying at ask prices, with accompanying losses or financial distress.
- **Operational Risk:** A risk of fraud, systems failures, trading errors (e.g., deal mispricing), and many other internal organizational risks.

Operational risk is an unsystematic risk, meaning it is unique to a specific industry and a business, and could be reduced through portfolio diversification. But, operational risk will change from industry to industry. It includes:

- ◦ Breakdowns in procedures and systems.
- ◦ Poor management for human error.

For example, when a mortgage application process fails to identify properly the riskiest applicants, because of the breakdown of the system or the human error. Furthermore, industries that have less human interaction tend to face less operational risks. Investors should consider operational risk carefully when weighing an opportunity Every investment comes with an uncertain risk along with a chance of earning the expected return.

- **Systemic Risk:** A risk of breakdowns in market wide liquidity or chain reaction default.
- **Regulatory and Legal Risk:** A risk that changes in regulations, accounting standards, tax codes, or the application of any of these, will result in unforeseen losses or a lack of flexibility. This includes the risk that the legal basis for financial contracts will change unexpectedly, as occurred with certain U.K. local authorities' swap positions in the early 1990s.

Risk measuring is introduced by Bodie et al. in Bodie & Merton, 2000 as a quantification of the associated cost of the risk. For instance, consider a single young woman, who has just graduated and starts her new job. During her studies, she was covered by the social security of her parents, but now she no longer has any social coverage. Therefore, she considers that her exposure to illness risk is high. To quantify this risk, she needs information. What is the probability that a person in her age and in the same socio-professional category falls ill? And what is the average cost of treatment?

This young woman, clearly needs information, which is costly to collect. One of the missions of companies is to provide this type of information. These companies employ actuaries, who are the specialized professionals in mathematics and statistics, whose role is to compute the data and to do statistical analysis, and to deduce the probabilities of illness, of accident and other analogous risks.

In the kingdom of the risks on the financial assets, households and companies need experts' advice to evaluate their exposure to some risks, and to measure the costs and the strategies' benefits in shares, bonds, etc. There are advisors specialized in investment, investment companies, and intermediate companies available to provide this information.

Measuring a risk is a complex computational process which needs an efficient team of financiers, statisticians, mathematicians, socioeconomists, etc. That is why the cost of the risk is specific and closely related to the financial institution in question.

Collateralized Debt Obligation (CDO)

As given in Duffie & Singleton, 2012, CDO structure is introduced as an asset-backed security, whose underlying collateral is typically a portfolio of bonds (corporate or sovereign) or bank loans. A CDO cash flow structure allocates interest income and principal repayments from a collateral pool of different debt instruments to a prioritized collection of CDO securities, which we shall call *tranches*.

A CDO is a type of financial portfolio; it is divided into assets tranches. An attachment point and a detachment point characterize each tranche; the attachment point defines the allowed minimum of losses, and the detachment point defines the allowed maximum of losses. The tranche is well designed in the case where the estimated losses are between the attachment point and detachment point.

CDO (Tavakoli, 2008) has been created by a financial institution, and is likely to have several risk levels related to different parts of a financial operation. Based on a risk analysis, assets are divided into different groups called tranches that are sold to investments. There are three types of tranches (Hager, 2008), which designate the preference level (or payment priority): Senior, Mezzanine and Equity. These types of tranches are defined as follows: if CDO's assets start deteriorating, losses are firstly borne by equity tranches, secondly by Mezzanine tranches, and finally by equity tranches.

For instance, consider the illustrated CDO in Figure 1 where a financial institution has a CDO portfolio type with \$100 of bonds portfolio and 7% interest.

Thus, the portfolio is divided into tranches:

1. Tranche A: rated AAA, senior tranche of \$75which yields 5.50%
2. Tranche B: rated AA, mezzanine tranche of \$10 which yields 5.80%
3. Tranche C: rated A, mezzanine tranche of \$5 of which yields 7.20%
4. Tranche D: rated BBB, mezzanine tranche of \$5which yields 9.10%
5. Tranche E: not rated, equity tranche of \$5 which yields 29.60%

Figure 1. Structure example of a CDO
Source: Inspired by (Ashwani, 2007)

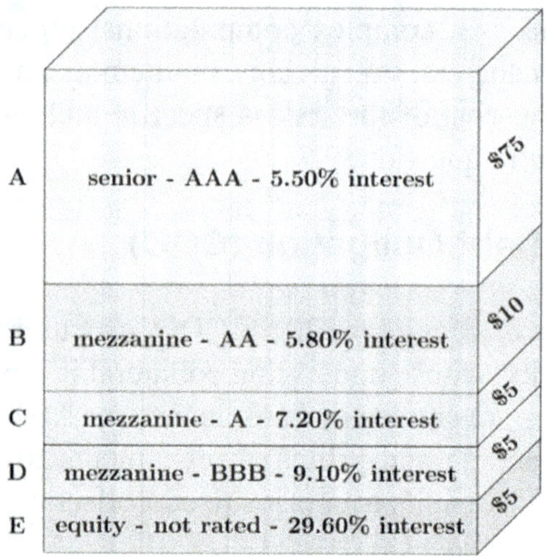

If we sum the realized interest rates over tranches, we obtain the total yield of $7:

5.50%.75+5.80%.10+7.20%.5+9.10%.5+29.60%.5=$7

We notice that E is the most attractive (29.60%), then D (9.10%), C (7.20%), B (5.80%) and A (5.50%). However, on the other hand, income and capital are paid in a sequential way, starting with the senior tranche and finishing with the equity tranche. The A tranche is the first one to be paid, then the B tranche, and so on, until the E tranche. Furthermore, if losses reach less than $5, only the E tranche will be affected. If losses are between $5 and $25, mezzanine tranches are also affected, but not the senior tranche. However, if losses exceed $25, the senior tranche is affected. If only $90 will be paid, A tranche makes $75, B tranche $10, C tranche $5, and finally nothing for the tranches D and E.

CDO structure is a financial invention, which offers more liquidity in the economy, by allowingfinancial institutions to sell their financial products by tranches.

Figure 2. A CDO's typical structure

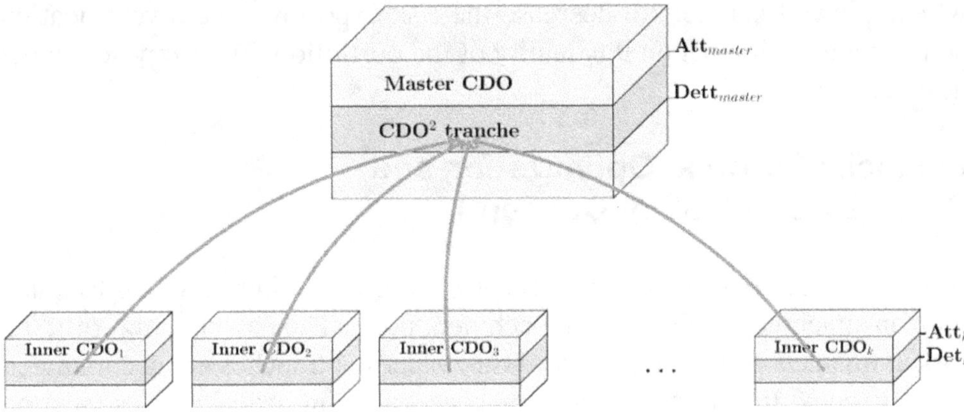

COLLATERALIZED DEBT OBLIGATION SQUARED (CDO SQUARED)

CDO Squared or CDO²(Gilkes& Drexler, 2003) is a CDO, whose underlying portfolio is invested in others CDOs' tranches[1]. In Guillaume, Jacobs & Shoutens (2008) it is defined as a double layer structure, supported by a CDOs' portfolio. A CDO² references a called master CDO (or outer CDO) portfolio composed of inner CDOs' tranches.

Figure 2 (Whetten & Adelson, 2005) illustrates the CDO with two layers of assets. The first layer represents the master CDO, which contains layers of the inner CDOs.

CDO squared was introduced in Guillaume, Jacobs & Shoutens (2008). It is a financial instrument that is similar to Credit Default Swaps (CDSs) and Collateralized Debt Obligations (CDOs), since the protection buyer of a CDO-squared pays periodic payments to the issuer in exchange for protection against the losses arising from default events of the underlying reference entities.

More precisely, a CDO-squared is a CDO where the underlying portfolio consists of CDO tranches. Hence, a CDO-squared, referred to as the outer CDO, is a two-layered product: the outer portfolio consisting of tranches of CDOs (called inner CDOs) and the inner portfolios composed of credit entities. The protection buyer makes periodic spread payments on the notional value of the outer tranche and receives compensation for the losses falling between the outer tranche attachment and detachment points(Guillaume, Jacobs & Shoutens, 2008).

This double layer architecture will allow a higher level of diversification, which allows financiers to decrease the risk exposure. The diversification concept and its impact on the quality of the portfolio will be exposed in the next section.

Financial Portfolio Optimization and CDO² (Diversification Concept)

CDO² is characterized by structured CDOs in tranches (Figure 3), each designed with an attachment point and a detachment point. The payment of profit, the loss at tranches and the maturity of all concerned tranches are accumulated and attributed to different CDO² tranches following priority rules (section Collateralized Debt Obligation) (Gilkes & Drexler, 2003).

Managing a CDO² is more complicated than a simple CDO (with one layer). But, the use of double layer structure is justified by various purposes (Whetten & Adelson, 2005; Guillaume et al., 2008), such as increasing the level of diversification. A double layer structure allows evoking a higher level of diversification, since in the majority of CDO², financial operations can reference several underlying CDOs. If these underlying CDOs share assets, so there are overlaps between these CDOs. The appearance of a high rate of overlapping between the portfolios implies immediately an important sharing of risks. Thus, minimizing this overlapping rate in a CDO² is a crucial criterion to minimize the risk profile.

Figure 3 shows the case where a CDO² portfolio includes two inner CDO portfolios. The number of shared assets is equal to two, which is the number of overlaps.

Assume that master CDO is composed of N underlying CDOs including no more than M financial assets. By construction, we have an overlap β_{ij}^{c} of two underlying CDOs i and j at the level of an asset c. β_{ij}^{c} is described as follows:

$$\forall i, j \in 1..N, c \in 1..M,$$

$$\beta_{ij}^{c} = \begin{cases} 0 \text{ if the asset } c \text{ does not belong in} \\ \quad \text{underlying } i^{th} \text{ and } j^{th} \text{ CDOs} \\ 1 \text{ otherwise} \end{cases}$$

Figure 3. Example of a CDO²'s structure
Source: Inspired from (Bhatt, Adams &Clunie, 2005)

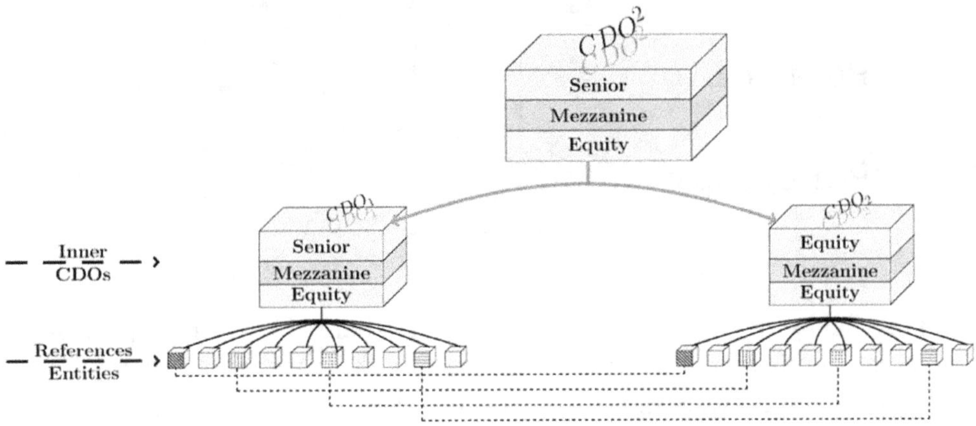

Figure 4. Example of shared asset by two CDO portfolios

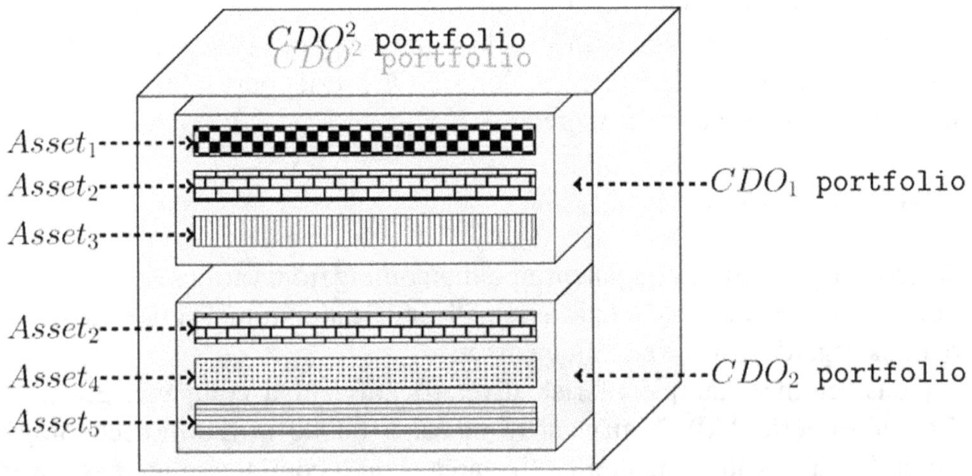

Consider a CDO² portfolio which includes two inner CDO portfolios. Each inner CDO includes four different assets (see Figure 4). In this example, we have N=2 and M=3.

The illustrated CDO² portfolio in Figure 4, according to the formula above, provides the following results:

$\beta_{12}^{1} = 0, \beta_{12}^{2} = 1, \beta_{12}^{3} = 0, \beta_{12}^{4} = 0$ and $\beta_{12}^{5} = 0$

Figure 5. A matricial structure of shared assets by two CDO portfolio

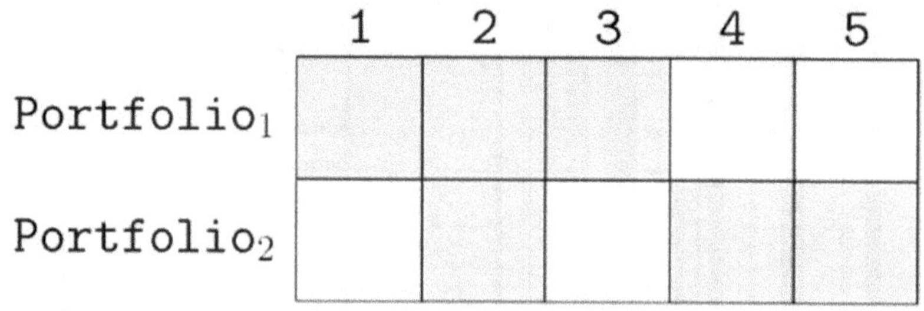

This means that assets 1, 3, 4 and 5 are not shared by the inner portfolios, and asset 2 is shared by the inner portfolios. In this case, we say that we have an overlapping between both inner portfolios $\lambda=1$. We have just one asset shared by the inner portfolios.

In Figure 5, we model the CDO Squared portfolio within a matricial design. The column indices represent the assets, the rows represent the CDO portfolios and the grey cells indicate the selected asset.

In this case we could not find another solution, where each portfolio contains of the five assets, with less than one overlap. Thus, this portfolio is optimized and the most efficient. As long as the overlapping rate is decreased, the rate of diversification is increased.

How to Diversify?

Diversifying is holding equivalent amounts coming from various risked assets, rather than investing in a unique asset. Diversification limits your exposition to a risk regarding a risked unique asset.

Consider the example of risk diversification of a company, given in (Bodie&Robert,2000). You want to invest $100000 in the biotechnology sector, because you estimate that this area should continue to increase over many years, due to new medicines which are discovered by genetic tools. You can invest your $100000 in one company. In this case your investment in biotechnologies would be concentrated and not diversified.

Diversification could be realized directly by the investor, or the company in which he invests, or by a financial intermediate. In your case, you can diversify your investment in biotechnology by adopting the following steps:

- Investing in several companies, each developing a new medicine.

- Investing in one company which develops various medicines.
- Investing in an Open-Ended Investment Company (OEIC)[2] which holds stakes in several companies developing new medicines.

How to Reduce Risk by Diversifying?

To understand how diversification can help to reduce the risk, take the example of biotechnology investment. Assume that investing in a medicine allows you to quadruple your invested money, but a failure means that you lose all your money. Compare these two situations:

1. The situation where you would invest the $100000 in one medicine development: in this case you end up with $400000 or nothing at all.
2. The situation where you divide your $100000 in two developments: you diversify in your investment by investing $50000 each time in two distinct medicines. You have three possible results:
   a. You have a chance to win $400000, if the both of the medicines are successful.
   b. You lose your money completely, if both of the medicines are failures.
   c. You end up in an intermediate situation, where one medicine is a success and another is a failure. In this case, you win $200000 (four times your investment $50000 in the successful medicine, and zero for the failed medicine).

When is Diversification Not Efficient in Reducing Risk?

The diversification will not reduce your risk, if the medicines in which you have invested will both become successes, or will both become failures. In this example with two medicines, if there is no chance that one medicine is a failure and the other a success, then there is no difference between investing $100000 in one medicine or in two medicines. In both cases, you have two possibilities:

1. Wining $400000, which is a common success.
2. Losing your total investment, which is a common failure.

In this particular case, we say that the success risks of both medicines are *correlated perfectly*.

Diversifying your investment may increase a household's security, because it contributes to reducing their risk exposure. Note that the fact of diversifying does not reduce the global uncertainty: if each year, 100 new medicines are discovered, the number of medicines which will be commercial successes will not be relayed to a greater or smaller repartition of the shares of the pharmaceutical companies. On the other hand, the effect of the uncertainty on the household's wealth can be limited by the diversification.

Big Winner, Big Loser or Medium Winner?

Consider the example of medicines given above. Assume that we have three investors who want to invest $100000 in two medicines A and B. Three situations should be presented:

- Investor 1 who puts all his money in the medicine A.
- Investor 2 who puts all his money in the medicine B.
- Investor 3 who puts $50000 in medicine A and $50000 in B.

We suppose that medicine A is a commercial success and B a commercial failure (Figure 6).

Each of the situations given above introduces a case of a specific type of investor according to his gains:

Figure 6. Investor's portfolio

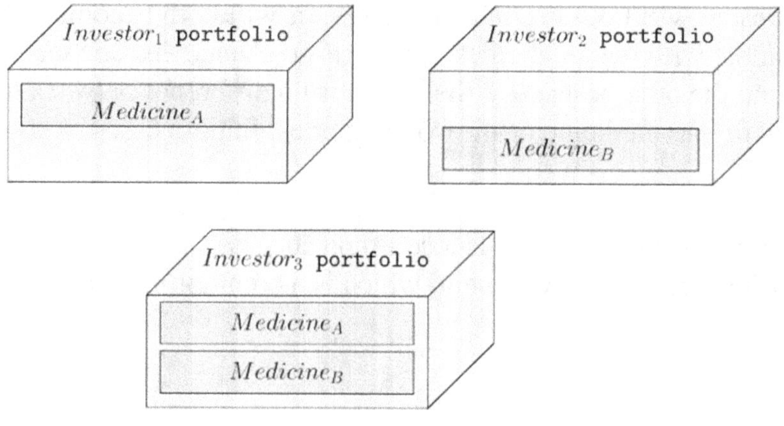

- Investor 1 is considered a big winner, since he wins \$400000. In other words:

$$\begin{cases} A(success) \\ Investor1 \text{ invests all \$100000 in A} \end{cases} \Rightarrow Investor1 \text{ is a big winner}$$

In this case, Investor 1 will be considered by the financial community as a genius, and he will be famous because his success.

- Investor 2 is considered a big loser, since he loses all his money. In the other words:

$$\begin{cases} B(failure) \\ Investor2 \text{ invests all \$100000 in B} \end{cases} \Rightarrow Investor2 \text{ is a big loser}$$

Suddenly, in this case, Investor 2 will be famous, not for his success but for his total failure.

- Investor 3 is a winner with a medium performance, since he wins just \$200000. In other words:

$$\begin{cases} A(success) \wedge B(failure) \\ Investor3 \text{ invests \$50000 in A and \$50000 in B} \end{cases} \Rightarrow Investor3 \text{ is a medium winner}$$

This case introduces the thoughtful and reasonable people who invests according to the accepted standards, by adopting the diversification concept to decrease the risks of a total failure.

A Big Question Is Highlighted in This Situation: Is Investor 1 A Genius or Just a Lucky Investor?

Comparing the performances of the investors through these three cases, the obvious and direct deduction is that the investors who have realized the most spectacular gains are most often not diversified. Although investing in one financial product induces a huge exposure of the investors to fail, people prefer to be considered geniuses. But according to their initial decision, they will be a big winner or a big loser. Thus, they should make a thoughtful decision, and choose a strategy which ensures a medium performance.

It's not uncommon to read stories about big losers on the stock exchange. These people are generally characterized as not talented or not sufficiently clever, because they did not choose suitable values. For instance, we have (Investopedia, n.d.):

- Nick Leeson, who was responsible for the failure of Barings Bank, the first investment bank in England. He lost about $1.3 billion, an amount which was reached after trading futures on the Nikkei 250, the main Tokyo index, on behalf of clients. His hopes of winning the money back were dashed in early 1995, when the Kobe earthquake hit Japan and the Nikkei fell sharply.
- John Rusnak, who was bullish on the yen, was responsible for losing $691 million in Allfirst Financial Bank. His luck held, until a series of policy changes in Asia. Thereafter, the crisis on the Asian Market appeared, and was followed by the fall of the yen. The process of Rusnak's bank fraud started in 1995.

Unfortunately, a fourth case should be highlighted and studied through our example. Imagine that both medicines are commercial failures. In this case, even the diversified investor will be a big loser. Thus, diversifying your portfolio should decrease your exposure to a disaster risk, without eliminating it. This point will be clarified in the next section.

SOLUTIONS AND RECOMMENDATIONS

Consider the example of investing in biotechnology, given above. We presented two types of investment: (1) undiversified investment and (2) diversified investment. In both cases, the investment can lead to the same result, which is the loss of the investor's entire portfolio. This result is achieved because of two reasons, according to the type of investment. Therefore, proposing and computing a solution of the problem depends on the investment's type.

In the first case, we deduce directly that the origin of the total loss is due to the diversification concept which is not being implemented. Thus, to avoid a financial disaster, the constructed portfolio should have a high level of diversification, unless the investor wants to take high risks for higher returns.

In the second case, the portfolio is a diversified one, but the problem of the total arises. A rigorous analysis of the situation should be carried out.

Actually, if we consider the diversification applied on the portfolio of Investor 3 (Figure 1.6), it is based only on the type of the medicine. Whereas, a real diversification should be founded on a real classification of the assets (or any financial product). A financial portfolio is well diversified if it is compounded from a set of assets coming from different classes. Thus, if both the medicines belong to the same financial class, they should have exposure to the same kind and degree of risks. Therefore they could be failures at the same time, which leads to a financial disaster as regards Investor 3, since he will lose all his money.

Many scientific works have addressed the classification of assets, following different reasonings and techniques. But, in essence, classifying a financial product is founded on the product's features, which are the type of risk, the degree of exposure to the risk, the behavior of the product in previous portfolios, etc. Sharpe introduced in (Sharpe,1991), an efficient approach which provides for a partitioning of the assets in classes, according to the assets' features and the result of the measurement of their risks. The set of these classes represents a classification of the assets founded on statistical and mathematical principles.

In addition to the classification problem, optimizing financial portfolios has drawn and is still drawing the attention of economists and financiers. First of all, Markovitz in (Markovitz,1991), introduced the foundations of portfolio theory. He highlighted the crucial uncertainty problem in building an effective portfolio. Indeed, compounding an investor's portfolio is like betting on the asset's future. Indeed, if the investor is certain about the success of a specific asset, diversifying his portfolio should not be necessary. In other words, measuring the risk exposure of an asset should be realized through complicated techniques coming from statistics and mathematics, and their classification problem is tackled via the asset's variance and covariance measuring. Markovitz addressed different notions of modern portfolio theory (MPT), which is more described in (Fabozzi, Gupta, & Markowitz, 2002). MPT foundations were given by Harry Markovitz in 1952. It is a dynamic approach based on: (1) a normative theory which describes the norm of the behavior which should be pursued by the investor, and (2) asset pricing theory such as the capital asset[3] pricing model, which leads to a formalizing of the relationship between asset returns and risk: returns should be maximized, in contrast to risks, which should be minimized. We have to remember that risky assets are the most profit-making if they are successful.

In Fernholz (2002), a Stochastic Portfolio Theory (SPT) is given. It consists of a stochastic approach proposed in building the optimized portfolio. Theoretically, Fernholz's tool is used in constructing portfolios with controlled behavior. Practically, it is applied in analyzing and optimizing the portfolio performance. It has been the basis of successful investment strategies for over a decade. KomSamo et al. introduced in KomSamo &Vervuurt (2016) machine learning techniques hybridized with the SPT approach, to solve the financial portfolio optimization problem. Like the SPT, it is used in analyzing the performance of a financial portfolio. Their approach learns investment strategies through the given results by SPT approach. The results provided through this approach outperform considerably existing SPT strategies in the US stock market.

In (Ray, Mukherjee, Dey, & Klepac, 2019), the authors represent the problem of portfolio optimization as a multi-objective problem, since we have to satisfy two objective functions: (1) maximizing returns, and (2) minimizing risk. They propose numerous techniques based on approximated methods such as Simulated Annealing (SA), Ant Colony Optimization (ACO), Evolutionary Computation (EC), Particle Swarm Optimization (PSO), Differential Evolution (DE) and Genetic Algorithms (GA). The proposed techniques are based on the Modern Portfolio Theory, which means that the optimized portfolio will be built from assets with controlled and analyzed behavior. Managing financial portfolios needs efficient techniques, which can manage tremendous data and tackle a multi-objective aspect of the problem. Thus, following the proposed methods is logically justified. The behavior of these methods applied to complex problems has proved their efficiency, whether in runtime or the quality of the results.

In (Grothey, 2009), a parallelizing approach to building an optimized portfolio is introduced. The author tackles the problem in the same way as Rey et al., but he proposes a parallel method instead approximate method. In his article, the parallelizing techniques are applied in the formulating model of the available computing platform.

In this book, we tackle another side of the portfolio optimization problem. We introduce a new formalism to the problem. We consider that the set of assets is previously classified by the specialists, and the adopted financial instrument is CDO Squared. The multi-objective portfolio problem is translated into a mono objective problem, by introducing the thoughtful notion of overlapping. This notion will be given in detail in Chapter 3. We expose numerous mathematical models and Operations Research techniques, which take into consideration the classification of the assets and the CDO^2

structure, since CDO^2 is considered a balanced financial instrument. We present different approximated and exact approaches to tackling the CDO^2 portfolio. We do not analyze and do not control the behavior of portfolios.

Consequently, the proposed models and techniques in this book could represent the intermediate step between the assets classification step and the portfolio analysis step. Nevertheless, in this book we prove that the obtained portfolios are really optimized and represent the most efficient portfolios, and the analyzing or controlling step should not be necessary.

FUTURE RESEARCH DIRECTIONS

As discussed above, the purpose of any financial institution is to improve its profit, which should be realized by ensuring its clients to be winners. That is why the financial institution applies a specific financial instrument in its management system. A good financial instrument must guarantee: (1) a good level of risk management and (2) a good level of diversification. The first point is very complicated, since the competent specialists involved come from different disciplines, and the computational process depends on the institution in question. The second point represents the following step of risk management. It has been studied in different research works, which were focused on the complex computations coming from complex mathematics and statistics formulas.

Financiers have created the CDO instrument, a simple structure with one level, then CDO squared with two layers and finally CDO cubed with three layers; from a simple, to a complicated, to a more complicated one. They focused on the diversification aspect of a financial portfolio and how to increase its level. Theoretically, the efficiency of CDO^2 and CDO^3 is proved, but their implementation has proven complicated.

A good implementation of CDO^2 in a financial institution should provide an optimized portfolio, that should be characterized by the best level of diversification. Thus, applying Information Technology (IT) and Operations Research (OR) techniques becomes essential.

In the following chapters, we introduce various mathematical models of the financial portfolio design problem, and various exact and approximated methods and algorithms. We then highlight the efficiency of the proposed models and techniques to provide the most optimized portfolio through the majority of cases.

In other words, we tackle the problem of portfolio design, based on the diversification concept. The results and analysis of performance given in this book show the success of the presented techniques.

CONCLUSION

In this chapter, first of all, we presented the financial disaster that appeared in 2008. Through a good understanding of the root causes of this financial disaster, we will be able to propose novel solutions. We presented different kinds of risks and their evaluation issues. The impact of the chosen and applied financial instrument on the improvement of the financial institution's profit is given through CDO and CDO^2 exposed structures. We concentrated on defining the diversification concept, which is the basic characteristic of an optimized financial portfolio.

The purpose of this book is to propose models and techniques to compute an optimized CDO^2 portfolio, through providing a high level of diversification. Thus, relying on a simple financial investment example, we laid out a diversification problem in detail.

We deduce from this chapter that the quality of the optimized financial portfolio depends on the degree of diversification in the selected assets. This diversification aspect will be modeled by mathematical constraints, called overlap constraints and will be solved by various techniques.

In the next chapter, we will introduce the state of the art of the useful different solving techniques coming from exact and approximate approaches. We will expose a panoply of methods and algorithms, which are applied and succeeded on the financial Portfolio Design (PD) problem.

REFERENCES

Anastasiu, L., Anastasiu, A., Dumitran, M., Crizboi, C., Holmaghi, A., & Nicoleta, R. M. (2017). How to Align the University Curricula with the Market Demands by Developing Employability Skills in the Civil Engineering Sector. *Education in Science*, *7*(3), 74. doi:10.3390/educsci7030074

Ashwani, B. (2007). Collateral Debt Obligations. Technical report. Planman Consulting.

Ashwani, B. (2007). *Collateral debt obligations. Technical Report*. Global Strategy and Investment Consulting.

Barnett-Hart, A. K. (2009). *The Story of the CDO Market Meltdown: An Empirical Analysis*. Harvard University. Retrieved from https://books.google.dz/books?id=ZBc9QwAACAAJ

Bhatt, R., Adams, A., & Clunie, J. (2005). *Hidden risks in the CDO squared market*. Working paper 05.03. Centre for Financial Markets Research, The Management School, University of Edinburgh.

Black, F., & Myron, S. (1973). The Pricing of Options and Corporate Liabilities. *Journal of Political Economy. University of Chicago Press*, *81*(3), 637–654. doi:10.1086/260062

Black, F., & Scholes, M. (1973). The pricing of options and corporate liabilities. *Journal of Political Economy*, *81*(3), 637–654. doi:10.1086/260062

Bodie, Z., & Merton, R. C. (Eds.). (2000). *Finance*. Prentice Hall.

Brigo, D., Pallavicini, A. & Torresetti, R. (2010). *Credit Models and the Crisis, or: How I Learned to Stop Worrying and Love the CDOs*. arXiv.org, Quantitative Finance Papers. Papers 0912.5427.

Clauss, P., Roncalli, T., & Weisang, G. (2009). Risk Management Lessons from Madoff Fraud, MPRA Paper 36754. University Library of Munich. doi:10.1108/S1569-3767(2009)0000010019

Cochran, J. P. (2012). A crisis of authority: Pierre Lemieux's somebody in charge: A solution to recessions? *Independent Review*, *16*, 591–598.

Duffie, D., & Singleton, K. J. (2012). *Credit Risk: Pricing, Measurement and Management*. Princeton University Press.

Dufour, M., & Orhangazi, Ö. (2014). *The United States Economy. After 2007-2008 Financial Crisis*. Academic Press.

Fabozzi, F. J., Gupta, F., & Markowitz, H. M. (2002). The Legacy of Modern Portfolio Theory. *Journal of Investing*, *11*(3), 7–22. doi:10.3905/joi.2002.319510

Fernholz, E. R. (2002). Stochastic Portfolio Theory - Applications of Mathematics. New York: Springer.

Gilkes, K., & Drexler, M. (2003). Drill-down approach for synthetic CDO squared transactions. Technical report, Standard & Poor's. New York: Ratings Direct. Structured Finance.

Graham, B., & Dodd, D. L. (1951). *Security analysis: Principles and technique*. New York: McGraw-Hill.

Grothey, A. (2009). Financial Applications: Parallel Portfolio Optimization. In R. Trobec, M. VajterÅ¡ic, & P. Zinterhof (Eds.), Parallel Computing (pp. 435-469). Springer London. doi:10.1007/978-1-84882-409-6_14

Guillaume, F., Jacobs, P., & Shoutens, W. (2008). Pricing and hedging of cdo-squared tranches by using a one factor levy model. Technical report, Section of Statistics-Department of Mathematics-Katholike Universitit Leuven. Belgium: Department of Mathematics, Celestijnenlaan.

Hager, S. (2008). Collateralized Debt Obligations: Structure and Valuation. In *Gabler Wissenschaft* (Ed.), *Pricing Portfolio Credit Derivatives by Means of evolutionary Algorithms* (pp. 7-39). Springer Science & Business Media. Retrieved from https://kar.kent.ac.uk/37473/

Investopedia. (n.d.). Retrieved from https://www.investopedia.com/

Kenton, W. (2020). *The Bernie Madoff Story*. Retrieved from https://www.investopedia.com/terms/b/bernard-madoff.asp

KomSamo, Y.-L., & Vervuurt, A. (2016). Stochastic Portfolio Theory: A Machine Learning Perspective. *Proceedings of the 32nd Conference on Uncertainty in Artificial Intelligence*. Retrieved from https://ssrn.com/abstract=2777631

Ksantini, M., & Boujelbène, Y. (2014). Impact of financial crises on growth and investment: An analysis of panel data. *Journal of International and Global Economic Studies*, *7*(1), 32–57.

Markowitz, H. (1952). Portfolio Selection. *The Journal of Finance*, *7*(1), 77–91.

Markowitz, H. M. (1991). Foundations of Portfolio Theory. *Journal of Finance. American Finance Association*, *46*(2), 469–477.

Numora Group. (2006). *The Evolution of Commercial Real Estate (CRE) CDOs. Technical Report.* New York, NY: Nomura Fixed Income Research, Nomura Securities International, Inc.

Papst, A. (Ed.). (2011). *The Crisis of Global Capitalism: Pope Benedict XVI's social encyclical and the future of political economy.* Eugene, OR: Wipf& Stock publishers.

Ray, J., Mukherjee, A., Dey, S. K., & Klepac, G. (2019). *Metaheuristic Approaches to Portfolio Optimization.* Hershey, PA: IGI-Global Publication. doi:10.4018/978-1-5225-8103-1

Rhee. (2009). The Madoff Scandal, Market Regulatory Failure and the Business Education of Lawyers. *Journal of Corporation Law, 35*, 363-391. Available at https://scholarship.law.ufl.edu/facultypub/486

Robinson, W. I. (2014). *Global capitalism and the crisis of humanity.* New York: Cambridge University Press. doi:10.1017/CBO9781107590250

Sharpe, W. F. (1992). Asset Allocation: Management Style and Performance Measurement. *Journal of Portfolio Management, 18*(2), 7–19. doi:10.3905/jpm.1992.409394

Tavakoli, J. M. (2008). *Structured finance and collateralized debt obligations new developments in cash and synthetic securitization.* John Wiley & Sons, Inc., Hoboken, New Jersey. doi:10.1002/9781118268230

U.S. Department of the Treasury. (2020). Retrieved from https://home.treasury.gov/

Whetten, M., & Aderson, M. (2005). CDOs-squared demystified. Technical report. Nomura Fixed Income Research.

Wong, S. (2012). *What Have Been the Impacts of World Bank Community-Driven Development Programs? CDD Impact Evaluation Review and Operational and Research Implications.* Washington, DC: World Bank.

ENDNOTES

1 "Tranche" is a French word, standing for a slice or a piece, and represents a different part of the same portfolio.

2 An open-ended investment company (OEIC) is a type of investment fund domiciled in the United Kingdom that is structured to invest in stocks and other securities. The company's shares are listed on the London Stock Exchange (LSE) and the price of the shares is based largely on the underlying assets of the fund. These funds can mix different types of investment strategies such as income and growth, and small cap and large cap and can constantly adjust their investment criteria and fund size (Investopedia, n.d).

3 Capital assets are significant pieces of property such as homes, cars, investment properties, stocks, bonds, and even collectibles or art (Investopodia, n.d.).

Chapter 2
Resolution Methods:
Applied Methods

ABSTRACT

The aim of this chapter is to introduce the different notions of the techniques used to solve the portfolio design problem. These techniques can be divided into two exact (or complete) methods and approached (or incomplete) methods. In the first part, the authors provide the exact approaches, namely linear programming and constraint programming, as well as the techniques of symmetry breaking, the modeling notions, and the different solving algorithms. The second part concerns approached methods, namely Simulated Annealing, IDWalk, Tabu Search, GWW, and Variable Neighborhood Search, including the techniques of studying the performance profiles of a method.

INTRODUCTION

This chapter presents the methods, the modeling and different solving tools, which will be exploited or projected to be applied to the Portfolio Design (PD) problem.

We describe the complete methods via Constraint Programming (CP) and Linear Programming (LP). Complete methods will be used to guarantee the optimality of the solution at the expense of the CPU time that is exponential.

Finally, we introduce local optimization methods, namely Simple Local Search (SLS) (e.g. Simulated Annealing, IDWalk, Tabu Search), population method GWW and Variable Neighborhood Search methods (VNS and SVNS).

DOI: 10.4018/978-1-7998-1882-3.ch002

These local methods will be used to get solutions quickly at the expense of their optimality.

The chapter is organized as follows. In Section 2, the notions of exact methods are detailed, considering Linear Programming and Constraint Programming. We present symmetry breaking techniques and their interest in solving symmetric problems. In section 3, we introduce the implemented approximate methods on the (PD) problem, namely Simulated Annealing, IDWalk, Tabu Search, GWW (Go With the Winners) and Variable Neighborhood Search (VNS and SVNS). We present principles and solving algorithms, techniques of landscape analysis and performance evaluation. Finally, we conclude the chapter.

BACKGROUND

Operations Research (OR) is a discipline which deals with computer science and applied mathematics to make decisions. During these last few years, (OR) has become omnipresent in many problems of optimization, namely financial portfolio optimization, scheduling, economics, industry, etc. Operations Research is conceived as a set of techniques of decision support; the solution (or the decision) is computed via rational bases and represents the best decision that should be taken by the human.

Combinatorial Optimization is a field coming from (OR). It includes all types of methods which are conceived to solve an optimized solution, such as maximizing the gain of a factory or minimizing its spending. It computes the optimal solution from an initial solution, within a set of realizable solutions (Definition 1.1).

Definition 2.1(Combinatorial Optimization Problem)
A combinatorial optimization problem *P(V,C,D)* is a problem which can be modeled in a graph or in an integer program, where:

- V: a set of variables $\{v_1,v_2,\ldots,v_n\}$, such that v_i is a continuous or a discrete variable.
- C: a set of constraints $\{c_1,c_2,\ldots,c_m\}$, such that c_j is a constraint defined on variables of$V$.
- D: a set of domains $\{D_1,D_2,\ldots,D_n\}$, such that D_i is a domain of the variable v_i.

Figure 1. Local optimum and global optimum in a search space (El-Ghazali, 2009)

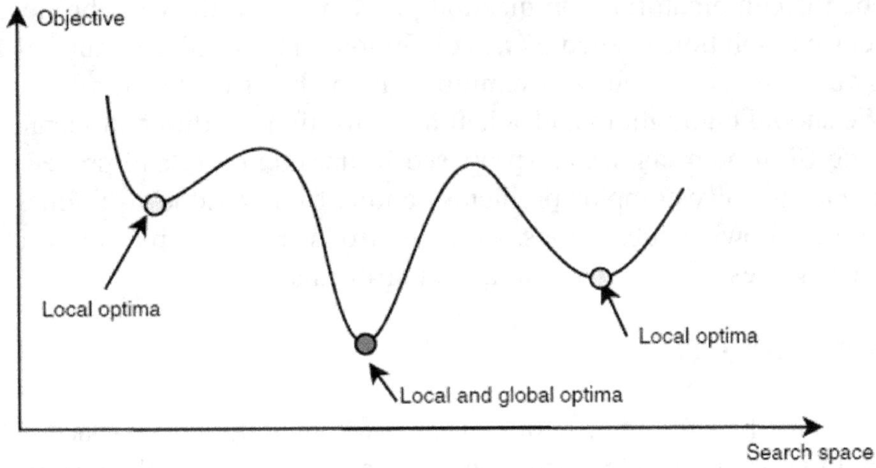

- An objective function of minimizing or maximizing noted *f*, such that: $f: D_1 \times D_2 \times \ldots D_n \rightarrow \mathbb{R}$

In the literature, we find different solving techniques coming from Operations Research, which seem to divide naturally into two categories: exact methods and approximate methods. The major difference between the both classes lies on finding the global optimum (Definition 1.2). Generally, optimization approaches start with initial solution s_0, computed randomly or by a greedy or exact algorithm, and attempt to improve s_0 (or the current solution), at each iteration until reaching the desired optimum (global or approximated)

Figure 1 shows a search space which contains three local optima, where only one corresponds to the global optimum.

The disadvantage of approximate methods is becoming stuck at a local optimum (Definition 2.3), due to searching for the best solution in the same neighborhood.

Definition 2.2 (Global Optimum)

Let be the combinatorial optimization problem *P* and the search space of *P* noted *S(P)*. A solution s^* is a global optimum of *P*if $\forall s' \in S(P): f(s^*) \leq f(s')$, where *f* is a minimization objective function.

Definition 3.3 (Local Optimum)
Let be the combinatorial optimization problem *P* and the neighborhood of the current solution *s* noted *N(s)*. A solution *s* is a local optimum of *P* if $\forall s' \in N(s): f(s) \leq f(s')$, where *f* is a minimization objective function.

We should highlight that efficient hybridizations of different techniques coming from both classes are proposed in the literature, and proved their efficiency to solve complex problems coming from various disciplines.

In the following subsections, we will introduce more explanations about both categories of solving optimization problems.

Exact Methods

An exact method allows browsing over the whole of the search space to find the optimal solution (global optimum). The efficiency and the termination of an exact algorithm should be proven. The weak point of these methods is that they are inefficient, applied to complex problems with large instances.

In the other words, an exact method is a method which should be able to find the optimum. Furthermore, such a method is not appropriate for a NP-Problem[1], except if its size, namely number of its decision variables or number of constraints, is small.

These methods are featured exact, in the sense that optimum solutions are searched by means of accurate, deterministic numerical algorithms; the convergence is generally proven for most of them. (Borne, Filip & Stefanoiu, 2013).

Exact algorithms are applied to solve a finite size instance of a combinatorial optimization problem within an instance-dependent run-time. Yet, due to the inherent complexity of combinatorial optimization problems, many of the problems are NP-hard and exact methods need exponential run-time in the worst case (Stützle, 1998).

Exact optimization has led to various exact techniques in solving combinatorial optimization problems, such as:

- Branch and bound/and Cut/ and price
- Constraint programming
- Dynamic programming
- Linear/Non-linear programming
- Continuous/Integer/Mixed integer Programming

In the following sections, we give more details about Linear Integer Programming and Constraint Programming, the proposed and the applied techniques on our problem in this book.

For more details on exact optimization see (Schrijver, 1986; Winston, 1991;Rossi, van Beek & Walsh, 2006; Borne, Filip & Stefanoiu, 2013; Anderson, Sweeney, Williams, Camm & Martin, 2011).

Approximate Methods

An approximate method is utilized naturally in two cases:

1. When no exact method exists to solve the considered problem. This type of problem is classified as NP-Complete or NP-Hard. In this situation, no exact and polynomial algorithm could be found.
2. When the approximate algorithm is faster than the exact algorithm, applied to the same problem.

Two classes of approximate methods may be distinguished:

1. Approximation algorithms: produce an optimum close to a global optimum at a fixed percentage noted ε.
2. Metaheuristics: produce a good optimum, without fixing how close the obtained solution should be to the optimal ones. In contrast to the exact method, an approximate method targets a good solution which should be close to the optimum.

The term metaheuristic derives from the composition of two Greek words: *Heuristic,* which derives from the verb *heuriskein,* which means “to find”, and the suffix *meta* which means “beyond, in an upper level”. This kind of methods is often called modern heuristics (Blum & Roli, 2003).

In the last 20 years, Combinatorial Optimization researchers have attempted to propose corresponding definitions of *Metaheuristic*.

Metaheuristics represent a family of approximate optimization techniques. They have gained a lot of popularity in the past two decades. They are among the most promising and successful techniques, especially on complex problems. Metaheuristics provide acceptable solutions, not necessarily the optimized ones, in a reasonable time (El-Ghazali, 2009). This kind of techniques is also used in the case where the desired solution is just a good solution, not necessary the best one. It is also used in computing the initial solution which should be essential to start-up an exact method.

Metaheuristics is a term which is also used to describe a major subfield, indeed the primary subfield, of stochastic optimization. Stochastic optimization is the general class of algorithms and techniques based on some degree of randomness to find an optimal (or as an optimal as possible) solution (Luke, 2013)

A *metaheuristic* is a high-level problem-independent algorithmic *framework*, which provides a set of guidelines or strategies to develop heuristic optimization algorithms. Numerous examples of metaheuristics include genetic/evolutionary algorithms, tabu search, simulated annealing, ant colony optimization, etc. (Sörensen & Glover, 2013). A metaheuristic is formally defined as an iterative generation process which is based on different heuristics and combines intelligently different concepts for exploring and exploiting the search space. Learning strategies are also used to structure information in order to find efficiently near-optimal solutions (Osman & Laporte, 1996).

The main goal of a metaheuristic is to avoid the disadvantages of iterative improvement and, in particular, multiple descent by allowing the local search to escape from local optima. This is achieved by using thoughtful and intelligent approaches such as neighborhood and evaluating algorithms. Many of the methods are characterized by the fact of providing a high quality solution quickly. Many of the metaheuristic approaches use probabilistic decisions during the search and the move decision (Voß, Martello, Osman, & Roucairol, 1999).

Approximate (not approximation) optimization has led to various approximate techniques in solving combinatorial optimization problems, such as:

- Single-state based metaheuristics like Simulated Annealing, Tabu Search, IDWalk, Variable Neighborhood Search, etc.
- Population based metaheuristics like Genetic Algorithm, Ant Colony Algorithm, Go With the Winners, etc.
- Problem-specific heuristics

In the following sections, we will introduce more details about simple, population and Variable Neighborhood search, the proposed and the applied approaches to our financial problem in this book.

For more details on approached optimization see (Stützle, 1998; eofilo, 2007; Xin-She Yang, 2010; Luke, 2013)

EXACT METHODS

The main principle of an exact method is to enumerate wisely, the set of all the solutions in the whole research space. Enumerating algorithms are conceived to detect earlier the failure assigning of the variables, and specific heuristics are generally adopted in the choice of the variable to instantiate and the value to affect. Applying this type of methods guarantees the optimality of the reached solution, if it exists, even if the realized CPU time reflects the slowness of the method.

An approached method is based on heuristics, which explore a part of the research space of the solutions and achieve a good solution in less time. However, this method cannot guarantee the optimality of the founded solution.

In the following sections, we introduce the modeling and solving techniques coming from exact and approached methods, which will be implemented and applied on our (PD) problem.

Linear Integer Programming

Linear Programming (LP) is a basic tool in Operational Research (OR)[1]. It offers powerful techniques, which allow modelling and solving many optimization problems. Solving an optimization problem with LP is to search the minimum (resp. maximum) of an *f* function, while ensuring the satisfaction of linear equations and inequalities system. The solving difficulty lies in two successive points:

1. To define the points set which satisfies the constraints,
2. To find their minimum.

In linear programming, we distinguish Continuous Linear Programming (CLP) (where the variables are continuous) and Integer Linear Programming (ILP) (where variables are discrete).

Integer Linear Programming (ILP) or Mixed-Integer Linear Programming (MIP) (Wolsey,1998)(Winston,2004) provides the most exploited effective methods in handling optimization problems, due in part to rich possibilities in modeling. An (ILP) program is a Linear Program (LP) where some variables should be integer, or even binary variables $\{0,1\}$. These variables are subject to integrality constraints. Generally, an ILP model contains:

- A set of decision variables.
- A set of linear constraints, that each constraint requires a linear expression of decision variables, either equal to, less than, or greater than a real value.
- A linear objective function, which assesses the solution cost.

Solving an ILP problem is to find the space of points satisfying all the constraints, whichever gives the smallest value to the objective function to minimize. In general, an ILP problem takes the following (2.1) form:

$$\begin{aligned}&\textit{Minimize } C^T X\\&\begin{cases}AX(\le,=,\text{ or }\ge)B\\x_i\in\mathbb{Z}, i=1..p\\x_i\in\mathbb{R}, i=p+1..n\end{cases}\end{aligned}\tag{2.1}$$

Where X represents the vector of decision variables, p is a positive integer value, c_j values, $\forall j=1\ldots n$, are called objective coefficients, A is an $n\times m$ matrix of coefficients, and B is an $m\times 1$ vector of second member associated to a system of linear constraints.

To solve ILP problems, we use a tree-search method called *branch-and-bound* derived from the Operational Research field. This method is essentially a *divide and conquer* approach, i.e., decomposing recursively the original problem into sub-problems until achieving problems easy to solve. For more details, we recommend the references (Winston,2004), (Wolsey,1998), (Papadimitriou & Steiglitz,1998) and (Lawer& Wood,1966).

Constraint Programming

Constraint Programming (CP) proposes a declarative programming paradigm, which designates at the same time a formalism and a strong algorithm for modeling and solving combinatorial problems (e.g., scheduling, planning, etc.). It has its origins in works of Laurière (Laurière, 1978) and it has had an important development (Hentenrick,2002; Rossi et al., 2006; Régin,1994; Lecoutre, 2013) between the 1990s and 2000s, especially by integrating new operational research techniques (Régin, 2003)(Régin, 2011).

CP is based on a notion of constraints network, or more generally Constraint Satisfaction Problem (CSP). A CSP *P* is defined by a triplet $P=\langle X,D,C\rangle$ where:

- *X*: a set of n variables $X=\{x_1,x_2,\ldots,x_n\}$.
- *D*: a set of *n* domains $D=\{D_1,D_2,\ldots,D_n\}$. *D* indicates the tuple $\langle D_1,D_2,\ldots,D_n\rangle$ of the variables' domains, with D_i the set of the defining values of the variable x_i.
- *C*: a set of *t* constraints $C=\{c_1,c_2,\ldots,c_t\}$ of the problem. The set vars(c_j) is used to denote the set of variables that occur in constraint c_j. A constraint c_j is defined by the set of authorized tuples $R(c_j)$ on the sequences of variables vars(c_j), called signature of the constraint. The size of vars(c_j) is the arity of the constraint c_j. $R(c_j)$ is the subset of the Cartesian product of the sequence variables vars(c_j).

An instantiation (or assignation) *I* of a variables' set *V* is a function that connects each variable $x_i \in V$ to a value $v(x_i) \in D_i$. A solution is a complete instantiation that satisfies all the constraints; also called consistent instantiation. Solving a *CSP* or searching a *CSP*'s solutions is an NP-Complete[2] problem. The set of a *CSP*'s feasible solutions is denoted by *sol(X,D,C)*.

Constraint programming (*CP*) proposes languages, and generic algorithms of solving based on filtering and propagation techniques, and decomposition of constraint satisfaction problems (Régin, 2004).

Filtering and Domains' Reduction

To define what is a filtering, we start by introducing the domains' consistency (Definition 2.4).

Definition 2.4 (Domains' Consistency)
Domains' consistency is linked to the notion of a feasible partial solution. A value *v* belonging to the domain of a variable x_i, verifies the domains' consistency, if and only if for any constraint c_j involving the variable x_i, there is an instantiation of variables belonging to *vars(c)* such that *c* is verified.

The filtering algorithm (definition 2.5) is to reduce the variables' domains, by deleting the values which will not belong to any solution.

Definition 2.5 (Filtering Algorithm)
A filtering algorithm is a reducing algorithm associated to a constraint c_j. Its role is to delete the inconsistent[3] values of the variables' definition domains in var(c_j).

Following the reduction of the variable's domain, other variables appearing in other constraints could become inconsistent. This is why it is important to use a propagation mechanism, to attempt all the possible reductions, due to the withdrawal of the contained values in the variables' domains.

For more details, we refer readers to (Rossi et al., 2006; Régin, 2011; Lecoutre, 2013).

CSP Solving Methods

A CSP solving method should identify an assignation of values to variables, so that all the constraints are satisfied (i.e. total and consistent instantiation). The general approach is to explore the research space defined by the domains' Cartesian product, and ends when a consistent instantiation is found, or when the absence of such instantiation is proven (inconsistent CSP).

The simplest method to look for a CSP solution is to generate all the variables' complete instantiations, and check later if each one of the generated candidate instantiations is a good solution of the problem. This strategy "generate and test" is very costly. Hence, we use elaborated schemes and more sophisticatedones to solve the problem more effectively.

The adopted scheme is that of "backtracking", which generates a consistent partial instantiation, and then extends this partial instantiation with a new variable's partial instantiation. In other terms, CSP variables are instantiated until:

- At least one constraint is violated. The algorithm backtracks to the last instantiation, and tests a new value on the most recent variable.
- If all the variable's values are tested without success, the algorithm realizes a back-track on the variable that precedes the most recent variable.
- This process stops once one solution is found, or the backtracking reaches the root of the research tree without finding a solution.

The resolution scheme by backtracking can be implemented in two ways:

1. **Prospective Strategy:** a strategy to take advantage of filtering algorithms (see the previous subsection) before each variable instantiation, in order to delete those cannot lead to a solution.
2. **Retrospective Strategy:** a strategy, in the failure case on a variable, instead of backtracking to the previous variable, we analyze the failure origin. Among the most elaborated retrospective methods we have the dynamic-backtracking method (Ginsberg,1993).

These two strategies are the most common used in constraint solvers, and particularly the intensive use of filtering algorithms to reduce drastically the research space.

SYMMETRIES ANALYSIS

Symmetry is one of critical subjects in Constraints Programming (CP) and Operational Research, becoming a research field in its own right. The origin of the symmetries handling, especially in CP, is due to the fact that the research process of solutions can revisit equivalent states many times, or even an exponential number of times. These equivalent states are called symmetric solutions. Breaking symmetries allows reducing the research tree handled by the algorithm. Hence, techniques of breaking symmetries can seriously boost the resolution process on symmetrical problems. In our case, we are interested in solutions' symmetries defined on variables' matrices.

Definition 2.6 (Symmetrical Problem)
A symmetrical problem is a problem allowing the management of other solutions by applying a symmetry type on the initial solution.

Example 2.1 (Symmetries in Chessboard) (Rossi et al., 2006)
Consider a 3×3 chessboard, where we mark the 9 boxes with numbers 1 to 9. We suppose the problem admits a solution designed by *sol* as follows:

1	2	3
4	5	6
7	8	9

(sol)

Numbers from 1 to 9 are the points to move via symmetries. We consider 9 natural symmetries on the chessboard which generate solutions satisfying the problem. Identity symmetry leaves each point unchanged, which is represented by the leftmost chessboard, noticed by *id*. Thereafter, we can realize clockwise rotations 90°, 180° and 270°. The points' locations resulting after each rotation degree are given by the chessboards rot90, rot180 and rot270. Finally, we have reflections: on vertical axis, on horizontal axis and on both diagonals illustrated by *v*, *h*, *d1*, *d2* chessboards, respectively.

1	2	3
4	5	6
7	8	9

(id)

7	4	1
8	5	2
9	6	3

(rot90)

9	8	7
6	5	4
3	2	1

(rot180)

3	6	9
2	5	8
1	4	7

(rot270)

3	2	1
6	5	4
9	8	7

(v)

7	8	9
4	5	6
1	2	3

(h)

1	4	7
2	5	8
3	6	9

(d1)

9	6	3
8	5	2
7	4	1

(d2)

The link between these symmetries is very direct via permutations. Each symmetry defines a permutations' set of points. We illustrate via the eight chessboards above, 5 types of symmetries: identity symmetry, rotational symmetry, column symmetry, row symmetry and diagonal symmetry.

We distinguish two types of breaking symmetries methods, namely static methods and dynamic methods. In Constraint Programming, there are various manners to break symmetries (Gent& Smith, 1999; Flener, Frisch, Hnich, Kiziltan,Miguel, Pearson & Walsh, 2002; Puget, 2006; Mears, de la Banda, Demoen & Wallace, 2014).

Generally, all of them start from the same principle,which is to add constraints to the CSP problem. These added constraints, called conditional constraints, should eliminate all variant symmetries, without eliminating non-generic solutions.

Since we will address in this manuscript a matricial model, we will bring forward, in the following subsections, the breaking of symmetries in relation with matrices (Flener, Frisch, Hnich, Kiziltan, Miguel, Pearson & Walsh, 2001)(Flener et al., 2002)

Static Symmetry Breaking

Static symmetry breaking is an approach based on adding new constraints to initial CSP, to eliminate all symmetrical solutions. In other words, these constraints allow breaking detected symmetries and lead to a new CSP without symmetries.

Row and column symmetries are the symmetries most handled by the static approach (Flener et al., 2002; Flener,Frisch, Hnich, Jefferson, Kiziltan, Miguel, Pearson& Walsh, 2003; Kiziltan, 2004). In order to break all row (or column) symmetries, we can order the rows (or the columns) in lexicographical order. The lines (or columns) of a 2-d matrix, are ordered in lexicographical order. If a row (resp. a column) is less than the next, then we notice $\leq_{lex}$, in the lexicographical order case. If a row (resp. a column) is greater than the next, then we notice $\geq_{lex}$, in the anti-lexicographical order case.

The example below illustrates a matrix representing row and column symmetries.

Example 2.2 (Row and Column Symmetries and Lexicographical Order)
Let be the following CSP P_1 (Flener et al., 2002).

$$P_1 \left| \begin{array}{l} X = \{x_{ij} \mid i \in 1..3, j \in 1..4\} \\ D_{X_{ij}} = \{0,1 \mid i \in 1..3, j \in 1..4\} \\ C = \{c_1, c_2\} \\ c_1 : \sum x_{ij} = 7 \mid \forall i \in 1..3, \forall j \in 1..4 \\ c_2 : \forall j \neq k, \sum x_{ik} x_{kj} \leq 1 \mid \forall i \in 1..3, \forall j \in 1..4 \end{array} \right. \quad (2.2)$$

This model represents row and column symmetries. A solution with lexicographical order on the rows is as given below:

$$\begin{pmatrix} 0 & 1 & 0 \\ 0 & 1 & 1 \\ 1 & 0 & 1 \\ 1 & 1 & 0 \end{pmatrix}$$

By applying a lexicographical order to columns of the first solution, we obtain the following matrix:

$$\begin{pmatrix} 0 & 0 & 1 \\ 0 & 1 & 1 \\ 1 & 1 & 0 \\ 1 & 0 & 1 \end{pmatrix}$$

However, this destroys the lexicographical order of the columns. By reordering the last two rows, we obtain a matrix (or a solution) with verified lexicographical order on rows and columns.

$$\begin{pmatrix} 0 & 0 & 1 \\ 0 & 1 & 1 \\ 1 & 0 & 1 \\ 1 & 1 & 0 \end{pmatrix}$$

In order to break row and column symmetries, Flener et al. propose adding two types of constraints in the initial CSP P_1: one for breaking row symmetry and the other to break column symmetry. Consequently, during the research, the lexical order constraints operate simultaneously, over both rows and columns. The theorem below (Flener et al., 2002) shows that if this order's type is realized sequentially or simultaneously, we will have a solution verifying the lexicographical order on rows and columns. Exploitation of this type of constraints will be given in chapter 5.

Theorem 2.1
In the matricial model having row and column symmetries in a 2-d matrix, each class of symmetries contains an element whose rows and the columns verify lexicographical order.

Unfortunately, the simultaneous application of lexicographical order over rows and columns can leave some symmetries in the 2-d matrix; this can be illustrated through the following example.

Example 2.3 (Row and Column Symmetries)
Let be the 3×3 matrix of x_{ij} 0-1 variables, which can be defined by the following CSP (Flener et al., 2002).

$$P_2 \left| \begin{array}{l} X = \{x_{ij} \mid i,j \in 1..3\} \\ D_{x_{ij}} = \{0,1 \mid i,j \in 1..3\} \\ C = \{c_1, c_2\} \\ c_1 : \sum_{j=1..3} x_{ij} \geq 1 \mid \forall j \in 1..3 \\ c_2 : \sum_{i=1..3} \sum_{j=1..3} x_{ij} = 4 \end{array} \right. \quad (2.3)$$

This model poses the two symmetries: row and column. Solving P_2 with constraints lexicographical order over the rows and the columns can generate the following solutions:

$$\begin{pmatrix} 0 & 0 & 1 \\ 0 & 1 & 1 \\ 1 & 0 & 0 \end{pmatrix}, \begin{pmatrix} 0 & 0 & 1 \\ 0 & 1 & 0 \\ 1 & 0 & 1 \end{pmatrix} and \begin{pmatrix} 0 & 0 & 1 \\ 0 & 1 & 0 \\ 1 & 1 & 0 \end{pmatrix}$$

Consequently, breaking row and column symmetries via lexicographical order application on rows and columns is a partial symmetry breaking.

Dynamic Symmetry Breaking

In contrast to static breaking, a dynamic symmetry breaking (Puget, 2006) is based on two points:

1. After each insertion of a new node in the research tree, new conditional constraints are added in order to eliminate symmetrical variables from the current partial assignment.
2. In order to avoid a repeated exploration of the symmetrical variant, each explored sub-tree is used as a no-good.

Among the most known methods in this type of breaking symmetries, we have SBDS (Symmetry Breaking During Search)(Gent & Smith, 1999), LDSB (Lightweight Dynamic Symmetry Breaking)(Mears, de la Banda, Demoen& Wallace, 2014) and SBDD (Symmetry Breaking by Dominance Detection) (Gent, Harvey, Kelsey & Linton, 2003). The dynamic method considered in this work is the LDSB method, which is why we propose more details about it.

LDSB is a method that does not interact with the used research's heuristics. It can be defined as an abbreviate descent from SBDS method. It requires providing the different symmetries and as soon as possible, it realizes a pruning of different symmetrical parts of the research tree.

The aim of this method is the ability to apply it on any kind of CSP and with any research strategy. This should be done by considering as a target the widespread groups of symmetries in practice, and could be represented in a compact way and handled with efficiency (Example 2.4).

Example 2.4 (Row, column and Diagonal Symmetries)

Consider a problem of 3×3 Latin square, where each cell from the 9 takes a value from the set {1,2,3}, such that each value appears once and only once through the row and the column (Mears et al., 2014).

The corresponding CSP can be given as follows:

$$P_3 = \left| \begin{array}{l} X = \{x_{11}, x_{12}, x_{13}, x_{21}, x_{22}, x_{23}, x_{31}, x_{32}, x_{33}\} \\ D_{x_{ij}} = \{1,2,3\}, with\ i,j \in 1..3 \\ C = \{x_{11} \neq x_{12}, x_{11} \neq x_{13}, x_{12} \neq x_{13}, \\ \quad x_{21} \neq x_{22}, x_{21} \neq x_{23}, x_{22} \neq x_{23}, \\ \quad x_{31} \neq x_{32}, x_{31} \neq x_{33}, x_{32} \neq x_{33}\} \end{array} \right. \tag{2.4}$$

The above P_3 CSP contains:

1. Column symmetries:

$$(x_{11}, x_{21}, x_{31}) \leftrightarrow (x_{12}, x_{22}, x_{32})$$
$$(x_{11}, x_{21}, x_{31}) \leftrightarrow (x_{13}, x_{23}, x_{33})$$
$$and\ (x_{12}, x_{22}, x_{32}) \leftrightarrow (x_{13}, x_{23}, x_{33})$$

2. Row symmetries.
3. Symmetries behind the diagonal.
4. Variable-value symmetry *f* which is defined by: $f(x_{i,j} = k) = (x_{k,j}, k = i)$.

The P_3 CSP admits the symmetries referred to above, since their application on every solution x_{sol} leads to new X'_{sol} solution, called symmetrical variant.

To break symmetries in a CSP *PX,D,X*, the method LDSB generates and handles the four symmetries groups summarized as follows (Mears et al., 2014):

- **Interchangeable Variables:** Let be the set of variables $W \subseteq X$, if f_r an extending of every permutation of the variable $r \in W$ keeps the variables unchanged in $X \setminus W$ then r is a symmetrical variable of P. We say the set's variables $W \subseteq X$ are interchangeable for P.
- **Interchangeable Values:** Let be the set of values $W \subseteq D$, if f_l an extending of every value $l \in W$ keeps the values unchanged in $D \setminus W$ then l is a symmetrical value of P. We say the set's values $W \subseteq D$ are interchangeable for P.
- **Interchangeable Variables Simultaneously:** Let be two variables' sequences $x_1,\ldots,x_n$ and $y_1,\ldots,y_2$ such that $x_1,\ldots,x_n, y,\ldots,y_n \in X$, if $x_1,\ldots,x_n \leftrightarrow y_1,\ldots,y_n$, i.e. if the bijection associates each variable x_i to y_i and vice versa, keeps the remaining variable in X unchanged, then the two sequences represent symmetrical variables for P. We say S is a set of interchangeable sequences for P, if $\forall s_1,s_2 \in S$, s_1 and s_2 are simultaneously interchangeable.
- **Interchangeable Values Simultaneously:** Let be two values' sequences $x_1,\ldots,x_n$ and $y_1,\ldots,y_2$ such that $x_1,\ldots,x_n, y,\ldots,y_n \in D$ are simultaneously interchangeable for P, if $x_1,\ldots,x_n \leftrightarrow y_1,\ldots,y_n$. We say S is a set of interchangeable sequences for P, if $\forall s_1,s_2 \in S$, s_1 and s_2 are simultaneously interchangeable.

The LDSB method is an advanced approach, that is a light version of the method SBDS. It is considered as the fastest and the efficient method, because it exploits an active symmetry which keeps the current partial instantiation, at the node n, unchanged (consistent). In other terms (Mears et al., 2014) the LDSB method has:

A mechanism allowing the composition of new symmetries belonging to the four types of symmetries, namely: interchangeable variables, interchangeable values, interchangeable variables simultaneously and interchangeable values simultaneously.

Very efficient algorithms to tackle these categories of symmetry.

Finally, LDSB is a dynamic and partial breaking symmetries method that gives performant results, in practice.

APPROXIMATE METHODS

In this section, we present modeling and solving methods and tools used in our approaches in handling the Portfolio Design (PD) problem.

We give a reminder about the optimizing local methods, namely simple local methods (e.g. Simulated annealing, IDWalk, Tabu Search) and GWW population method. These methods will be used to get solutions quickly but at the expense of their optimality.

Simple Local Search (SLS)

Simulated Annealing

Simulated Annealing (Kirkpatrick, Jr. & Vecchi, 1983) is a method proposed by Kirkpatrick et al. inspired by the physical annealing process in metallurgy. It is characterized by the temperature T, an important measure in the cooling metal. The method steps may be summarized as follows:

1. Start with initial solution S_0, whose evaluation is $f(S_0)$.
2. Choose a new random solution S_1 in the neighborhood of S_0 noted by $val(S_0)$.
   (a) If $f(S_0) \geq f(S_1)$ (minimization problem) then S_1 is adopted while improving the current solution S_0.
   (b) If $f(S_0) < f(S_1)$ we compute $v = e^{-\frac{f(S_1)-f(S_0)}{T}}$. We choose randomly a value p in $[0,1]$. If $p \leq v$ then S_0 is replaced by S_1.
3. At each iteration, T is decreased slowly.
4. If $T < \varepsilon$ then the algorithm is stopped with S_0 optimal solution, else go to step 2.

The algorithm 1 produces the algorithmic steps of simulated annealing method.

Algorithm 1 Simulated Annealing

```
Input: S0 initial solution; k∈]0,1[ cooling parameter; ε fixed
threshold close to 0; T temperature; MaxIter maximum number of
iterations
Iter←0
Choose randomly an initial solution S0
Repeat
Iter←Iter+1
 Choose randomly a solution S1 in V(S0)
δf=f(S1) - f(S0)
if δf≤0 then
```

```
S0←S1
else
        pick randomly p in [0,1]
        if p ≤ e^(-δf/T) then
        S0←S1
        endif
        endif
        T←k×T
        until (T≤ε) or (Iter=MaxIter)
        return S0
```

IDWalk Method

IDWalk (Intensification and Diversification Walk) (Neveu, Trombettoni & Glover, 2004) has been proposed by Neveu et al. in 2004. It is characterized by two parameters: *MN* which is the maximum neighbors to cover and *SN* (spare neighbor) which is the type of diversification. Consider the current solution *CS* and the best solution *BS*, this method is defined in two steps:

- **Intensification:**
    a. Starting with an initial solution S_0, and evaluate *val*(S_0) where *val* is the objective function. S_0 is considered as the current solution *CS*.
    b. The *MN* neighbors of the current solution are explored.
    c. We choose the best neighbor *BN*, by flipping the variable $Var_{conflict}$ (as given in section 4),
    d. if *BN* is better than the current solution, *CS* is replaced by *BN* and *val-conflict* is updated.
- **Diversification:**
  If *BN* does not improve *CS* then we choose the best one in *SN* first neighbors. In the case of *SN=1* we choose a randomized neighbor.
  Idwalk is a simple and effective metaheuristic requiring only one parameter, which is the maximum number of candidate neighbors.

Algorithm 2 IDWalk

```
Input: S moves' number; Max neighbors' number; SP diversification type
   Compute an initial random solution x
   x_opt←x x_opt ← x
```

```
for i∈1..S do
Nb_sol←1; Sol_rejected ←∅ ; Sol_accepted←false;
while (Nb_sol≤Max) and (Sol_accepted=false) do
        Choose a solution x'∈V(x)
if f(x')≤f(x) then
Sol_accepted←true
else
        Sol_rejected ← Sol_rejected ∪ {x'}
        endif
        Nb_sol←Nb_sol+1
        endwhile
        if Sol_accepted then
        x←x'
        else
        if SP≠0 then
        x←SELECT(Sol_rejected, SP)
        endif
        endif
        if f(x)<f(x_opt) then
        x_opt←x
        endif
        enfor
        return x_opt
        procedure SELECT(Sol_rejected, SP)
        if SP=1 then
              Choose randomly a solution x'∈Sol_rejected
        else
              Choose the solution x' in the SP first candidates in Sol_rejected
        endif
        return x'
        Endprocedure
```

Tabu Search

Tabu method (Algorithm 3) was introduced by Glover (Glover & Laguna, 1997). It is characterized by a tabu list T, which contains the tabu solutions. In a tabu search, we start by an initial solution x, and we search the best solution x' which is in the neighborhoods $V(x)$ of x and does not appear in T. We update the best solution if x' is better than the current optimal solution. The algorithm stops when the list T is full. Other stop conditions may be adopted (e.g. see (Prins, 1994)).

Algorithm 3 Tabu

Input: x initial solution; T tabu list; $V(x)$ neighborhood of x; x_{opt} the best solution

1. $T \leftarrow \varnothing$
2. $LT \leftarrow 0$
3. Compute a random initial solution x
4. $x_{opt} \leftarrow x$
5. **while** stop condition not reached **do**
6. Let be the configuration $x' \in V(x)$ such that $\forall x'' \in V(x), f(x') \leq f(x'')$ and $x'' \notin T$
7. **if** $f(x') \leq f(x'')$ **then**
8. $x_{opt} \leftarrow x'$
9. endif
10. Update the list T with the element x'
11. $x \leftarrow x'$
12. end while
13. **return** x_{opt}

Population Local Search (PLS)

Algorithm 4, GWW (Go With the Winners)(Aldous & Pitman,1994), is a population method that explores different configurations at the same time in the research space by handling a population of particles (solutions). At the beginning, the particles are distributed randomly and the threshold is fixed above the worst solution.

At each iteration, the threshold value is decreased. The particles whose values are above the threshold are called dead particles, otherwise they are called living particles. After the threshold is decreased, the dead particles are redistributed on the living particles.

In (Neveu&Trombettoni, 2003), the random walk was replaced by a local method (e.g. tabu method, simulated annealing, etc.). **Algorithm** 4 as well as other incomplete methods were implemented in the library INCOP (Neveu&Trombettoni,2004).

Algorithm 4 GWW-LS

Input: B particles' number; S walk length; T threshold parameter; WP walk parameter;

1. Each particle is randomly placed on a configuration and stored in the

```
    table Particles
T← the least cost particle in Particles
while Truedo
T← decreas T
   ifBest(Particles)>Tthen
returnBest(Particles)
else
   Redistribute Particles by putting each particle having a higher cost to T
       on a chosen living particle randomly
for p∈Particles do
       for i∈1..S do
              Move the particle p on the best neighbor by exploiting a local
       search with parameter WP
       end for
       endif
       end while
```

Variable Neighborhood Search (VNS)

Variable Neighborhood Search (VNS) (Mladenovic & Hansen, 1997) is a recent metaheuristic or a platform, conceived to construct heuristics by exploiting systematically the neighborhood changes in the descent to the local optimum, in order to exit the valley that contains it.

Based Variable Neighborhood Search (VNS)

VNS method is described in Algorithm 5 and illustrated in Figure 2. As shown the basic scheme of the method:

1. The neighborhood structure, that defines the neighborhoods surround every point $x \in X$ in the solutions' space, is specified.
2. A local search is applied, in order to lead to a local optimum x.
3. A point x' is randomly selected in the neighborhood $N_1(x)$ of x. A downhill is realized from x' by a local search method, which leads to a new local optimum x''. At this level, three results are possible:
   (a) $x'' = x$, i.e. the obtained solution is also at the bottom of the valley; in this case the procedure is reiterated by using a new neighborhood $N_k(x)$, $k \geq 2$.
   (b) $x'' \neq x$ and $f(x'') < f(x)$, i.e. another local optimum better than the last obtained one; In this case, the research is refocused around x'' and restarts with the new neighborhood. The last neighborhood may

be scanned without leading to a solution better than the solution found already: in this case, the research is again relaunched on the first neighborhood $N_1(x)$ until reaching the stop condition (e.g. the maximum runtime, the maximum number of iterations, or the maximum number of iterations starting from the last adopted solution).

Algorithm 5 VNS

```
Input: x initial solution; K_max VNS parameter; LS local search method;
Compute a random initial solution x
while stop condition is not reached do
k←1
    while k≤K_max do
x' ← SHAKE(x,k)
x" ← LS(x')
            if f(x") < f(x') then
x ← x"
k←1
        else
        k←k+1
        end if
        end while
         end while
        return x
         procedure SHAKE(x,k)
        Generate randomly a solution x' in the k^th neighborhood of the solution x;
        return x'
        end procedure
```

Skewed Variable Neighborhood Search (SVNS)

Generally, VNS method gives better results, compared to a descent local search (called multistart). VNS is much better when the solutions' landscape represents several local optima. VNS makes it easy to visit far neighbors. Consequently, it is possible that VNS has practically the same behavior as a multistart method. Thus, we have a new variant of VNS, called SVNS (Skewed VNS), allows avoiding the multistart behavior by intensifying the research without changing the neighborhood.

Figure 2. VNS research illustration (Hansen & Mladenovic, 2009)

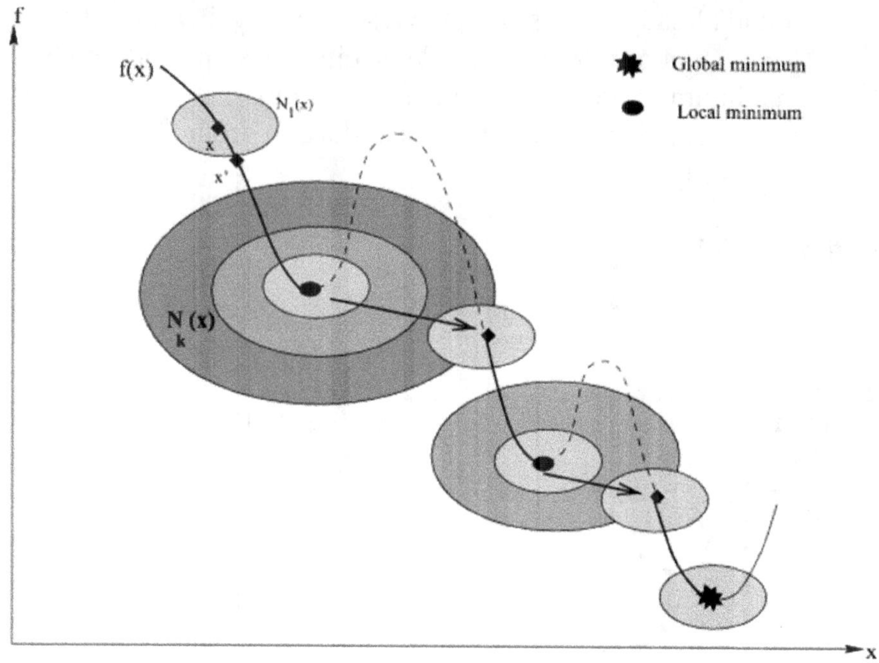

The modified neighborhood Skewed VNS (SVNS) (Mladenovic & Hansen, 1997), is given through the algorithm 6. The relaxation rule refocuses the research by using instead of $f(x'')$, an evaluation's linear function $\alpha\rho(x,x'')$, where $\rho(x,x'')$ is the distance between x and x'' and α a parameter. The measure of the distance between two solutions is practically easy to compute, e.g. the Hamming distance when the solutions are defined by Boolean vectors, or the Euclidian distance in the case of continuous solutions.

Algorithm 6 SVNS

```
Input: x initial solution; K_max SVNS parameter; LS local search method;
    Compute a random initial solution x
    while stop condition is not reached do
    k←1
        while k≤K_max do
    x'← SHAKE(x,k)
    x"← LS(x')
            if f(x") < f(x) then
    x← x"
```

```
else
    if f(x") − αρ(x,x") < f(x) then
    x ← x"
    k←1
                        else
    k←k+1
        end if
        end if
    end while
     end while
    return x
```

Landscape Analysis

The landscape of the handled problem depends on the used approach of neighborhood function and the evaluation function (Marmion, Dhaenens, Jourdan, Liefooghe&Verel, 2013)(Jarboui, Siarry&Teghem, 2013). It represents the evolution of the realized moves, as well as the evolution of the found solutions, whose goal is to find the global optimum. The analysis of a solution neighborhood or a valley in the landscape is linked to the found local optimum. Algorithm 7, Hill Climbing, gives the behavior of the local method in the intensification step, with an initial solution, generally computed through the diversification step.

Algorithm 7 HillClimbing

```
Input: S solutions' set; V(s) neighbors set of the solution s;
   Choose a random initial solution s∈S
   repeat
   choose s'∈V(s) such as eval(s') < eval(s)
   s ← s'
   until s is a local optimum
```

The kind of landscape is distinguished relatively to the observed distance between two different solutions s and s'. This distance noted by $dist(s,s')$, represents the number of necessary moves to go from s to s'. Three types of landscape are identified in (Marmion, Jourdan,Dhaensen,2013): smooth landscape, rough landscape and neutral landscape.

Smooth Landscape

Figure 3 illustrates a smooth landscape. In this situation, an heuristic with good exploration ability should allow a good exploration of the neighborhood of a solution *s* and reach the global optimum.

Figure 3. Smooth landscape (Marmion et al., 2013)

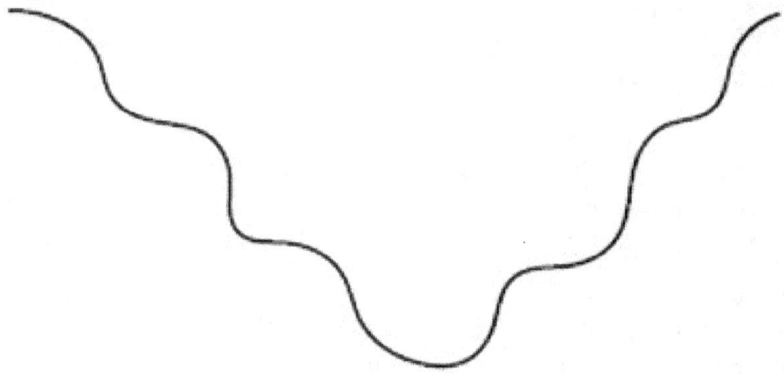

Rugged Landscape

Figure 4 shows a rugged landscape, a typical case of the local optimums problem, posed by the incomplete approaches. Consequently, a good exploration technique is recommended to move from neighborhood to neighborhood, and to avoid becoming trapped at the bottom of one of the valleys in the landscape.

Figure 4. Rugged landscape (Marmion et al., 2013)

Neutral landscape

Neutral landscape (Marmion et al., 2012) is a landscape with a tray form. It represents the case of no improvement of the current solution. This phenomenon occurrs when the metaheuristic considers the neutral solutions. Therefore, we obtain a sequence of movements, which provide solutions with equal evaluations.

Figure 5. Neutral landscape

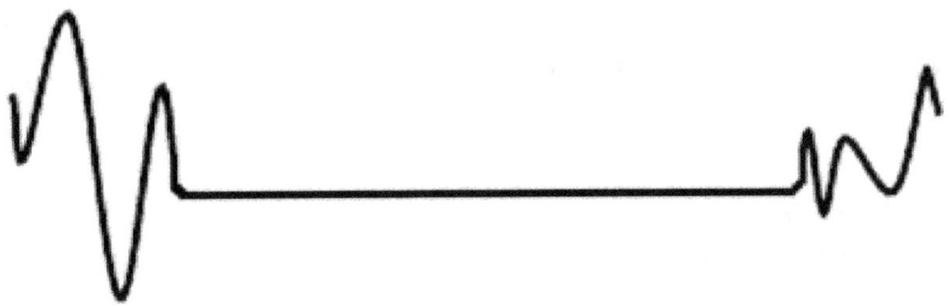

In other terms, the applied metaheuristic stagnates, and takes a long time without making improvements. Accordingly, a good exploration technique should be included in the implemented metaheuristic.

PERFORMANCE EVALUATION

To realize the high quality of synthesis of the performances of the different realized approaches, we will use the performance profile proposed in (Dolan &Moré, 2002) (Chapter 6 and Chapter 7).

Let *p* be a set of problems, and *M* a set of applied methods. Let $p_i \in P$ be a problem, and $m_j \in M$ the applied method to solve p_i. Consider the measure *t* which $t(p_i,m_j)$ evaluates the performance of the method m_j to solve the problem p_i in terms of t. The performance ratio $r(p_i,m_j)$ compares the performance of the method m_j with the performance of the best method that resolves p_i. The smallest value $t(p_i,m_j)$ represents the best quality of the method.

Definition 2.7 (Performance Ration)
Let be

$$r(p_i,m_j)=\frac{t(p_i,m_j)}{\min\{t(p_i,m_k)|m_k\in M\}} \tag{2.5}$$

If $r(p_i,m_j)=1$, then m_j is the best method to solve the problem p_i. Let be τ_{max}, the highest computed ratios $r(p_i,m_j)$. In order to evaluate the performance of all the methods in M on the problems P, we use the fractional performance $\rho_{m_j}:[1,\tau_{max}]\rightarrow[0,1]$.

Definition 2.8 (Fractional Performance of the Method m_j)
Let be

$$\rho_{m_j}(\tau)=\frac{|p_i\in P:r(p_i,m_j)\le\tau|}{|P|} \tag{2.6}$$

$\rho_{m_j}(\tau)$ is the fraction of problems in P that m_j is able to solve with a factor $\tau\geq 1$ of the best method. Consequently, the methods with the highest value $\rho_{m_j}(\tau)$ will be the best.

CONCLUSION

In this chapter, we presented different approaches, which will be exploited to solve the portfolio design problem set out in Chapter 1. We started by introducing complete approaches, namely Linear Programming and Constraint Programming, highlighting the techniques of symmetry breaking. Thereafter, we described the implemented incomplete approaches, where three types of methods were described, namely Simple Local Search (SLS) methods, population local search method and Variable Neighborhood Search (VNS) methods.

The implementation and the analysis of the complete and the incomplete proposed approaches and algorithms, will be presented and detailed respectively in Chapters 4 and 5, and analyzed in Chapters 6 and 7.

In the next chapter, we will broach different proposed portfolio design models and their properties. We will particularly describe the matrix model that we will exploit to solve the portfolio design problem.

REFERENCES

Aldous, D., & Pitman, J. (1994). *Brownian bridge asymptotics for random mappings. Random Structures & Algorithms Journal, 4*, 487-512.

Anderson, D. R., Sweeney, D. J., Williams, T. A., Camm, J. D., & Martin, K. R. (2011). *An Introduction to Management Science: Quantitative Approaches to Decision Making* (13th ed.). South-Western College Publishing.

Benhamou, B. (1994). Study of symmetry in constraint satisfaction problems. *Proceedings of CP-94, Lecture Notes in Computer Science*, 246-254.

Benhamou, B., & Saïdi, M. R. (2007). Local symmetry breaking during search in CSPs. *Principles and Practice of Constraint Programming - CP 2007, 13th International Conference, CP 2007, Proceedings*, 195-*209*. 10.1007/978-3-540-74970-7_16

Blum, C., & Roli, A. (2003, September). Metaheuristics in combinatorial optimization: Overview and conceptual comparison. *ACM Computing Surveys, 35*(3), 268–308. doi:10.1145/937503.937505

Borne, P., Filip, F. G., & Stefanoiu, D. (2013). *Optimization in engineering sciences: exact methods*. Wiley Publishing.

Dolan, E. D., & Moré, J. J. (2002). Benchmarking optimization software with performance profiles. *Mathematical Programming, 91*(2), 201–213. doi:10.1007101070100263

El-Ghazali, T. (2009). *Metaheuristics: From Design to Implementation*. Wiley Publishing.

Flener, P., Frisch, A., Hnich, B., Jefferson, C., Kiziltan, Z., Miguel, I., ... Walsh, T. (2003). Breaking symmetries in matrix models: A brief overview. *Proceedings of the Tenth Workshop on Automated Reasoning*, 27-28.

Flener, P., Frisch, A. M., Hnich, B., Kiziltan, Z., Miguel, I., Pearson, J., & Walsh, T. (2001). Symmetry in matrix models. *Proceedings of the CP'01. Workshop on Symmetry in Constraints*, 41-48.

Flener, P., Frisch, A. M., Hnich, B., Kiziltan, Z., Miguel, I., Pearson, J., & Walsh, T. (2002). Breaking row and column symmetries in matrix models. In Lecture Notes in Computer Science. Springer. doi:10.1007/3-540-46135-3_31

Gent, I. P., Harvey, W., Kelsey, T., & Linton, S. (2003). Generic SBDD using computational group theory. *Principles and Practice of ConstraintProgramming - CP 2003, 9th International Conference, CP 2003, Proceedings*, 333-*347*.

Gent, I. P., & Smith, B. (1999). Symmetry breaking during search in constraint programming. *Proceedings ECAI'2000*, 599-603.

Ginsberg, M. L. (1993). *Dynamic backtracking. Journal of Artificial Intelligence Research*, 1, 25–46.

Glover, F., & Laguna, M. (1997). *Tabu Search*. Norwell, MA: Kluwer Academic Publishers. doi:10.1007/978-1-4615-6089-0

Gonzalez. (2007). Handbook of Approximation Algorithms and Metaheuristics. Chapman & Hall/CRC.

Hansen, P., & Mladenovic, N. (2009). Variable neighborhood search methods .In Encyclopedia of Optimization, Second Edition, (pp. 3975-3989). doi:10.1007/978-0-387-74759-0_694

P. V. Hentenryck (Ed.). (2002). Principles and Practice of Constraint Programming - CP 2002. In *Proceedings of 8th International Conference, CP 2002* (vol. 2470). Ithaca, NY: Springer. 10.1007/3-540-46135-3

Kirkpatrick, S., Jr., & Vecchi, M. P. (1983a). Optimization by simulatedannealing. *Science*, *220*, 671-680.

Kiziltan, Z. (2004). *Symmetry Breaking Ordering Constraints* (Doctoral dissertation). Retrieved from www.diva-portal.org/smash/get/diva2:164039/FULLTEXT01.pdf

Laurière, J. (1978). A language and a program for stating and solving combinatorial problems. *Artificial Intelligence*, *10*(1), 29-127.

Lawler, E. L., & Wood, D. E. (1966). Branch-and-bound methods: A survey. *Operations Research*, *14*(4), 699–719. doi:10.1287/opre.14.4.699

Lecoutre, C. (2013). Constraint Networks: Targeting Simplicity for Techniques and Algorithms. ISTE. Wiley.

Luke, S. (2013). *Essentials of Metaheuristics*. Lulu. Available at https://cs.gmu.edu/~sean/book/metaheuristics/

Marmion, M., Jourdan, L., & Dhaenens, C. (2013). Fitness landscape analysis and metaheuristics efficiency. *Journal of Mathematical Modelling & Algorithms, 12*, 3-26.

Marmion, M.-E., Dhaenens, C., Jourdan, L., Liefooghe, A., & Verel, S. (2012). Conception de recherche locale en présence de neutralité. In Proceedings ROADEF 2012: 13rd congres of the French Society of Operational Research and Decision Support (Société Française de Recherche Opérationnelle et d'Aide à la Décision). Angers, France: Academic Press.

Marmion, M.-E., Jourdan, L., & Dhaensen, C. (2013). Fitness Landscape Analysis and Metaheuristics Efficiency. *Journal of Mathematical Modelling and Algorithms*, *12*(1), 3–26.

Mears, C., de la Banda, M. G., Demoen, B., & Wallace, M. (2014). Lightweight dynamic symmetry breaking. *Constraints*, *19*(3), 195–242. doi:10.100710601-013-9154-2

Mladenovic, N., & Hansen, P. (1997). *Variable neighborhood search. Computers & Operations Research Journal, 24*, 1097-1100.

Neveu, B., & Trombettoni, G. (2003). Incop: An open library for incompletecombinatorial optimization. In Proceedings CP, (909-913). Springer.

Neveu, B., Trombettoni, G., & Glover, F. (2004). Idwalk: A candidate liststrategy with a simple diversification device. In Proceedings CP (pp. 423-437). Springer Berlin Heidelberg.

Osman, I. H., & Laporte, G. (1996). Metaheuristics: A bibliography. *Annals of Operations Research*, *63*(5), 513–623. doi:10.1007/BF02125421

Papadimitriou, C., & Steiglitz, K. (1998). *Combinatorial Optimization: Algorithms and Complexity*. Dover Publications.

Puget, J.-F. (2006). An efficient way of breaking value symmetries. AAAI, 117–122.

Régin, J.-C. (1994). A filtering algorithm for constraints of difference in CSPs. Proceedings AAAI-94, 362-367.

Régin, J-C. (2003). Global Constraints and Filtering Algorithms. In *Constraints and Integer Programming Combined*. Kluwer.

Régin, J-C. (2011). Global Constraints: a survey. In *Hybrid Optimization*. Springer.

Rossi, F., van Beek, P., & Walsh, T. (2006). *Handbook of Constraint Programming. Foundations Artificial Intelligence*. New York, NY: Elsevier Science Inc.

Schrijver, Z. (1986). *Theory of Linear and Integer Programming*. New York, NY: John Wiley & Sons, Inc.

Sörensen, K., & Glover, F. W. (2013). Metaheuristics. In S. I. Gass & M. C. Fu (Eds.), *Encyclopedia of Operations Research and Management Science*. Boston, MA: Springer. doi:10.1007/978-1-4419-1153-7_1167

Stützle, T. (1998). *Local Search Algorithms for Combinatorial Problems -- Analysis, Improvements, and New Applications* (PhD thesis). Darmstadt University of Technology, Department of Computer Science.

Voß, S., Martello, S., Osman, I. H., & Roucairol, C. (1999). *Metaeuristics-Advances and Trends in Local Search Paradigms for Optimization*. Dordrecht, The Netherlands: Kluwer Academic Publishers.

Winston, W. (1991). Introduction to mathematical programming: applications and algorithms. Business Statistics. PWS-Kent Publishing Company.

Winston, W. L. (2004). *Operations Research. Applications and Algorithms*. Thomson Business Press.

Winston. (2002). Book reviews: Introduction to mathematical programming, applications and algorithms (second edition). Math. Comput. Educ., 36(1), 85-87.

Wolsey, L. (1998). Integer Programming. Wiley-Interscience Publication.

Xin-She, Y. (2010). *Engineering Optimization: An Introduction with Metaheuristic Applications* (1st ed.). Wiley Publishing.

ENDNOTE

1 NP-Problem is a problem whose no polynomial algorithm is given; its resolution time is characterized unbounded or exponential.

Chapter 3
Portfolio Design Models:
Mathematical Models Proposal

ABSTRACT

This chapter applies different models to the financial portfolio design problem that affect assignment of assets to portfolios subject to a compromise between maximizing gains and minimizing losses. This practical problem appears in financial engineering, such as in the design of a CDO Squared portfolio. The aim of the authors is to propose and to solve a general model corresponding to the problem, within well classified assets. The authors express the diversification problem through a panoply of models such as the set model, matricial model, and MiniZinc model. These models represent an optimized problem of building efficient financial portfolios by maximizing the diversification rate. As long as the diversification rate is increased, the profit is increased, and the risk rate is decreased.

INTRODUCTION

Beyond our complex world and the highly complicated problems which need a resolution, scientists focus on efficient solving techniques to make our lives easier. Before solving, the first and basic step of the resolution process is understanding the problem, followed by the step of modeling, which should provide a thoughtful and equivalent model.

DOI: 10.4018/978-1-7998-1882-3.ch003

It is amazing when we succeed in translating a long text that describes a complicated problem, into a model composed of variables and constraints. It is very helpful when a problem which is described through a text, is represented by a mathematical model. This model will allow us to apply an appropriate resolution, to reach the desired solution.

In this chapter, we present modeling tools of the Portfolio Design (PD) problem, namely set models, matricial model and MiniZinc model. These models are the result of a good understanding of the complex financial problem, which consists in building an optimized CDO Squared portfolio. As given in Chapter 1, the resolution problem is based on statistical and probabilistic approaches, which makes a degree of uncertainty in the computed portfolio. The proposed models in this chapter should add an exact aspect which is founded on the notions of proved Operations Research.

In this chapter, we describe mathematical models which are applied to a model which is firstly revealed in (Flener, Pearson & Reyna, 2004), where Constraint Programming techniques are applied to solve the portfolio design problem.

The reader will find a detailed description of all the proposed models. We start by presenting the set model, which interprets the main problem of diversification in a financial portfolio design. This model is based on BIBD structure (Charles & Jeffrey, 2006). Thereafter, we introduce the matricial model, which is based on a 0-1 matrix structure. This model represents thoroughly the description of the problem. The strongest symmetrical aspect of the problem offers the opportunity to solve it by applying various techniques of symmetry breaking. This 0-1 model highlights different symmetry properties of the Portfolio Design Problem. It allows us to tackle the different symmetries by applying symmetry breaking techniques coming from the Constraint Programming discipline. Since the majority of Operations Research solvers admits the MiniZinc models, we introduce the corresponding model of the 0-1 model in MiniZinc language (Flener & Monette, 2015). In the other words, having the MiniZinc model is generally a meaningful input in the implementation phase. As cited below, the (PD) problem is strongly symmetrical, therefore definitions of some types of symmetries and some symmetry breaking techniques are introduced. Breaking symmetries should boost the applied approaches to yield optimized results while minimizing the CPU-time.

This chapter is organized as follows. In section 2, we introduce the set model which is based on BIBD model. In the second section, the adopted and tackled model is described in detail. We propose a matricial model, which verifies the original problem via linear and quadratic constraints. A translation of the model into MiniZinc language is also given in this section. In section 3, the symmetrical nature of the (PD) problem is highlighted, by introducing the noticed symmetries on the matricial model. Finally, we conclude the chapter.

BACKGROUND

The majority of proposed models for CDO or CDO squared are based on the analysis of the financial portfolio, more than on the portfolio building. Generally, financiers use many complex formulas coming from mathematics, statistics and probabilities, which are difficult to handle during the portfolio manipulation. Moreover, the pricing step is more highlighted than the way that the portfolio should be built (Rubinstein,2002; Reza,Banafsheh, Meisam &Fatemeh, 2016; Markowitz, 1952; Markowitz, 1959; Ida, 2003; Maknickiene, 2013; Nasr,, Sobhiyah & Yousefi, 2016; Spuchľakova, Frajtova & Mišanková, 2015)

Measuring the rate risks takes much space in the research works of financiers, economists and mathematicians. Thus, each proposed specialized article, technical report or book, generally takes into account the type of risks and the type of the financial institution. In this book, we propose models and solving techniques to build a balanced portfolio in its general definition. The model that we propose in this chapter should be very useful for all kinds of financial institutions.

First of all, Flener et al. worked on the general CDO Structure and how to exploit its two-layer structure, to construct a balanced financial portfolio (Flener, Pearson & Reyna, 2004; Olof,2005; Flener, Pearson, Reyna & Sivertsson, 2007). They proposed a mathematical model based on sets and different exact approaches to solve the problem.

They highlighted the existing similarities between (PD) problem and the well-known problem Balanced Incomplete Block Design (BIBD), which is defined as follows:

Figure 1. Incidence matrix for the $BIBD\langle 7,7,3,1\rangle$ *(Flener et al., 2007)*

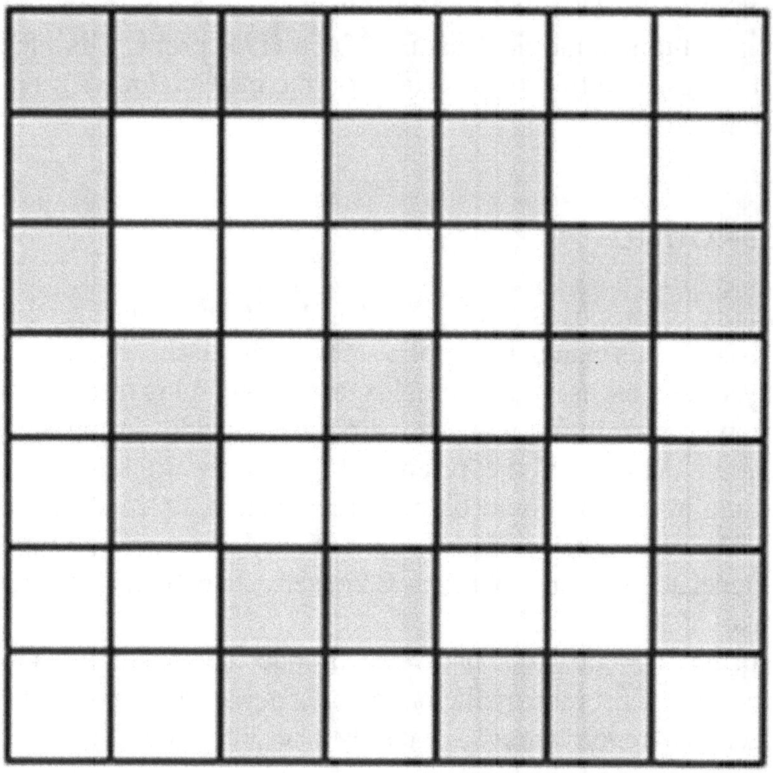

Definition 3.1 (Balanced Incomplete Block Design BIBD)
Let $V=\{1,\dots,v\}$ be any set of v elements, called *varieties*. Let $B=\{1,\dots,b\}$. A *balanced incomplete block design* $BIBD\langle v,b,r,\lambda\rangle$ consists of b sets $B_1,\dots,B_b$, called *blocks*, each being a k-element subset of V, with $2\leq k<v$ such that each pair of distinct varieties occurs together in exactly λ blocks. This is called the *balancing condition* and we here call λ the *overlap*.

Figure 1 shows the incidence matrix representing the $BIBD\langle 7,7,3,1\rangle$ instance of the BIBD problem. Where the columns are called blocks and rows co-blocks, grey cells represent $M_{ij}=1$ and white cells represent $M_{ij}=0$.

According to Definition 3.1 and Figure 1, $BIBD\langle v,b,r,\lambda\rangle$ could be modeled by a set model (Model 3.1), where the relationships on and between the sets V and B are as follows:

V_i: called co-block is the set of the indices of the blocks $V_i=\{j\in B|\ i\in B_j\}$.
$|V_i|=r$: the r elements of V_i constitute a subset of B.

$|B_j|=b$: the b elements of B_j constitute a subset of V.
$|V_i \cap V_k| = \lambda$: the sets V_i and V_k share exactly λ elements.

More formally, a $BIBD\langle v,b,r,\lambda\rangle$ problem consists in the following set model:

$$BIBD\langle v,b,r,\lambda\rangle \left| \begin{array}{l} \forall j \in B : B_j \subseteq V \\ \forall i \in V : V_i \subseteq B \\ \forall j \in B : |B_j| = k \\ \forall i \in V : |V_i| = r \\ \forall i \neq k \in V : |V_i \cap V_k| = \lambda \end{array} \right. \quad (3.1)$$

If we project the definition of the *BIBD* problem on the instance $BIBD\langle 7,7,3,1\rangle$ given in Figure 3.1, we deduce that:

- $\forall i \in 1..7$, $|V_i|=r=3$, with $V_1=\{1,2,3\}$, $V_2=\{1,4,5\}$, $V_3=\{1,6,7\}$, $V_4=\{2,4,6\}$, $V_5=\{2,5,7\}$, $V_6=\{3,4,7\}$ and $V_7=\{3,5,6\}$
- $\forall j \in 1..7$, $|B_j|=k=3$, with $B_1=\{1,2,3\}$, $B_2=\{1,4,5\}$, $B_3=\{1,6,7\}$, $B_4=\{2,4,6\}$, $B_5=\{2,5,7\}$, $B_6=\{3,4,7\}$ and $B_7=\{3,5,6\}$
- $\forall i,k \in 1..7, i \neq k : |V_i \cap V_j| = \lambda = 1$

There are some properties or admissibility conditions which should be verified for BIBDs (Hall, 1964; Colbourn & Dinitz, 1996), which are given in the mathematical relations (3.3), (3.4) and (3.5), given below:

$$\lambda < r \quad (3.3)$$

$$vr = bk \quad (3.4)$$

$$r(k-1) = \lambda(v-1) \quad (3.5)$$

The pairwise overlap between any two co-blocks V_i and V_k with $i \neq k$ is captured by the matrix product:

$$MM^T = \begin{pmatrix} r & \lambda & \lambda & \cdots & \lambda \\ \lambda & r & \lambda & \cdots & \lambda \\ \lambda & \lambda & r & \cdots & \lambda \\ \vdots & \vdots & \vdots & r & \vdots \\ \lambda & \lambda & \lambda & \cdots & r \end{pmatrix}$$

From MM^T, the Fisher's inequality (Relation (3.6)) for BIBDs is deduced, as given in Proposition 3.1 (Hall, 1964) as follows:

Proposition 3.1
For any $BIBD\langle v,b,r,\lambda\rangle$ *we must have*

$$b \geq v \tag{3.6}$$

When the M is a square matrix or v = b, the following Proposition 3.2 (Hall, 1964) can be proved by using Lagrange's four-squares theorem.

Proposition 3.2
For any $BIBD\langle v,b,r,\lambda\rangle$ *with v = b, we must have*

for v even: $\exists x \in \mathbb{Z} : x^2 = k - \lambda$ (3.7)

for v odd: $\exists x, y, z \in \mathbb{Z} : z^2 = (k-1)x^2 + (-1)^{(v-1)/2} \lambda y^2, \text{with } x \neq 0$ (3.8)

BIBD is a structure which represents two types of symmetries: row symmetries and column symmetries in order of $v!b!$. Breaking all these symmetries can be realized by adding $v!b!-1$ lexicographical ordering constraints (Flener, Frisch, Hnich, Jefferson, Kiziltan, Miguel, Pearson & Walsh, 2003).

From the BIBD structure, the authors proposed in (Flener et al., 2004) a set mathematical model to designate the Optimization Portfolio Design (OPD) problem as follows (Definition 3.2):

Definition 3.2
Let $V=\{1,\ldots,v\}$ be any set of v elements, called varieties. Let $B=\{1,\ldots,b\}$. A portfolio design $(PD)\langle v,b,r,\lambda\rangle$ consists of v sets $V_1,\ldots,V_v$, called co-blocks, each being an r-element subset of B, such that any two co-blocks with distinct

indices share at most λ elements. This is called the balancing condition and we call λ the maximum overlap.

A $PD\langle v,b,r,\lambda\rangle$ problem consists in the following five set constraints, given in Model (3.9).

$$(PD)\langle v,b,r,\lambda\rangle \left| \begin{array}{l} \forall j \in B : B_j \subseteq V \\ \forall i \in V : V_i \subseteq B \\ \forall j \in B : |B_j| \leq v \\ \forall i \in V : |V_i| = r \\ \forall i \neq k \in V : |V_i \cap V_k| \leq \lambda \end{array} \right. \tag{3.9}$$

$PD\langle v,b,r,\lambda\rangle$ differs from $BIBD\langle v,b,r,\lambda\rangle$ by two points:

- Two co-blocks share at most, rather than exactly λ elements.
- The cardinalities of the blocks B_j can have the values in the interval 0,…,*v*, rather than exactly a fixed value *k*.

By considering S_{BIBD} and S_{PD} respectively, the search spaces of $BIBD\langle v,b,r,\lambda\rangle$ and $PD\langle v,b,r,\lambda\rangle$, we deduce that *BIBD* can be seen as a special case of *PD*, since $S_{BIBD} \subset S_{PD}$. Nevertheless, some *PD*s are actually *BIBD*s, which occurs when *b* divides *rv* and any two co-blocks with distinct indices share exactly λ elements. The observed similarities and differences, existing between the both structures, are exploited successfully, which yields satisfactory results.

Solving a $PD\langle v,b,r,\lambda\rangle$ is considered as a Constraint Satisfaction problem, with *v*, *b* and *r* the fixed parameters, and λ a minimum value to find. Thus, an OPD problem is introduced via Definition 3.3, as an Optimization Constraint problem.

Definition 3.3

Let *V*={1,…,*v*} be any set of v elements, called varieties. Let *B*={1,…,*b*}. An optimal portfolio design $(OPD)\langle v,b,r,\lambda\rangle$ consists of v sets $V_1,\ldots,V_v$, called co-blocks, each being an r-element subset of B, such that any two co-blocks with distinct indices share at most λ elements, where λ is minimal.

From Definition 3.3, we propose formally the (OPD) problem through the following model (3.10).

$$(OPD)\langle v,b,r\rangle \left| \begin{array}{l} \min(\lambda) \\ \hline \forall j \in B : B_j \subseteq V \\ \forall i \in V : V_i \subseteq B \\ \forall j \in B : |B_j| \leq v \\ \forall i \in V : |V_i| = r \\ \forall i \neq k \in V : |V_i \cap V_k| \leq \lambda \end{array} \right. \tag{3.10}$$

The researches succeeded in computing a lower bound on λ as given by Constraint (3.11) in Theorem 3.1[1].

Theorem 3.1

Let $V_1,\ldots,V_v$ be r-element sets and B be their union, with $b=|B|$. If $|V_i \cap V_j| \leq \lambda$ for all $i \neq j$, then

$$\lambda \geq \frac{\left\lceil \frac{rv}{b} \right\rceil^2 \bmod(rv,b) + \left\lfloor \frac{rv}{b} \right\rfloor^2 (b - \bmod(rv,b)) - rv}{v(v-1)} \tag{3.11}$$

Thus, they come back to a constraint satisfaction problem by modifying the last constraint of the model (3.10), which gives rise to the following model (3.12).

$$(PD)\langle v,b,r,\lambda\rangle \left| \begin{array}{l} \forall j \in B : B_j \subseteq V \\ \forall i \in V : V_i \subseteq B \\ \forall j \in B : |B_j| \leq v \\ \forall i \in V : |V_i| = r \\ \forall i \neq k \in V : |V_i \cap V_k| = \lambda \end{array} \right. \tag{3.12}$$

For several reasons, Flener et al. have suggested that a tighter lower bound ought to exist, though it is considered an open question whether there is a tighter lower bound that is easy to compute.

They have proposed many approaches based on Constraint Programming techniques to solve the (PD) problem. In Background section in Chapter 5, we will introduce an overview of all these approaches, and more details will be given in the next section.

SET MODEL

The *(PD)* - Portfolio Design - model describes existing relationships between different tranches of the CDO^2. The CDO^2 Squared portfolio is divided into v tranches and each tranche contains r assets. Any two tranches share at most λ assets, called overlap.

In the given models in this book, the financial features of the CDO Squared instrument are verified. In the other words, financially, the size of the universe of assets is $250 \leq b \leq 500$. A typical portfolio is constrained by $4 \leq v \leq 25$ tranches, each of which is sized $r \approx 100$. The formal definition of the *(PD)* problem is given by Definition 3.2 and Model (3.9). The number of the selected assets from the existing assets' set, and the number r of the selected assets within a tranche, should be fixed by the financier.

The (OPD) optimization problem consists in minimizing λ such that given within Model (3.10). Nevertheless, after computing a lower bound of λ, subject to the *(PD)* constraints, as given in formula (3.11), a good bound makes *(PD)* model consistent, and λ is surely the best overlap value between the co-blocks.

In constraint programming, *(BIBD)* is well solved, even on large instances, due to an efficient exploitation of many symmetries in this problem. The (PD) problem is translated into BIBD problem, which is well solved by Constraint Programming techniques. Since solving big instances of (PD) proves difficult, a second proposition consists in decomposing a large instance of *(PD)* into multiple *(PD)* (Formula (3.13)) having small dimensions. $PD\langle v,b,r,\lambda\rangle$ is decomposed into m occurrences of $PD\langle v,b_1,r_1,\lambda_1\rangle$ and one occurrence $PD\langle v,b_2,r_2,\lambda_2\rangle$,which is denoted by:

$$PD\langle v,b,r,\lambda\rangle = m.PD\langle v,b_1,r_1,\lambda_1\rangle + PD\langle v,b_2,r_2,\lambda_2\rangle \tag{3.13}$$

This decomposition must respect some conditions:

- $0 \leq r_i \leq b_i \geq 1$ for $i=1,2$
- $b=m.b_1+b_2$
- $r=m.r_1+r_2$
- $\lambda \leq m.\lambda_1+\lambda_2$

For more details, we refer the reader to (Wetzel & Zabbata, 1998; Flener, Pearson & Reyna, 2004; Flener et al., 2007). Practically, when it succeeds,

Figure 2. Structure of ith inner portfolio

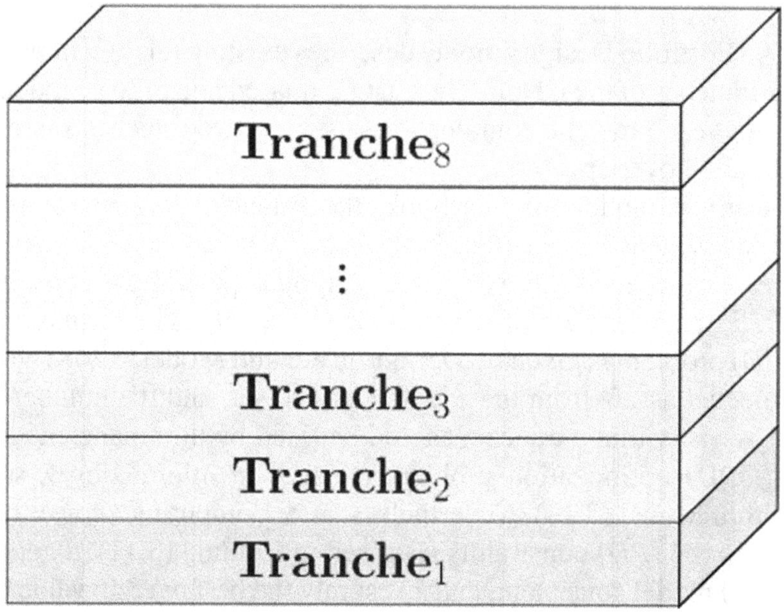

this decomposition based method enables finding one solution. When the applied resolution technique fails (no solution is found), there is nothing to say about the consistency of the problem. This is exactly the behavior of local search approaches. Therefore, a general framework of local search algorithms is investigated in this book (Chapters 6 and 7) to solve the problem within its matricial version.

MATRICIAL 0-1 MODEL OF THE PORTFOLIO DESIGNS

Starting from a set model, we deduce the corresponding matrix model, based on quadratic constraints and defined on 0-1 domain. The portfolio design *OPD* consists of v tranches of assets $V_1, V_2, \ldots, V_v$; in each tranche there are r assets chosen from b portfolios, called row constraint. We call balanced condition or overlap constraint, each pair of tranches have at most λ elements in common, called overlaps. Solving *(PD)* consists in finding the matrix $M(v \times b)$, such that each row contains at most r units, and the overlapping between any two rows is less than λ. As given above, the parameters v, b and r must be fixed by a specialized financier.

Figure 3. Optimized of selecting assets through eight inner portfolios and ten tranches

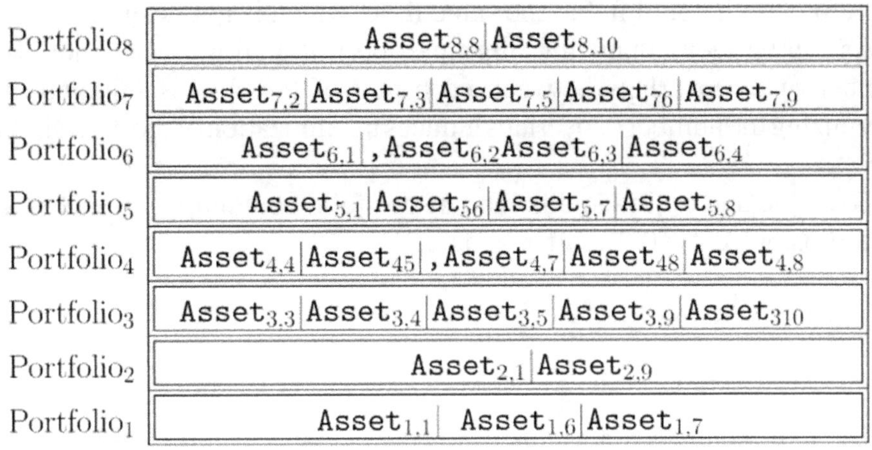

For a better understanding, let be a small instance of CDO Squared portfolio which includes 8 inner CDO portfolios (b=8). Each inner portfolio constituted of 10 tranches (v=10). Each tranche corresponds to a specific class of assets.

The ith inner portfolio as illustrated in Figure 2 is well diversified since the containing assets come from various tranches. This structure gives the first level of diversification.

To increase the diversification rate, in the building of an optimized portfolio, we have to select assets from:

- different inner portfolios to yield the highest diversification rate of CDO Squared portfolio.
- different tranches, which provides a high diversification rate over each inner CDO portfolio.

From a financial point of view, if the CDO Squared portfolio contains 8 inner portfolios, which are each structured in 10 tranches, we should necessarily and exactly choose 3 assets from each tranche coming from different 3 inner portfolios. Thus, the CDO Squared portfolio will be composed of 3×10=30 diversified assets. This portfolio is described by $OPD\langle 8,3,2\rangle$.

In Figure 3.3, we illustrate a selection of assets which should be contained in the studied portfolio. We define by $Asset_{i,j}$ the asset that belongs to the portfolio i and the tranche j. To maximize the diversification rate, we should minimize the assets shared by each pair of tranches, which is called minimizing the number of overlaps of each pair of tranches. Indeed, selecting two assets from the same portfolio implies that the assets share critical financial features. Therefore, both could fall at the same time, which is not desired.

As can be seen, analyzing this small portfolio allows verification if the number of the overlaps between each pair of tranches is minimal. Thus, minimizing the number of overlaps induces maximization of the diversification rate.

To tackle and optimize this kind of portfolio containing v tranches and b portfolios, we use a 0-1 matrix, where:

$$M_{i,j} = \begin{cases} 1 \text{ if the } Asset_{i,j} \text{ is selected} \\ 0 \text{ else} \end{cases}$$

The row indices I represents the ith tranche and the column indices j the jth inner portfolio.

In Figure 3.4, we have the matricial structure of the illustrated solution of $OPD\langle 8,3,2 \rangle$ in Figure 3.3. In this figure, we notice the overlapping rate is λ=2. Thus, we obtain the portfolio $PD\langle 10,8,3,2 \rangle$, which is the optimized one because the overlapping is optimum, according to Formula (3.11).

As we can see, in Figure 3.2 we have one overlap between tranches 1 and 2, two overlaps between tranches 7 and 8 and 0 overlap between tranches 8 and 9.

Consequently, optimizing a CDO Squared portfolio structured characterized by v tranches, b portfolios, r selected assets per tranche and λ optimized overlapping, noted by $PD\langle v,b,r,\lambda \rangle$,is formally modeled via the 0-1 matricial model (Model (3.14)) as follows:

$$PD\langle v,b,r,\lambda \rangle \begin{cases} \forall i \in 1..v, \sum_{j \in 1..b} M_{ij} = r \\ \forall i \in 1..v, \forall k > i, \sum_{j \in 1..b} M_{ij} M_{kj} \leq \lambda \\ \hline \forall i \in 1..v, \forall j \in 1..b, M_{ij} \in \{0,1\} \end{cases} \tag{3.14}$$

The (OPD) optimization problem consists in minimizing λ -- the number of overlaps, under the constraints of (PD)(Model(3.15)):

$$(OPD\langle v,b,r,\lambda \rangle) \begin{cases} \min \lambda \\ \hline (PD) \end{cases} \tag{3.15}$$

Figure 4. Example of matricial structure of (PD) model

	$Portfolio_1$	$Portfolio_2$	$Portfolio_3$	$Portfolio_4$	$Portfolio_5$	$Portfolio_6$	$Portfolio_7$	$Portfolio_8$
$Tranche_1$	1	1	0	0	0	1	0	0
$Tranche_2$	0	0	0	0	1	1	1	0
$Tranche_3$	0	0	1	0	0	1	1	0
$Tranche_4$	0	0	1	0	1	1	0	0
$Tranche_5$	0	0	1	1	0	0	1	0
$Tranche_6$	1	0	0	0	1	0	1	0
$Tranche_7$	1	0	0	1	1	0	0	0
$Tranche_8$	0	0	0	1	1	0	0	1
$Tranche_9$	1	1	0	0	0	0	1	0
$Tranche_{10}$	0	0	1	1	0	0	0	1

The *(PD)* problem is a Constraint Satisfaction Problem, whereas *(OPD)* is an optimization problem. The *(OPD)* problem is the most challenging, where minimizing the overlaps between the rows (tranches) makes the constructed CDO-squared tranches stronger. As known in the Operations Research field, this model is hard to solve because it contains quadratic constraints and is defined on {0,1} domain. Therefore, we propose in the next chapter, an efficient linearization to the model.

Since MiniZinc modeling is supported by various solvers coming from Operations Research, we introduce below the corresponding MiniZinc model conceived for the model (3.15) (Flener &Monette,2015).

MINIZINC-Model OPDModel

```
include "lex_greatereq.mnz";
%instance data
int: v;
int: b;
int: r;
set of int: rows = 1..v;
set of int: cols = 1..b;
%computing a lower bound for lambda
int: rv = r*v;
int: rvmdb = rv mod b;
int: floorrv = rv div b;
int: ceilrv = rv div b + bool2int(rv mod b != 0);
int: num = (ceilrv*ceilrv*rvmod+floorrv*floorrv*(b-rvmodb)-rv);
int: denom = v*(v-1);
int: lb_lambda=num div denom + bool2int(num mod denom !=0);

%lambda is called objective for the minizinc challenge
var lb_lambda..b: objective;

array [rows, cols] of var 0..1: m;

%every row must sum to r
constraint forall (i in rows) (sum (j in cols) (m[i,j])=r);

%the dot product of every pair of distinct rows must be at most
lambda for e
an opd and pd, and equal to lambda for a bibd
constraint forall (i_a, i_b in rows where i_a < i_b) (
sum (j in cols) (m[i_a,j]*m[i_b,j]) <= objective);

%break row symmetry in the incidence matrix
constraint symmetry_ breaking_constraint(
  forall(i in rows diff {max(rows)})(
    lex_greatereq([m[i,j] | j in cols], [m[i+1,j]| j in cols]
  )
);
%break column symmetry in the incidence matrix
constraint symmetry_breaking_constraint(
  forall(j in cols diff {max(cols)})(
    lax_greatereq([m[i,j] | i in rows], [m[i,j+1] | i in rows])
  )
);

Solve:: seq_search([int_search([m[i,j] | i in rows, j in cols],
input_order, indomain_max,complete),
int_search([int_search([objective], input_order, indomain_min,
```

```
complete)]
minimize objective;
;
```

The 0-1 matrix model allows us to apply a panoply of techniques coming from different categories, and to exploit their strong points. For instance, applying local search techniques proves very efficient compared to the systematic approach, regarding the efficiency of the resulted portfolio and the realized CPU-time. The symmetric nature of the problem is well observed and modeled within the matricial model, which is easily considered and tackled by Linear programming and Constraint Programming disciplines. We highlight that applying symmetry breaking techniques allows minimizing the CPU-time.

Expressing the (OPD) problem in MiniZinc language (OPDModel), allows application of Constraint Based Local Search techniques, which often outperform exact methods in numerous cases, even on large instances.

SYMMETRIES ANALYSIS

Symmetry is one of the critical topics in Constraint Programming (CP) and Operational Research (OR), becoming a research field in its own right; as introduced previously, the (PD) model is strongly symmetrical. We have detected three symmetries:

- Column symmetry, which is expressed and proved in chapter 4 and chapter 5. This symmetry can be broken statically, by integrating new constraints in the original model. We integrate constraints to impose the lexicographical order between the matrix column (Kiziltan, 2004).
- Row symmetry, described in chapter 4 and chapter 5. This symmetry is modelled by constraints imposing lexicographical order onthe matrix rows(Kiziltan, 2004).
- 180° rotation symmetry, which will be eliminated by dynamic techniques (Gent& Smith,1999).

Including symmetry breaking techniques in resolution approaches should decrease the run-time realized before. All the detected symmetries will be described and proved in Chapter 5. The corresponding symmetry breaking techniques will be implemented and described in detail in chapters 4 and 5.

$$OPD_{sym}\langle v,b,r\rangle = \begin{cases} \min \lambda \\ \forall i \in 1..v, \sum_{j\in 1..b} M_{ij} = r \\ \forall i \in 1..v, \forall k > i, \sum_{j\in 1..b} M_{ij}M_{kj} \leq \lambda \\ \forall i \in 1..v, \forall j \in 1..b, M_{ij} \in \{0,1\} \\ \hline \forall i \in 1..v-1, \sum_{j=1}^{b} M_{ij}2^{(j-1-b)} \leq \sum_{j=1}^{b} M_{i+1,j}2^{(j-1-b)} \\ \forall j \in 1..b-1, \sum_{i=1}^{v} M_{ij}2^{(i-1-v)} \leq \sum_{i=1}^{v} M_{i,j+1}2^{(i-1-v)} \end{cases} \quad (3.16)$$

All these observed symmetries on the (PD) problem, precisely within the matricial model, are detailed and proved in Chapter 4 and Chapter 5.

CONCLUSION

In this chapter, we described different mathematical models corresponding to the Portfolio Design (PD) problem, which consists in a process of the selection of assets in order to build an optimized portfolio. The contrast of minimizing risks and maximizing gains, is solved by giving a balance between the risk rate and the portfolio profit. This balance is modelled via an objective function which aims to minimize the overlapping. As overlapping is decreased, the diversification rate is increased. The optimum diversification guarantees the optimality of the portfolio.

To tackle the problem of the trade-off research risks and profitability, we presented a 0-1 matricial model which is easier to tackle by different techniques coming from the Operations Research discipline. This model stands for many types of symmetries, which could be exploited to reduce the run-time and improve the efficiency of the applied approaches.

We introduced the (OPD) model extended with lexicographical ordering constraints, to eliminate statically the detected row and column symmetries. The 180° rotation symmetry was not handled in this chapter, because it should be broken by dynamic techniques based on Constraint Programming techniques (Chapter 2). It will be further detailed in Chapter 5.

In this book we focused on the utilization of the 0-1 model (matricial model), because of its flexibility to be tackled by numerous approaches coming from different categories of methods. Thereby, the symmetric property of (OPD) is easily and specifically handled by Constraint Programming techniques.

The following chapter will outline the state of the art of the exact methods, such as Linear Programming and Constraint Programming approaches.

REFERENCES

Benhamou, B. (1994). Study of symmetry in constraint satisfaction problems. *Proceedings of CP-94, Lecture Notes in Computer Science*, 246-254.

Benhamou, B., & Saïdi, M. R. (2007). Local symmetry breaking during search in CSPs. *Principles and Practice of Constraint Programming - CP 2007, 13th International Conference, CP 2007 Proceedings*, 195-*209*. 10.1007/978-3-540-74970-7_16

Colbourn & Dinitz. (2006). Handbook of Combinatorial Designs (2nd ed.). Chapman & Hall/CRC.

Flener, P., Frisch, A., Hnich, B., Jefferson, C., Kiziltan, Z., Miguel, I., ... Walsh, T. (2003). Breaking symmetries in matrix models: Abrief overview. *Proceedings of the Tenth Workshop on Automated Reasoning*, 27-28.

Flener, P., Frisch, A. M., Hnich, B., Kiziltan, Z., Miguel, I., Pearson, J., & Walsh, T. (2001). Symmetry in matrix models. *Proceedings of the CP'01. Workshop on Symmetry in Constraints*, 41-48.

Flener, P., Frisch, A. M., Hnich, B., Kiziltan, Z., Miguel, I., Pearson, J., & Walsh, T. (2002). Breaking row and column symmetries in matrix models. Lecture Notes in Computer Science, 462–476. doi:10.1007/3-540-46135-3_31

Flener, P., & Monette, J. N. (2015). *Problem 065: Optimal Financial Portfolio Design*. Retrieved 2015, from http://www.csplib.org/Problems/prob065/

Flener, P., Pearson, J., & Reyna, L. G. (2004). Financial portfolio optimization. *LNCS, 3258*, 227–241.

Flener, P., Pearson, J., Reyna, L. G., & Sivertsson, O. (2007). Design of financialcdo squared transactions using constraint programming. *Constraints, 12*(2), 179–205. doi:10.100710601-006-9014-4

Gent, I. P., Harvey, W., Kelsey, T., & Linton, S. (2003). Generic SBDD using computational group theory. *Principles and Practice of ConstraintProgramming - CP 2003, 9th International Conference, CP 2003, Proceedings*, 333-*347*.

Gent, I. P., & Smith, B. (1999). Symmetry breaking during search in constraint programming. *Proceedings ECAI'2000*, 599-603.

Ida, M. (2003). Portfolio Selection Problem with Interval Coefficients. *Applied Mathematics Letters*, *16*(5), 709–713. doi:10.1016/S0893-9659(03)00071-5

Kiziltan, Z. (2004). *Symmetry Breaking Ordering Constraints* (Doctoral dissertation). Retrieved from www.diva-portal.org/smash/get/diva2:164039/FULLTEXT01.pdf

Maknickiene, N. (2013). Selection of Orthogonal Investment Portfolio Using Evolino RNN Trading Model. *Procedia: Social and Behavioral Sciences*, *110*. doi:10.1016/j.sbspro.2013.12.962

Markowitz, H. (1952). Portfolio Selection. *The Journal of Finance*, *7*(1), 77–91. doi:10.2307/2975974

Markowitz, H. M. (1959). *Portfolio Selection: Efficient Diversification of Investments*. New York: John Wiley & Sons.

Marshall Hall, J. (1964). *Block Designs*. Wiley.

Mears, C., de la Banda, M. G., Demoen, B., & Wallace, M. (2014). Lightweight dynamic symmetry breaking. *Constraints*, *19*(3), 195–242. doi:10.100710601-013-9154-2

Nasr, E. H., Sobhiyah, M. H., & Yousefi, V. (2016). Project Portfolio Selection via Harmony Search Algorithm and Modern Portfolio Theory. *Procedia: Social and Behavioral Sciences*, *226*, 51–58. doi:10.1016/j.sbspro.2016.06.161

Puget, J.-F. (2006). An efficient way of breaking value symmetries. AAAI, 117–122.

Reza, R., Banafsheh, F., Meisam, S., & Fatemeh, R. (2016). Study of the Relationship between Credit Diversification Strategy and Banks' Credit Risk and Return: Evidence from Tehran Stock Exchange (TSE). *Procedia Economics and Finance*, *36*, 62–69. doi:10.1016/S2212-5671(16)30016-8

Rodriguez, D., Cotta, C., & Fernandez, A. J. (2009). Finding Balanced Incomplete Block Designs with Metaheuristics. *Evolutionary Computation in combinatorial optimization: 9th European Conference, EvoCOP*, 156-167. 10.1007/978-3-642-01009-5_14

Rubinstein, M. (2002). Markowitz's "Portfolio Selection": A Fifty-Year Retrospective. *The Journal of Finance*, *57*(3), 1041–1045. doi:10.1111/1540-6261.00453

Spuchľakova, E., Frajtova, M. K., & Mišanková, M. (2015). Risk of the Collective Investment and Investment Portfolio. *Procedia Economics and Finance*, *26*, 167–173. doi:10.1016/S2212-5671(15)00910-7

Wetzel, G., & Zabbata, F. (1998). A constraint programming approach to portfolio selection. In H. Prade (Ed.), *13th European Conference on Artificial Intelligence, Proceedings*. John Wiley and Sons.

ENDNOTE

1 For more details, the proof is given in Flener, Pearson, and Reyna (2004).

Chapter 4
Linear Integer Programming Techniques for Portfolio Design Problem:
Linear Programming Approaches

ABSTRACT

This chapter introduces Integer Linear Programming (ILP) approaches for solving efficiently a ðnancial portfolio design problem. The authors proposed a matricial model in Chapter 3, which is a mathematical quadratic model. A linearization step is considered necessary to apply linear programming techniques. The corresponding matricial model shows clearly that the problem is strongly symmetrical. The row and column symmetries are easily handled by adding a negligible number of new constraints. The authors propose two linear models, which are given in detail and proven. These models represent the problem as linear constraint systems with 0-1 variables, which will be implemented in ILP solver. Experimental results in non-trivial instances of portfolio design problem are given.

INTRODUCTION

As given in Chapter 3, the financial problem tackled in this book is modeled in a 0-1 matricial model, which is linear and has quadratic constraints. Since the problem is quadratic, applying linear programming techniques turns out

DOI: 10.4018/978-1-7998-1882-3.ch004

to be impossible without transforming the problem into a linear problem. A linear model which is thoroughly equivalent to the quadratic model, without relaxing the space of solutions. Applying Linear Programming (LP) complete techniques provides us the desired optimum of the financial portfolio, which is a critical and crucial problem in finance. Financial institutions and clients should be satisfied through an optimized profit.

In this chapter, via the 0-1 quadratic model all the features of the portfolio are totally and precisely modeled, which allows us to reach the best overlapping rate. An efficient linearization method is applied to the model, in order to solve the problem with (LP) approaches.

Due to the strong symmetrical nature of the problem, we found that breaking the corresponding symmetries is achievable if we apply the Constraint (CP) static Symmetry Breaking techniques, which should be efficient in eliminating the no consistent values, and thus minimizing the CPU time.

This chapter is organized as follows. In section 2, we present the Linear Programming discipline and especially Simplex algorithm, the most useful algorithm on LP problems. In section 3, we present the linearization approach and its application result on the quadratic (PD) model. Row and column symmetries are broken and handled via lexicographic ordering constraints. In section 4, experimental results are presented and analyzed in depth. Finally, we conclude the chapter.

BACKGROUND

Linear Programming was used implicitly by Fourier in the early 1800s. However, it was at first formalized and applied to economic problems, by Leonid Kantorovich in the 1930s. Later, it was rediscovered and applied by Tjalling Koopmans, by tackling shipping problems in the 1940s. The first complete algorithm to solve linear programming problems was published by George Dantzig in 1947. Nevertheless, Koopmans was the one who proposed the name "Linear Programming" in discussion with Dantzig in 1948. Kantorovich and Koopmans shared the 1975 Nobel Prize in Economics for their contributions to the theory of optimum allocation of resources (Erickson, 2015). Whereas George Dantiz, who is the recognized inventor of the Simplex algorithm, was simply passed over by the Nobel awards committee, an act of stunning omission. Dantzig, the inventor of Linear Programming, was honored with the National Medal of Science in 1975. (Erickson, 2015; Nahin, 2007)

To apply linear programming techniques to solve a specific problem, we should model it in a Linear Program (LP) which is based on a linear function (Definition 4.1) and linear inequations (Definition 4.2) (Winston, 2004).

Definition-4.1 (Linear-Function)
A function $f(x_1,x_2,\ldots,x_n)$ of $x_1,x_2,\ldots,x_n$ is a linear function if and only if for some set of constants $c_1,c_2,\ldots,c_n$, $f(x_1,x_2,\ldots,x_n) = c_1x_1,c_2x_2,\ldots,c_nx_n$.

Definition 4.2 (Linear-Constraint)
For any linear function $f(x_1,x_2,\ldots,x_n)$ and any number b, the inequalities $f(x_1,x_2,\ldots,x_n)\leq b$ and $f(x_1,x_2,\ldots,x_n)\geq b$ are linear inequalities.

More precisely, an (LP) is composed of three parts as follows:

- n decision variables $x_1,x_2,\ldots,x_n$, which verify the condition $x_j \geq 0, j=\overline{1,n}$,
- an objective function, which interprets the optimization aspect of the problem. It can be:
  - a minimization function $\min Z=\sum_{j=1}^{n} c_j x_j$. It is used for instance in the case of optimizing the manufacturing time or manufacturing costs.
  - a maximizing function $\max Z=\sum_{j=1}^{n} c_j x_j$. It is used for instance in the case of optimizing the profit of the production or the production quantity.
- m linear constraints, which are linear equations or inequations as follows: $\sum_{j=1}^{m} a_{ij} x_j \leq b_i, i=\overline{1,m}$.

Consequently, a Linear Program is characterized by *1* objective function sub *m* linear constraints and *n* decision variables, which gives us the following model:

$$\max Z=\sum_{j=1}^{n} c_j x_j$$
$$s.c\begin{cases}\sum_{j=1}^{m} a_{ij} x_j \leq b_i, i=\overline{1,m} \\ x_j \geq 0, j=\overline{1,n}\end{cases} \quad (4.1)$$

The matricial version of Model (4.1) is deduced and introduced below:

$$\max\ z = CX$$
$$s.c\begin{cases} AX \le B \\ X \ge 0 \end{cases} \tag{4.2}$$

With:

$X = [x_1, x_2, \ldots, x_n]^T$

$C = [c_1, c_2, \ldots, c_n]$

$$A = \begin{bmatrix} a_{11} & a_{12} & \cdots & a_{1n} \\ a_{21} & a_{22} & \cdots & a_{2n} \\ \vdots & \vdots & \ddots & \vdots \\ a_{m1} & a_{m2} & \cdots & a_{mn} \end{bmatrix}$$

and B= $[b_1, b_2, \ldots, b_m]^T$

Example 4.1 (Graphical Resolution)
Let be a factory (Charon, Germa & Hudry, 1996) that produces two types of product P_1 and P_2 by using two machines M_1 and M_2. Each product must successively pass through M_1 and M_2, in indifferent order and taking the following times, in minutes:

	P_1	P_2
M_1	30	20
M_2	40	10

In addition, the machine M_1 is available for 6000min/month and M_2 is available for 4000min/month.

Monthly, the production of *1* product of P_1 provides \$400 and 1 product of P_2 provides \$200, of profit.

The head of the factory hopes to find the monthly manufacturing plan which allows him to maximize the factory profit.

To solve this problem, we must follow three steps:

1. Modeling the problem with PL format:
   We design the decision variables x and y which represent, respectively the number of products of P_1 and the number of P_2 product.
   The PL includes 2 decision variables, 1 objective function to maximize the profit, 1 constraint on the time of M_1 availability and 1 constraint on the time of M_2 availability. Thus, the corresponding PL is given by (PL_1) as follows:

$$\max\ z=400x+200y$$
$$\text{s.c}\begin{cases}30x+\ \ 20y\ \ \leq 6000\\40x+\ \ 10y\ \ \leq 4000\\ \quad x,\quad\ \ y\quad\ \ \geq 0\end{cases}\qquad (PL_1)$$

2. Solving the corresponding PL (PL_1):
   Since the problem has been modeled in two variables, we give the graphical resolution as follows:
   a. We start by drawing the constraints graphically, as illustrated in Figure 1.
      The points (x,y) belonging to the quadrilateral in gray ABCO represent the points which satisfy both of the constraints.
   b. The lines set $\Delta_\lambda = \{(x,y) |\ 400x+200y=\lambda\}$ is a set of parallel lines. If we fix λ to 40000 we obtain, as illustrated in Figure 4.2 the line in bold, which crosses the quadrilateral.
   c. We move the traced Δ_λ upwardly to approach more and more (Figure 2) the optimal solution. The last line among the lines Δ_λ which intersect the quadrilateral passes by the point B(20,240). This line represents the biggest value of λ=64000.
   d. The optimum of the problem is (x^*,y^*)=(20,240) with z^*=64000.
3. Interpreting the solution:
   According to the provided results, the factory should produce 20 products of P_1 and 240 products of $P_{2,}$ to have the optimal profit of $64000.

Through Example 4.1, we introduce a little of the terminology of linear programing. The quadrilateral in gray represents the feasible region (Definition 4.3) since all the points inside verify all the constraints. The optimal solution is the point of the feasible region which gives the biggest value to the objective function (Definition 4.4) (Winston, 2004).

Figure 1. Graphical representation of the constraints of (PL_1)

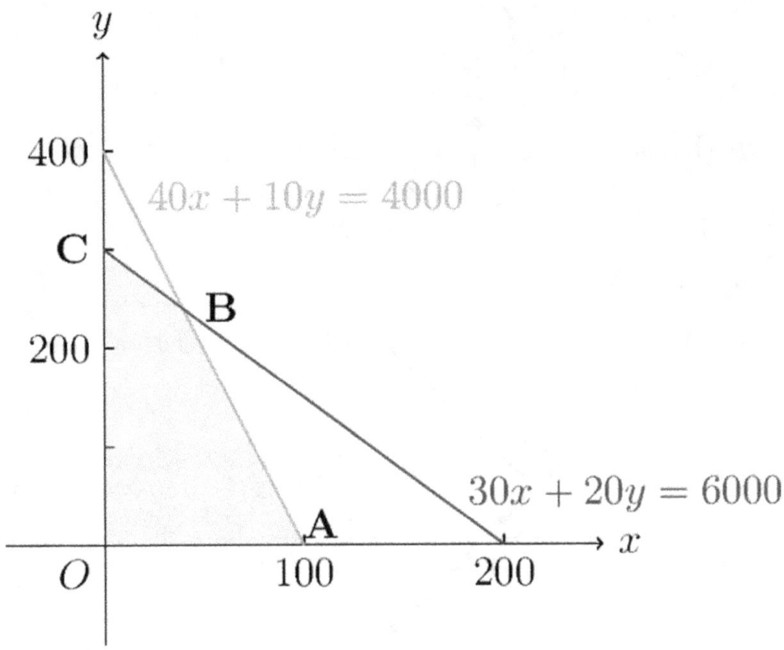

Definition 4.3 (Feasible Region)
The feasible region for an LP is the set of all points that satisfies all the LP's constraints and sign restrictions.

Definition 4.4 (Optimal Solution)
For a maximization problem, an optimal solution to an LP is a point in the feasible region with the largest objective function value. Similarly, for a minimization problem, an optimal solution is a point in the feasible region with the smallest objective function value.

Generally, LPs have only one optimal solution, but some particular situations deserve to be cited:

- An LP with an infinite number of optimal solutions (*alternative* or *multiple optimal solutions*).
- An LP with no feasible solutions, called infeasible problem.
- LPs with the unbounded feasible region, called unbounded problem.

Graphical resolution could be realized only on the problem with at most three variables. Thus, we need an algorithm which allows us to handle big

Figure 2. Graphical representation of the objective function of (PL_1)

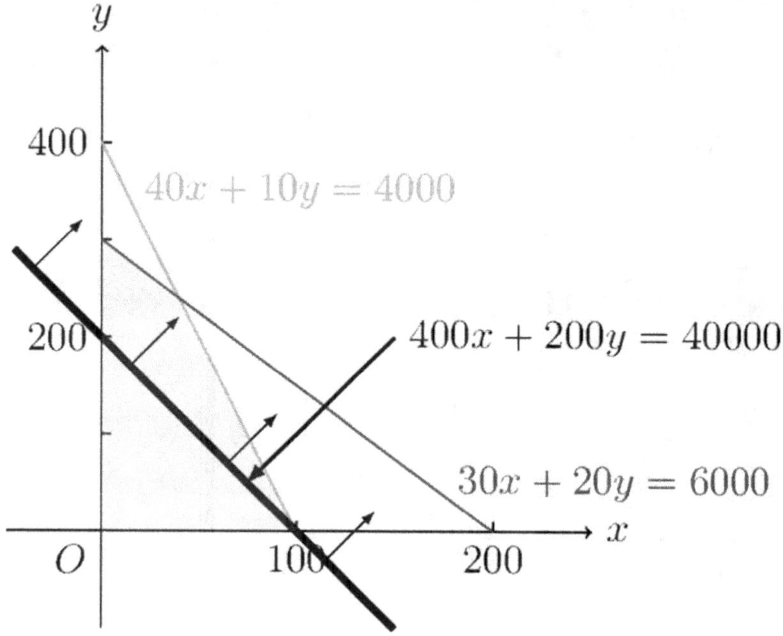

Figure 3. Graphical representation of the optimum of (PL_1)

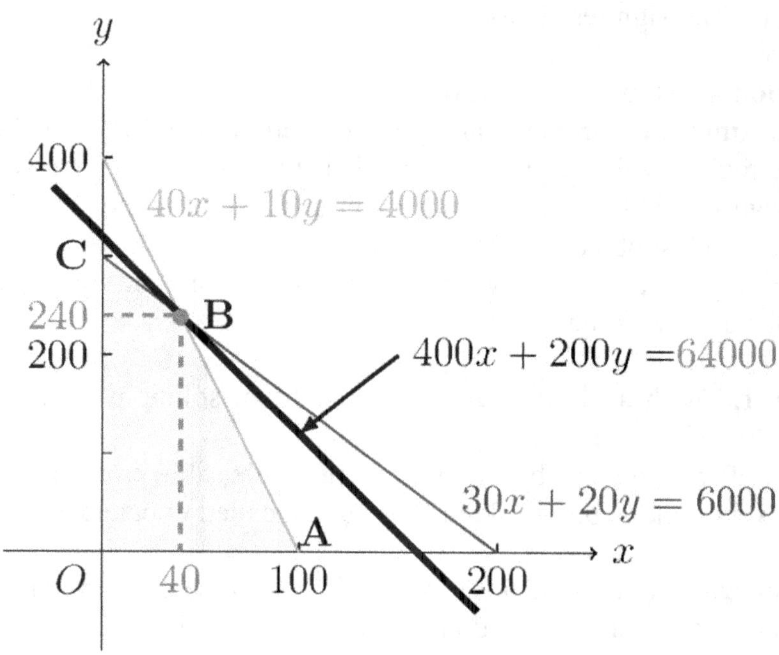

problems. Until now, the most efficient algorithm in linear programming has been the Simplex algorithm (Algorithm 4.1), which has a polynomial complexity in the average case. We mention that Simplex is conceived to tackle Linear Programs with continuous variables, but it still applies on discrete variables.

Algorithm 4.1 SIMLEX

Input: The(PL) in Model (4.1)
Output: The optimal solution of (PL)
1: Add the slack variables to build the first dictionary:

$$\frac{x_{n+i} = b - \sum_{j=1}^{n} a_{ij}x_j, i = 1,...,m}{z = \sum_{j=1}^{n} c_j x_j} \qquad (D_1)$$

2: Compute the initial satisfied solution:

$$(x_1^*,\cdots,x_n^*,x_{n+1}^*,\cdots x_{n+m}^*) = (0,\cdots,0,b_1,\cdots b_m)$$

3: **if** ($\exists c_j$>0| i=1..n) **then**
4: Compute the entering variable x_e:

$$x_e, r \in 1..n \left| c_e = \max_{j=1..n}(c_j) \right.$$

5: **else**
6: Go to 11
7: **end if**
8: Compute the departing variable x_d such as:

$$\frac{b_d}{a_{di}} = \min_{i=1..m}\left(\frac{b_i}{a_{ie}}\right) \| a_{ie} > 0$$

9: Write the following dictionary, replace:

- a_{ij} by $a_{ij} - a_{je}\frac{a_{ei}}{a_{er}}$
- b_i by $b_i - b_i\frac{a_{dj}}{a_{dr}}$

10: Go to 3
11: **END**(The optimum is found).

In order to understand the algorithm, we consider Example-4.1 with some modifications.

Example 4.2 (Simplex Resolution) (Winston, 1991)[1]
The factory produces 4 types of products P_1, P_2, P_3 and P_4. Each product must successively pass through M_1, M_2 and M_3, in indifferent order and taking the following times (in hours):

Table 1. The following times (in hours) for P_1, P_2, P_3 and P_4 to successively pass through M_1, M_2 and M_3

	P_1	P_2	P_3	P_4
M_1	2	4	5	7
M_2	1	1	2	2
M_3	1	2	3	3

In addition, the machine M_1 is available for 42h/week, M_2 is available for 17h/week and M_2 is available for 24h/week.

Weekly, the production of *1* product of P_1 provides \$7,1 product of P_2 provides \$9, 1 product of P_3 provides \$18 and 1 product of P_4 provides \$17, of profit.

The head of the factory hopes to find the weekly manufacturing plan which allows him to maximize the factory profit.

To find the best plan for this factory, we follow the same steps:

1. Modeling the problem:
   The corresponding PL (PL_2) to the problem is given below.

$$\max z = 7x_1 + 9x_2 + 18x_3 + 17x_4$$

$$s.c\begin{cases} 2x_1 + 4x_2 + 5x_3 + 7x_4 \leq 42 \\ x_1 + x_2 + 2x_3 + 2x_4 \leq 17 \\ x_1 + 2x_2 + 3x_3 + 3x_4 \leq 24 \\ x_1, x_2, x_3, x_4 \geq 0 \end{cases} \qquad (PL_2)$$

2. Solving the PL with Simplex algorithm:
   a. Integrating the slack variables (instruction 1 of the Algorithm 4.1). We obtain the PL (PL_3), thus the dictionary (D_1).

$$\max z = 7x_1 + 9x_2 + 18x_3 + 17x_4$$

$$s.c\begin{cases} 2x_1 + 4x_2 + 5x_3 + 7x_4 + x_5 = 42 \\ x_1 + x_2 + 2x_3 + 2x_4 + x_6 = 17 \\ x_1 + 2x_2 + 3x_3 + 3x_4 + x_7 = 24 \\ x_1, x_2, x_3, x_4, x_5, x_6, x_7 \geq 0 \end{cases} \qquad (PL_3)$$

$$\begin{array}{llllll} x_5 & 42- & 2x_1 - & 4x_2 - & 5x_3 - & 7x_4 \\ x_6 & 17- & x_1 - & x_2 - & 2x_3 - & 2x_4 \\ x_7 & 24- & x_1 - & 2x_2 - & 3x_3 - & 3x_4 \\ \hline z= & & 7x_1 + & 9x_2 + & 18x_3 + & 17x_4 \end{array} \quad (D_1)$$

b. There are positive coefficients in the last row of the previous dictionary (D_1) (instruction 3), then we compute the entering and the departing variables (instructions 4 and 8), to obtain the new dictionary (D_2) (instruction 9).

$$\begin{array}{llllll} x_5 = & 2- & \frac{1}{3}x_1 - & \frac{2}{3}x_2 - & 2x_4 - & \frac{5}{3}x_7 \\ x_6 = & 1- & \frac{1}{3}x_1 + & \frac{1}{3}x_2 + & & \frac{2}{3}x_7 \\ x_3 = & 8- & \frac{1}{3}x_1 - & \frac{2}{3}x_2 - & x_4 - & \frac{1}{3}x_7 \\ \hline z= & 144+ & x_1 - & 3x_2 - & 4x_4 - & 6x_7 \end{array} \quad (D_2)$$

c. There are positive coefficients in the last row of the previous dictionary (D_2) (instruction 3), then we compute the entering and the departing variables (instructions 4 and 8), to obtain the new dictionary (D_3) (instruction 9).

$$\begin{array}{llllll} x_5 = & 1- & x_2 - & 2x_4 + & x_6 + & x_7 \\ x_1 = & 3+ & x_2 - & & 3x_6 + & 2x_7 \\ x_3 = & 7- & x_2 - & x_4 + & x_6 - & x_7 \\ \hline z= & 147- & 2x_2 - & x_4 - & 3x_6 - & 4x_7 \end{array} \quad (D_3)$$

d. There are no positive coefficients in the last row of the last dictionary (D_3), then the optimum is reached. The optimal solution of (PL2) is $(x_1^*,x_2^*,x_3^*,x_4^*) = (3,0,7,0)$, $(x_5^*,x_6^*,x_7^*) = (1,0,0)$ and $z^*=147$.

3. Interpretation of the solution:
The obtained Simplex Solution means that the factory should produce 3 units of P1, 0 units of P2, 7 units of P3 and 0 units of P4, to have the maximal profit of $147. Additionally, the values of the slack variables give us information about the remaining hours on each machine; in this case the head of the factory has just 1 hour not consumed on the M_1.

According to the type of the decision variables, Linear Programs are divided into three categories:

- Linear Programs defined on continuous variables, noted LP.
- Integer Linear Programs defined on integer/discrete variables, noted ILP.
- Mixed Integer Linear Programs defined on a set of discrete variables and a set of continuous variables, noted by MILP.

For each category, we find algorithms which are conceived according to the nature of the decision variables.

As given in the previous chapter, the Portfolio Design problem is modeled under a matricial model, including 0-1 variables. If a linearization technique is applied to the model, we will have an Integer Linear Program (ILP), or Integer Program (IP) (Bisschop, 2006), which should be solved by appropriate algorithms, such as:

1. Branch and Bound methods, which is based on dividing the problem into subproblems' feasible regions, and finding the optimal solution to an IP by efficiently enumerating the points in each feasible region. As given in (Winston, 2004), a Branch-and-Bound method for solving pure IPs can be given in two steps:
   Step 1: If it is unnecessary to branch on a subproblem, then it is fathomed. The following three situations result in a subproblem being fathomed: (1) The subproblem is infeasible; (2) the subproblem yields an optimal solution in which all variables have integer values; and (3) the optimal z-value for the subproblem does not exceed (in a max problem) the current LB.
   Step 2: A subproblem may be eliminated from consideration in the following situations: (1) The subproblem is infeasible; (2) the LB (representing the z-value of the best candidate to date) is at least as large as the z-value for the subproblem.
2. Column Generation, which is applied when an LP has many variables. It is very time-consuming to price out each non basic variable individually. The column generation approach lets us determine the not basic variable that prices out most favorably by solving a subproblem.

As cited in the website NEOS Solvers, there are many solvers conceived to be applied to Linear/Integer Linear Programs. As an example, we can cite:

- BDMLP, Clp, CPLEX, Gurobi and SoPlex80bit in Linear Programming.
- CPLEX, Gurobi, Proxy and scip in Mixed Integer Linear Programming.

LINEARIZATION OF (PD) MODEL

To apply the ILP techniques, a step of linearization should be realized on the model. Many techniques of linear relaxation exist in the literature (Sherali & Adams, 1999; Sahinidis & Twarmalani, 2002).

Linearization Principle

In (Gharibi & Xia, 2012) the authors introduce the linearization of the quadratic terms. We have to formulate the zero-one quadratic with additional binary variables and/or continuous variables and continuous constraints. It is a simple approach which linearizes a zero-one quadratic minimization problem. Since the quadratic term of zero-one variables has two equivalent piece-wise formulations, convex and concave cases, small linearization is obtained by reformulating the corresponding convex piece-wise objective function and/or constraints.

In (Bisschop, 2006), the author proposes a linearization algorithm for quadratic terms, which are in the following form:

$$\begin{cases} \sum_{i=1..n} x_i y_i \le p \\ x_i, y_i \in \{0,1\} \end{cases}$$

Each term in $\{x_i, y_i\}$ is replaced by the variable z_i, which should verify the conditions:

$$\begin{cases} z_i \le x_i \\ z_i \le y_i \\ z_i \ge x_i + y_i - 1 \end{cases}$$

Which provides the linear system below:

$$\begin{cases} \sum_{i=1..n} z_i \le p \\ z_i \le x_i \\ z_i \le y_i \\ z_i \ge x_i + y_i - 1 \\ x_i, y_i, z_i \in \{0,1\} \end{cases}$$

The most relevant advantage of this algorithm of linearization is to have the same feasible region.

Linear Model of (PD) Problem

By applying the linearization intended for quadratic constraints defined on 0-1 variables, we obtain the linear model (4.1) given in the following proposition.

Proposition 4.1
Consider the portfolios optimization problem $PD\langle v,b,r,\lambda\rangle$ defined by the quadratic model (3.6) (Chapter 3). Linear reformulation of the model (4.1) is given by:

$$PD_{Lin}\langle v,b,r,\lambda\rangle \begin{cases} \forall i \in 1..v, \sum_{j\in 1..b} M_{ij} = r \\ \forall i \in 1..v, \forall k > i, \sum_{j=1}^{b} Z_{ikj} \le \lambda \\ \forall i \in 1..v, \forall j \in 1..b, M_{ij} \in \{0,1\} \\ \hline \forall i \in 1..v, \forall k > i, Z_{ikj} \le M_{ij} \\ \forall i \in 1..v, \forall k > i, Z_{ikj} \le M_{kj} \\ \forall i \in 1..v, \forall k > i, Z_{ikj} \le M_{ij} + M_{kj} - 1 \\ \forall i \in 1..v, \forall j \in 1..b, \forall k, Z_{ikj} \in \{0,1\} \end{cases} \tag{4.1}$$

Proof: Consider the quadratic constraints (4.2), which model the overlap constraint.

$$\begin{cases} \forall i \in 1..v, \forall t > i, \sum_{j=1}^{b} M_{ij} M_{kj} \le \lambda \\ with\ M_{ij}, M_{tj} \in \{0,1\} \end{cases} \tag{4.2}$$

Let be the additional variable $Z_{ikj} \in \{0,1\}$, such as $Z_{ikj} = M_{ij} \times M_{kj}$. The linear constraints (4.3) force the variable Z_{ikj} to take the value of $M_{ij} \times M_{kj}$, if the constraints (4.3) are verified.

$$\begin{cases} Z_{ikj} \le M_{ij} \\ Z_{ikj} \le M_{kj} \\ Z_{ikj} \ge M_{ij} + M_{kj} - 1 \end{cases} \tag{4.3}$$

We can easily prove the constraints system (4.3) is equivalent to the constraint $Z_{ikj}=M_{ij}\times M_{kj}$. We just have to verify that both systems have the same solutions, by enumerating the eight cases of the truth table corresponding to $Z_{ikj}=M_{ij}\times M_{kj}$.

Applying the linearization in question on Model (3.6) yields the Integer Linear Program Model (4.1). Thereby, Model (4.3) contains exactly:

- $\frac{v(v-1)}{2}b$ linearization variables in addition of vb variables of the quadratic constraints, which gives $\frac{v(v-1)}{2}b+vb$, or $\frac{v^2b+vb}{2}$ variables.
- $\frac{3}{2}v(v-1)b$ linearization constraints in addition of $v+\frac{v(v-1)}{2}$ constraints of the initial model, which gives totally $\frac{(1+3b)v^2+(1-3b)v}{2}$ constraints.

SYMMETRY BREAKING ON THE LINEAR MODEL

In this section, we exploit the particular semantic of the problem, linked directly to row and column constraints, in order to break row and column symmetries. Static symmetry breaking is realized by adding linear constraints to the model. Specifically, the ILP model will include, in addition to its original constraints, the lexicographical ordering constraint $\geq_{Lex}$ described in Chapter 3.

Proposition 4.2 expresses the model (4.4) that enriches the model (4.1) with two constraints of lexicographical ordering over the rows and the columns.

Proposition 4.2

Consider the linear model (4.1). Applying the symmetry breaking $\leq_{Lex}$ on the rows and the columns of the (PD) problem, gives as the following model:

$$PD_{LinLex}\langle v,b,r,\lambda\rangle = \begin{cases} \forall i \in 1..v, \sum_{j\in 1..b} M_{ij} = r \\ \forall i \in 1..v, \forall k > i, \sum_{j=1}^{b} Z_{ikj} \le \lambda \\ \forall i \in 1..v, \forall k > i, Z_{ikj} \le M_{ij} \\ \forall i \in 1..v, \forall k > i, Z_{ikj} \le M_{kj} \\ \forall i \in 1..v, \forall k > i, Z_{ikj} \ge M_{ij} + M_{kj} - 1 \\ \forall i \in 1..v, \forall j \in 1..b, M_{ij} \in \{0,1\} \\ \forall i \in 1..v, \forall j \in 1..b, \forall k, Z_{ikj} \in \{0,1\} \\ \hline \forall i \in 1..v-1, \sum_{j=1}^{b} M_{ij} 2^{(j-1-b)} \le \sum_{j=1}^{b} M_{i+1,j} 2^{(j-1-b)} \\ \forall j \in 1..b-1, \sum_{i=1}^{v} M_{ij} 2^{(i-1-v)} \le \sum_{i=1}^{v} M_{i,j+1} 2^{(i-1-v)} \end{cases} \tag{4.4}$$

Proof: Let M be the matrix $v\times b$ of 0-1 variables handled in the model (4.1). Any permutation between any row and another row keeps intact all solutions of the (PD) model. Similarly, if we swap two columns the set of solutions will be preserved. Consequently, given a solution of (PD) problem, we can obtain other symmetrical solutions by swapping the rows and/or columns.

We suppose that $M_{i,1..b}$ and $M_{i+,1..b}$ are the vectors which represent the successive rows of the indices *i* and *i+1* within *M*. Likewise, on the columns, let be $M_{1..v,j}$ and $M_{1..v,j+1}$ the vectors which represents the successive columns within *M*. By applying lexicographical ordering relation $\le_{Lex}$ introduced in chapter 2, we obtain the following constraints:

$$\forall i \in 1..v-1, M_{i,1..b} \le_{Lex} M_{i+1,1..b} \tag{4.5}$$

$$\forall j \in 1..b-1, M_{1..v,j} \le_{Lex} M_{1..v,j+1} \tag{4.6}$$

We inject this set of Lex constraints in the linear model, to avoid the symmetrical solutions over the rows and the columns. We have to prove that the previous constraints (4.5) and (4.6) are respectively equivalent to the two constraints added to the model (4.4):

$$\forall i \in 1..v-1, \sum_{j=1}^{b} M_{ij} 2^{(j-1-b)} \le \sum_{j=1}^{b} M_{i+1,j} 2^{(j-1-b)} \tag{4.7}$$

$$\forall j \in 1..b-1, \sum_{i=1}^{v} M_{ij} 2^{(i-1-v)} \leq \sum_{i=1}^{v} M_{i,j+1} 2^{(i-1-v)} \tag{4.8}$$

Due to the binary nature of the variables M_{ij}, the two lexicographic orderings (4.5) and (4.6) are numerically translated into the two constraints (4.7) and (4.8). The reverse is also true.

The number of the added constraints to break row and column symmetries, is $(v-1)+(b-1)$, which is negligible compared to the contained constraints in Model (4.1).

In the experimental section of this chapter, Table 4.3 clearly shows on each instance of the problem the number of the added constraints.

EXPERIMENTS

The machine used has the following configuration: Linux-Ubuntu 12.04, Intel CPU E5-2603 and 8 GB/RAM, and the time out is fixed to 3600 seconds.

SCIP Environment

SCIP (Solving Constraint Integer Programming) (Achterberg,2005; Achterberg, Berthold, Heinz,Koch & Wolter,2008a; Achterberg, Berthold, Heinz, Koch & Wolter,2008b) is a framework to solve Constraint Integer Programs (CIPs) and Mixed-Integer Nonlinear Programs (MIP). SCIP proposes a new paradigm, which incorporates ILP (Integer Linear Programming) techniques and CP (Constraint Programming) techniques. SCIP is an open source solver and accessible for academic use at *scip.zib.de*.

The exploited approach in the solver differs from those realized previously over the integrating level. Indeed, SCIP combines the techniques of CP (Constraint Programming), SAT (Boolean SATisfiability Problem) and MIP (Mixed-Integer Programming) at the lowest level of the platform. Particularly, all the research algorithms operate on the same research tree, which allows a close integration between these techniques. For instance, the IP's (Integer Programming) components can exploit decision heuristics, based on statistics collected by the CP algorithms, and vice versa. The two paradigms IP and CP can use the dual information given by LP after the relaxation of the ongoing sub-problem. In other terms, SCIP allows us to exploit different algorithms from different techniques, namely:

- Propagation of the variables' domains by specific applied algorithms in CP.
- Solving linear programs after relaxing the model representing the problem.
- Enhancing the LP model with Branch & Cut techniques.
- Analyzing the infeasible sub-problems to deduce a global knowledge, and using the handled instance of the problem.

Combining modeling and solving techniques stemming from the CP and the IP is not a new idea. Many authors have proved that an integrated approach can be more efficient in solving optimization problems, which were insoluble with one method.

Experimental Results

Table 2 describes each instance by giving its parameters and the contained variables' number. We introduce, for each model (4.1) and (4.4) via the respective columns PD_{Lin} and PD_{LinLex}, the number of the contained constraints as well as the realized CPU time in seconds. The first column introduces different instances of the financial Portfolio Design problem.

The column PD_{Lin} shows the failure of SCIP in solving some instances, SCIP solver exceeds the time-out fixed to 3600s. If we consider row and column symmetry breaking, we have only two instances solved on PD_{LinLex} and not on PD_{Lin}, which are $\langle 10,8,3,1 \rangle$ and $\langle 16,8,3,1 \rangle$. According Table 4.1, applying SCIP on PD_{LinLex} turns out to be inefficient, especially on big instances.

To analyze deeply the given results in Table 4.1, we introduce Figure 4 which shows the CPU time evolution under the SCIP environment, according to variable number of the instances. The curves PD and PD-Lex represent respectively, the resolution of the PD_{Lin} (Model (4.1)) and PD_{LinLex} (Model (4.4)).

According to Figure 4, we notice the both LPs (4.1) and (4.4) are very close in CPU time until the instance Inst6 PD$\langle 10,15,6,2 \rangle$, the CDO Squared portfolio composed of 10 tranches and 15 inner portfolios, where the curve PD_{LinLex} diverges, which expresses the slowness of symmetry breaking under SCIP. Thus, PD_{Lin} resolution was faster and provided just 5 failures out of 16.

Table 2. Experimental results by SCIP solver

Instance	NBR-VAR	PD_{Lin}		PD_{LinLex}	
		NBR-CONST	CPU-TIME	NBR-CONST	CPU-TIME
⟨7,7,3,1⟩	169	469	1.67	481	0.14
⟨10,8,3,1⟩	440	1135	>3600	1151	91.51
⟨8,14,7,3⟩	504	1212	33.53	1232	32.18
⟨11,11,5,2⟩	726	1881	47.50	1901	191.03
⟨16,8,3,1⟩	1088	3016	>3600	3038	14.77
⟨10,15,6,2⟩	825	2080	178.92	2130	229.39
⟨9,18,8,3⟩	810	1989	96.22	2014	320.75
⟨9,24,8,2⟩	1080	2637	304.33	2668	313.74
⟨15,15,4,1⟩	1800	4845	>3600	4873	>3600
⟨10,25,8,2⟩	1375	3430	1860.47	3463	>3600
⟨10,30,9,2⟩	1650	4105	2658.31	4143	>3600
⟨9,37,12,3⟩	1665	4041	1260.36	4085	>3600
⟨10,37,14,6⟩	2035	5050	588.80	5095	>3600
⟨10,38,10,2⟩	2090	5185	6204.09	5231	>3600
⟨19,20,9,4⟩	3800	10450	>3600	10487	>3600
⟨15,350,100,25⟩	42000	110370	>3600	110733	>3600

CONCLUSION

In this chapter, we introduced Linear Programming aspects, such as the Linear Program form and the resolution techniques. We described the processes of the graphics resolution and the Simplex algorithm, via two simple examples. As mentioned above, Simplex remains the most useful exact method to solve a linear problem.

An equivalent linear mathematical model to the 0-1 quadratic model of the (PD) problem is computed through an efficient and proved method. Thus, a 0-1 linear model called PD_{Lin} was given to be solved by SCIP solver which combines various linear programming techniques. The provided CDO Squared portfolios from the PL techniques were not really efficient, especially in the large instances of the PD problem.

Since the linear model has been formulated, breaking the counted symmetries in the problem became feasible. New constraints were added to PD_{Lin} to break the row and column symmetries in a static way, which provide a new linear model called PD_{LinLex}. We launched the same solver on PD_{LinLex}, but

Figure 4. Comparison of CPU time realized under SCIP, with and without row and column symmetry breaking

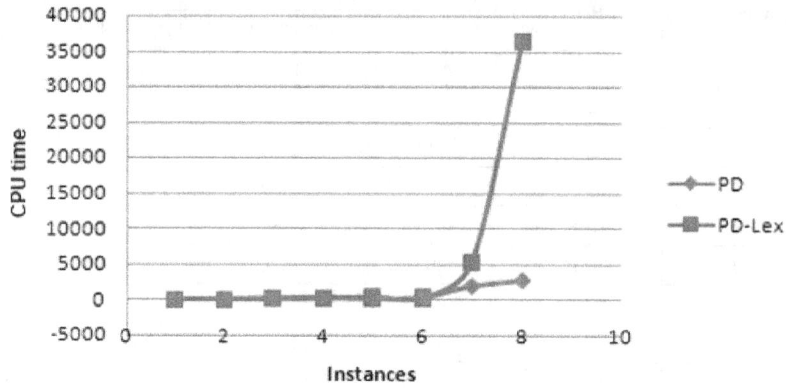

the obtained results represent a real failure, especially on the large instances of CDO Squared portfolio, having equal or more than 150 variables such as a portfolio with 10 tranches and 15 inner portfolios, or portfolios with 15 tranches and 350 inner portfolios that is modeled by 15×350=5250 variables.

If we compare SCIP results on PD_{Lin} and PD_{LinLex}, symmetry breaking becomes inefficient on the large instances. PD_{Lin} resolution was faster and provided just 5 failures out of 16.

As a general conclusion, launching the SCIP solver on the Linear Programs PD_{Lin} and PD_{LinLex} turns out not to be very efficient, particularly on a CDO Squared portfolio containing large numbers of tranches and inner CDOs. That is due to the algorithms used in the SCIP solver to tackle PD_{Lin} and PD_{LinLex}. Indeed, the models that we have to solve are ILPs with 0-1 variables, and SCIP uses relaxing techniques which widen generally the feasible region of the problem, and the Simplex algorithm via the Soplex solver, which is intended basically to tackle continuous variables.

Consequently, to take advantage of the generated linear models in this chapter, we should take into consideration the discrete aspect of the problem and apply the appropriate algorithms such as Branch-and-bound and cutting-plane.

In the next chapter, we explore the Constraint Programming discipline to solve the PD problem and to build the optimized CDO Squared portfolio.

REFERENCES

Achterberg, T. (2005). SCIP-A framework to integrate constraint and mixed integer programming. Technical Report, ZIB. *Takustr, 7*, 14195.

Achterberg, T. (2009). SCIP: Solving Constraint Integer Programs. *Math. Program. Comput., 1*(1), 1-41.

Achterberg, T., Berthold, T., Heinz, S., Koch, T., & Wolter, K. (2008a). Constraint Integer Programming: Techniques and applications. Technical Report 08-43, ZIB. *Takustr, 7, 14195.*

Achterberg, T., Berthold, T., Koch, T., & Wolter, K. (2008b). Constraint integer programming: A new approach to integrate CP and MIP. *Integration of AI and OR Techniques in Constraint Programming for Combinatorial Optimization Problems, 5th International Conference, CPAIOR 2008*, 5015, 6-20. 10.1007/978-3-540-68155-7_4

Bisschop, J. (2006). *AIMMS-Optimization Modeling*. Paragon Decision Technology.

Bisschop, J. (2006). *Aimms Optimization Modeling*. Paragon Decision Technology. Retrieved from https://books.google.dz/books?id=oHR8vSZFMvgC

Charon, I., Germa, A. & Hudry, O. (1996). *Méthodes d'optimisation combinatoiores*. Collection pédagogique de télécommunication. Elsevier Masson.

Erickson, J. (2015). *Algorithms*. Retrieved from https://www.cs.illinois.edu/~jeffe/teaching/algorithms/

Gharibi, W., & Xia, Y. (2012). A Tight Linearization Strategy for Zero-One Quadratic Programming Problems. *International Journal of Computer Science Issues, 9.*

Nahin, P. (2007). *When Least Is Best: How Mathematicians Discovered Many Clever Ways to Make Things as Small (or as Large) as Possible*. Princeton, NJ: Princeton University Press. Retrieved February 1, 2020, from www.jstor.org/stable/j.ctt7rh9x

NEOS Solvers. (n.d.). Retrieved from https://neos-server.org/neos/solvers/index.html

Reischuk, R. M., Schulte, C., Stuckey, P. J., & Tack, G. (2009). Maintaining state in propagation solvers. In *Fifteenth International Conference on Principles and Practice of Constraint Programming*, (vol. 5732, pp. 692-706). Lisbon, Portugal. Springer-Verlag.

Sahinidis, V., & Twarmalani, M. (2002). *Convexification and Optimization in Continuous and Mixed-Integer Nonlinear Programming*. Kluwer Academic Publishers Group.

Schulte, C. (2002). Programming Constraint Services, volume 2302 of Lecture Notes in Artificial Intelligence. Springer-Verlag.

Schulte, C., & Stuckey, P. J. (2008). Efficient constraint propagation engines. *ACM Transactions on Programming Languages and Systems*, *31*(1), 111. doi:10.1145/1452044.1452046

Schulte, C., & Tack, G. (2006). Views and iterators for generic constraint implementations. Lecture Notes in Artificial Intelligence, 3978, 118-132.

Schulte, C., Tack, G. & Lagerkvist, M. Z. (2010). *Modeling and programming with GECODE*. Academic Press.

Sherali, H., & Adams, W. (1999). *A Reformulation-Linearization Technique for Solving Discrete and Continuous Nonconvex Problems*. Kluwer Academic Publishing. doi:10.1007/978-1-4757-4388-3

Winston, W. L. (1991). *Introduction to mathematical programming: applications and algorithms*. PWS-Kent Publishing Company.

Winston, W. L. (2004). *Operations Research: Applications and Algorithms*. Thomson Brooks/Cole. Retrieved from https://books.google.dz/books?id=tg5DAQAAIAAJ

ENDNOTE

1 The example is inspired by the Giapetto problem given in Winston (1991).

Chapter 5
Constraint Programming Applied to Portfolio Design Problem:
Modelling and Solving

ABSTRACT

This chapter introduces Constraint Programming (CP) approaches for solving efficiently a financial portfolio design problem. The CP includes powerful techniques for modeling and solving complex problems. Symmetry breaking coming firstly from CP has proved its efficiency in minimizing CPU times when the problem is symmetric. The authors have adopted CP techniques to model the problem in a constraints system to capitalize on the flexibility of the CP paradigm and to take into consideration the symmetric aspect of the problem. The authors propose different CP models and different hybridizations of symmetry breaking techniques to tackle the problem. Experimental results on non-trivial instances of the problem show the effectiveness of the CP approach.

INTRODUCTION

Building an optimized financial portfolio is a critical problem. It must verify different constraints and should be tackled with precision, without forgetting the strong symmetrical nature of the problem. Consequently, we introduce

DOI: 10.4018/978-1-7998-1882-3.ch005

different notions and techniques coming from the Constraint Satisfaction discipline.

In this chapter, we start by giving an overview of Constraint Programming and its strong points, such as the flexible algorithms used and the global constraint aspect.

We provide a CSP (Constraint Satisfaction Problem) which represents perfectly the portfolio design problem. To capitalize on the CP techniques, we apply static and dynamic symmetry breaking methods, and we propose different combinations of these methods.

The experiments are realized on non-trivial instances of CDO Squared portfolio, under the GECODE solver which is a conceived solver to solve CSP/CD problems. The results of the experiments are given and analyzed in detail. The techniques of symmetry breaking stemming from the Constraint Programming field have had real success in speeding up the constraint systems resolution, especially the dynamic technique.

In section 1, we provide the indispensable notions of Constraint Programming, illustrated by figures. In section 2, we introduce two CP model corresponding respectively to a model without taking into consideration the symmetry nature of the problem, and to the CP model with added constraints to break the symmetries statically. In section 3, the proposed approaches in this chapter are experimented and analyzed. A detailed synthesis is given in this section. In section 4, we conclude the chapter and we give some perspectives.

BACKGROUND

Constraint Programming (CP) (Rossi, van Beek & Walsh, 2006) is a powerful paradigm which is the result of many scientific works focusing on the resolution of the problems coming from Combinatorial Optimization. It is the result of exploiting a wide range of techniques coming from Artificial Intelligence, Information Technology, databases, programming languages and Operations Research. Nowadays, CP is a field providing many techniques which succeed in solving problems within different fields such as scheduling, planning, vehicle routing, automation, networks and bioinformatics.

Constraint Programming provides a strong modeling tool based on formulating a problem in constraints. CP handles all kinds of constraint, namely logical constraints, linear constraints, non-linear constraints, and sets constraints. CP resolution algorithms based on filtering and propagation algorithms have proven their efficiency in solving large instances of complex problems. A Constraint Satisfaction Problem is a set of variables and a set of constraints which states simply the relation between variables.

A Constraint Satisfaction Problem (CSP) is defined as follows (Definition 5.1) (Rossi, van Beek & Walsh, 2006)

Definition 5.1 (Constraint Satisfaction Problem)
A CSP P is triple $P\langle X,D,C\rangle$ where X is an n-tuple of variables $X=\{x_1,x_2,\ldots,x_n\}$, D is an n-tuple of domains $D=\{D_1,D_2,\ldots,D_n\}$ such that $x_i \in D_i$ and C is a t-tuple of constraints, $C=\{c_1,c_2,\ldots,c_n\}$.

$$P\left|\begin{array}{l} X=\{x_i \mid i=1..n\} \\ D=\{D_i \mid i=1..n\} \\ C=\{c_j \mid j=1..t\} \end{array}\right. \tag{5.1}$$

A constraint c_j is a pair $\langle R_{S_j},S_j\rangle$ where R_{S_j} is a relation on the variables in S_j=scope(c_j). In other words, R_{S_j} is a subset of the Cartesian product of the domains of the variables in S_i.

Let be a problem with three variables $x_1 \in \{1,3\}$, $x_2 \in \{1,3\}$ and $x_3 \in \{2,3\}$, which must be pairwise distinct.

The problem can be represented by a 3-ary constraint (Figure 1) or by n-ary constraints (Figure 2). The corresponding CSP to Figure 2 is given by *P'* (Model 5.2) as follows:

$$P'\left|\begin{array}{l} X=\{x_1,x_2,x_3\} \\ D_{x_1}=\{1,3\},D_{x_2}=\{1,3\},D_{x_3}=\{2,3\} \\ C=\{c_1,c_2,c_3\} \\ c_1: x_1 \neq x_2 \\ c_2: x_1 \neq x_3 \\ c3: x_2 \neq x_3 \end{array}\right. \tag{5.2}$$

Definition 5.2 (Constraint Arc-consistency)
A CSP $P\langle X,D,C\rangle$ is arc consistent iff: $\forall x_i \in X$, $\forall a_i \in D_i$, $\forall c_j \in C$ constraining x_i, $\forall x_j,\ldots,x_k \in X_C$, $\exists a_j,\ldots,a_k$ such that $C(a_j,\ldots,a_i,\ldots,a_k)$ holds.

As given in Chapter 2, CSP resolution is based on three basic algorithms, namely propagation, filtering and backtrack algorithms.

Thus, to solve *P'*, we are called to apply these algorithms on the model, which gives us the following steps:

- Instantiating x_1 with a value from D_{x_1}, for instance x_1=1.
- Filtering the variables which appear in the same constraints with x_1:
  - x_2={2,3}
  - x_3={2}
- Propagation on x_2; since x_1=1 we instantiate x_2 according to the shared constraint c_1; x_2=2.
- Filtering the variable x_3 which appears in the same constraint c_3 with x_2:
  - $x_3 = \varnothing$
- Propagation on x_3; since $x_3 = \varnothing$, no instantiation is possible of x_3, thus a backtrack must be realized.
- Backtrack on x_2 with:
  - x_2={3}
  - x_3={2}
- Instantiating x_2 with a value from D_{x_3}, for instance x_2=3.
- Filtering the variable x_3 which appears in the same constraint c_3 with x_2:
  - x_3={2}
- Propagation on x_3; since x_3={2}, the unique and possible instantiation is x_3=2.

After instantiating x_3, we notice that all the constraints are verified. Thus, the configuration (x_1,x_2,x_3) = (1,2,3) is a solution of *P'*. In other words, P' is arc consistent (Régin, 1994) with (x_1,x_2,x_3) = (1,3,2) (Definition 5.2).

There are many backtrack, propagation and filtering algorithms in the literature (Rossi, van Beek & Walsh, 2006; Nadel, 989). Utilization of a high level of thoughtful algorithms represents the first highlight of solving CSP problems.

The second highlight of CSP discipline is the global constraint concept. A global constraint is a constraint which models the behavior of many constraints. All the global constraints coming from Constraint Programming have been regrouped by Nicolas Beldiceanu et al. in (Beldiceanu, Carlsson, Demassey & Petit, 2007).

For instance, in (Régin, 1994), the constraints c_1, c_2 and c_3 of difference, the author realized the global constraint called *Alldiff*, such as *Alldiff*$(x_1,x_2,\ldots,x_n)$

Figure 1. Graph model $G = \langle X, D, E \rangle$ of Alldiff global constraint

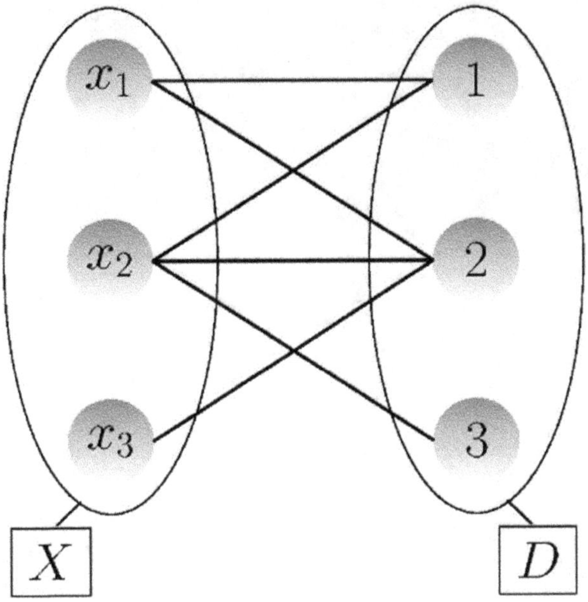

expresses that all the variables $x_1, x_2, \ldots, x_n$ must be pairwise distinct. This global constraint is solved by using a maximum matching concept coming from Graph Theory.

Consequently, the CSP *P'* is replaced by *P"*, as follows:

$$P'' \left| \begin{array}{l} X = \{x_1, x_2, x_3\} \\ D_{x_1} = \{1,3\}, D_{x_2} = \{1,3\}, D_{x_3} = \{2,3\} \\ C = \{c_1\} \\ c_1 : Alldiff(x_1, x_2, x_3) \end{array} \right. \quad (5.3)$$

The constraint c_1 is modeled graphical by a bipartite graph $G = \langle X, D, E \rangle$ (Figure 1), such that $X = \{x_1, x_2, \ldots, x_n\}$ the set of variables, $D = \{1,2,3\}$ the union of all the variables' domains and $E = \{(x_1,1), (x_1,2), (x_2,1), (x_2,2), (x_3,3), (x_3,2)\}$ the set partial instantiations.

Since the graph is bipartite, the application of the appropriate algorithm to compute the maximum matching (Ahuja, Magnanti & Orlin, 1993;Régin,1994) become feasible. In Figure 2, the given edges in bold, represent a maximum matching $G = \langle X, D, E \rangle$, which provides the instantiation of the variables $(x_1, x_2, \ldots, x_n) = (1,3,2)$.

Figure 2.: Solving Alldiff(x_1,x_2,...,x_n) Constraint with a maximum matching

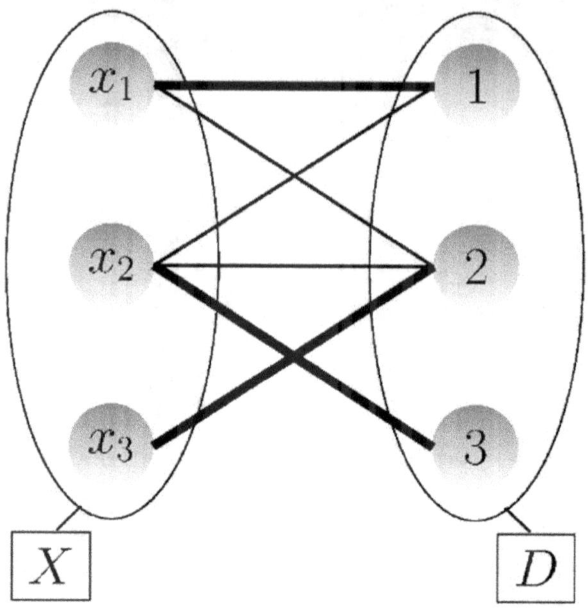

Constraint Programming is really a paradigm of modeling and solving *CSP* and *CP* problems. It offers a large platform of constraints and algorithms, such as global constraints and filtering, propagation and backtrack algorithms, which are developed to tackle critical problems coming from various fields and requiring exact solutions. Such as Linear Programming, different types of Constraint Satisfaction Program exist in the literature, namely Constraint Program (CP) which is tackled in the case of optimization problems, Boolean SATisfiability problem (SAT) which is used to determine if a solution of Boolean formula exist, and Mixed Integer Program (MIP) which is composed of discrete variables and continuous variables, and a set of constraints.

In addition, CSP is the first discipline which integrated static and dynamic techniques to break symmetries, which can be used as strong and thoughtful filtering techniques of the variables.

To solve a CSP, a panoply of specific constraints and algorithms coming from Operations Research is reliably utilized, such as Branch and Bound, Branch and Cut, Columns Generation and Simplex. This discipline provides exact approaches to solve complex problems.

The tackled (PD) problem, in this book, is a complex and critical problem in Finance, since the problem is difficult to be appropriately modeled and solved, which justifies the use of CSP techniques. Indeed, the corresponding

0-1 matricial model of the problem is modeled by a CSP that contains global constraints. Different types of symmetries are considered on the problem and broken by different algorithms.

CONSTRAINT PROGRAM

On the basis of global constraints catalog proposed in (Beldecianu, Carlsson, Demassey & Petit, 2007), we reword the (PD) model (3.7) (given in Chapter 3) in the form of a CP model, which is introduced through the proposition 5.1.

Proposition 5.1
The (PD) model expressed in the formulation (3.7) is equivalent to the following CP:

$$CP_{PD}\begin{cases} X=\{X_{ij} \mid i\in 1..v, j\in 1..b\}\cup\{P_{itj} \mid i\in 1..v, j\in 1..b, i<t\le b\} \\ D_{X_{ij}}=D_{P_{itj}}=\{0,1\},\text{ with } i\in 1..v, j\in 1..b \text{ and } i<t\le b \\ c_1: LINEAR(Row_X(i),=,r), \forall i\in 1..v \\ c_2: AND(P_{itj},(X_{ij},X_{tj})), \forall i\in 1..v, \forall t>i, \forall j\in 1..b \\ c_3: LINEAR(P_{itj}\{j=1..b\},\le,\lambda), \forall i\in 1..v, \forall t>i \end{cases} \quad (5.1)$$

The proposed CP_{PD} contains the variables' matrix X and the matrix of reification variables P. We use two global constraints known in *CP*:

1. The global constrain *LINEAR*, whose the syntax is *LINEAR(VECTOR,CTR,VAL)* where:
   - *VECTOR* is the vector that the components should be assumed,
   - *CTR*$\in\{<,>,=,\le,\ge\}$. The relation *CTR* should be verified between the realized summation and the value VAL,
   - *Row*X(*i*) designates the row *i* of the matrix *X*.
2. The global constraint *AND* whose the syntax is *AND(VAR,VARIABLES)* where:
   - VARIABLES is the series of 0-1 variables: $VAR_1, VAR_2, \ldots, VAR_n (n>2)$,
   - VAR is the variable which is defined by the equality $VAR = VAR_1 \wedge VAR_2 \wedge \ldots VAR_n$.

In fact, the constraints c_1, c_2 and c_3 express the usual form:

$$\begin{cases} c_1 : \sum_{j \in 1..b} X_{ij} = r, \forall i \in 1..v \\ c_2 : P_{itj} = X_{ij} X_{tj}, \forall i \in 1..v, \forall t > i, \forall j \in 1..b \\ c_3 : \sum_{j \in 1..b} P_{itj} \leq \lambda, \forall i \in 1..v, \forall t > i \end{cases}$$

The constraint c_1 expresses the row constraint of the (PD) model. The constraint c_3 expresses the overlapping constraint in function of the vector P which is the result of the multiplication of pairs of rows.

STATIC AND DYNAMIC BREAKING OF SYMMETRIES

As already mentioned in the previous chapter, the (PD) problem contains row and column symmetries, which were expressed in proposition 4.2 (chapter 4). In CP, we can express these symmetries by using the global constraint of lexicographical ordering:

Definition 5.1
Let be two vectors X and Y vectors of size n:

$$X = [X_0, \ldots X_{n-1}]$$
$$Y = [Y_0, \ldots Y_{n-1}]$$

We say that the vector X is lexicographically less than or equal to Y, denoted by $X \leq_{Lex} Y$*, if and only if* $X_0 < Y_0$ *or (*$X_0 = Y_0$ *and* $[X_1, \ldots X_{n-1}] \leq_{Lex} [Y_1, \ldots Y_{n-1}]$*).*

The symmetries are tackled by the lexicographical ordering relation (or anti-lexicographical) between the rows and between the columns, which are described in details in the following subsections.

In addition to these two symmetries, columns and rows, already mentioned in chapter 4, we introduce another symmetry detected on our problem: the relationship symmetry of 180° rotation described in the following proposition.

Proposition 5.2
The Portfolio Design problem (PD) described by the model 3.6 in chapter 3 contains a 180° rotation symmetry.

Proof

The matrix M of size $v \times b$ solving the problem (PD). Let be M^{180} the obtained after a 180° rotation. In fact, M^{180} is gathered from M by applying the following operations:

1- Row swapping: in the matrix M, the row v is swapped with the row 1, the row v-1 with the row 2, … the row $\frac{v}{2}$ with the row [if v is even then $\frac{v+2}{2}$ else $\frac{v+3}{2}$]. We obtain the intermediate matrix M', by applying these $\frac{v}{2}$ swaps.

2- Column swapping: in the matrix M', the column b is swapped with the column 1, the column b-1 with 2, … the column $\frac{b}{2}$ with the column [if v is even then $\frac{b+2}{2}$ else $\frac{b+3}{2}$]. We obtain the intermediate matrix M'', by applying these $\frac{b}{2}$ swaps.

3- The matrix M'' is obviously the matrix M^{180}.

In other words, we have three symmetries in the model (PD): row, column and 180° rotation. In CP, three techniques are developed to break symmetries: static, dynamic and mixed. For more details, refer to chapter 3.

According to the model CP_{PD} and the symmetries contained in the problem, we apply four strategies of symmetry breaking, namely:

1- Static row and column symmetry breaking by using the lexicographical ordering (Flener, Frisch, Hnich, Kiziltan, Miguel, Pearson & Walsh, 2002;Flener, Pearson, Sellmann, Hentenryck & Agren, 2009). This is done by integrating two additional constraints in CP_{PD}.

2- Dynamic row and column symmetry breaking by applying the LDSB method (Mears, de la BANDA, Demoen & Wallace, 2014) described in Chapter 3.

3- Row and column symmetry breaking via the methods Lex and LDSB, by applying:
   - The relation $\leq_{Lex}$ on the rows (or on the columns).
   - The method LDSB to break row symmetry (or column symmetry).

4- We introduce in last position, the 180° rotation symmetry to break with LDSB.

Static Symmetry Breaking

As indicated previously in chapter 2, static symmetry breaking implies integrating supplementary constraints to the CP modeling the problem, in order to express the lexicographical ordering between rows and between columns. This gives rise to CP_{PDLEX} as follows:

$$CP_{PDLEX}\left|\begin{array}{l}CP_{PD}\\ c_4: LEX\_GREATEREQ\left(Row_X(i), Row_X(i+1)\right), \forall i \in 1..v-1\\ c_5: LEX\_GREATEREQ\left(Column_X(j), Column_X(j+1)\right), \forall j \in 1..b-1\end{array}\right. \quad (5.2)$$

CP_{PDLEX} feeds the model CP_{PD} with two supplementary constraints to break row and column symmetries. These two added constraints appeal to the global constraint LEX_GREATEREQ whose syntax is:

$LEX\_GREATEREQ(VECTEUR_1, VECTEUR_2)$

which expresses the relationship $VECTEUR_1 \geq_{LEX} VECTEUR_2$.

Consequently, we have the constraints:

c_4: $LEX\_GREATEREQ(Row_X(i), Row_X(i+1))$, $\forall i \in 1..v-1$,

that expresses the relationship $Row_X(i) \geq_{LEX} Row_X(i+1)$ with $Row_X(i)$ and $Row_X(i+1)$ which designate respectively the ith row and the $i+1^{th}$ row of X.

c_5: $LEX\_GREATEREQ(Column_X(j), Column_X(j+1))$, $\forall j \in 1..b-1$,

that expresses the relationship $Column_X(j) \geq_{LEX} Column_X(j+1)$ with $Column_X(j)$ and $Column_X(j+1)$ which designate respectively the jth column and the $j+1^{th}$ column of X.

Dynamic Symmetry Breaking

We will also appeal to the dynamic method LDSB to break the symmetries. The method's intake will be highlighted in the experimental part of this chapter.

EXPERIMENTS

The used machine has the following configuration: Linux-Ubuntu 12.04, Intel CPU E5-2603 and 8 GB/RAM, and the time out is fixed to 3600 seconds.

GECODE Environment

GECODE is a development environment of systems and applications based on constraints (Schulte, Tack, & Lagerkvist, 2019). It is an open source tool available from GECODE, which is accessible and efficient in solving combinatorial problems. GECODE provides a rich library in modeling, containing techniques of propagation, of filtering, of symmetry breaking, etc. The power of the solver is the access to its source code and the ability to integrate new propagation algorithms, new branching strategies, new search engine and new types of variables. For more details, see (Schulte, 2002; Schulte & Tack, 2005; Reischuk, Schulte, Stuckey & Tack, 2009).

Experimental Results

The implementation of different CPs (e.g. CP_{PD}, CP_{PDLEX}) with or without symmetry breaking are realized in the GECODE environment.

In table 1, we introduce the CPU times obtained via different realized experiments under GECODE, namely:

1. Solving CP_{PD} without considering any symmetry. This is noted PD.
2. Solving CP_{PDLEX} with breaking row and column symmetries by using Lex method. This is noted PDLEX.
3. Solving CP_{PD} with breaking row and column symmetries by using LDSB method. This is noted PDSym2LDSB.
4. Solving CP_{PD} with breaking row symmetry by using Lex, and column symmetry by using LDSB. This is noted PDLexLDSB.
5. Solving CP_{PD} with breaking all symmetries by using LDSB. This is noted PDSym3LDSB.

The first column in the experimental table introduces the tackled instances, in ascending order by number of variables. The columns 2, 3, 4 and 5 introduce the runtimes realized on the previous cited types of experiments.

Table 1.Experimental results with GECODE

Instance	PD	PDLex	PDSym2LDSB	PDLexLDSB	PDSym3LDSB
⟨7,7,3,1⟩	0.001	0.001	0.001	0.001	0.001
⟨10,8,3,1⟩	0.002	0.004	0.003	0.001	0.003
⟨8,14,7,3⟩	0.089	2.744	0.018	0.049	0.031
⟨11,11,5,2⟩	0.027	1.354	0.013	0.020	0.025
⟨16,8,3,1⟩	>3600	>3600	>3600	>3600	>3600
⟨10,15,6,2⟩	8.641	39.468	0.071	0.476	0.147
⟨9,18,8,3⟩	6.955	2009.371	0.156	0.955	0.321
⟨9,24,8,2⟩	1.298	3269.871	0.086	1.043	0.178
⟨15,15,4,1⟩	350.293	>3600	2.173	0.318	4.683
⟨10,25,8,2⟩	182.292	>3600	1.362	11.276	2.994
⟨10,30,9,2⟩	9.945	>3600	1.045	8.168	2.173
⟨9,37,12,3⟩	>3600	>3600	>3600	>3600	>3600
⟨10,37,14,6⟩	524.930	>3600	84.055	522.907	90.353
⟨10,38,10,2⟩	35.067	>3600	2.093	49.140	2.248
⟨19,20,9,4⟩	10.571	>3600	8.914	5.376	9.224
⟨15,350,100,25⟩	>3600	>3600	>3600	>3600	>3600

Table 1 compares the realized runtime between different symmetry breaking techniques. Applying Lex method to break row and column symmetries fails to solve half of the instances in less than an hour.

Figure 3 shows the runtime comparison between the most profitable CP implementations: PD, PDSym2LDSB, PDLexLDSB and PDSym3LDSB.

Through the given curves in Figure 5.1, we reach two conclusions:

1. The curves -PD- and -PDLexLDSB- represent respectively the resolution without symmetry breaking and with combined symmetry breaking (static/dynamic), which are less stable than the others.
2. Applying LDSB to break the row and column symmetries PDSym2LDSB, and the symmetries row, column and 180° rotation PDSym3LDSB, give the best results according to the CPU time and the curves are stable.

Table 1 provides three failure instances: ⟨16,8,3,1⟩ a financial portfolio with 16 tranches and 8 inner portfolios; ⟨9,37,12,3⟩ a financial portfolio with 9 tranches and 37 inner portfolios; and ⟨15,350,100,25⟩ a financial portfolio with 15 tranches and 350 inner portfolios through the five columns.

Figure 3. Runtime comparison on CP implementations according to the number of variables

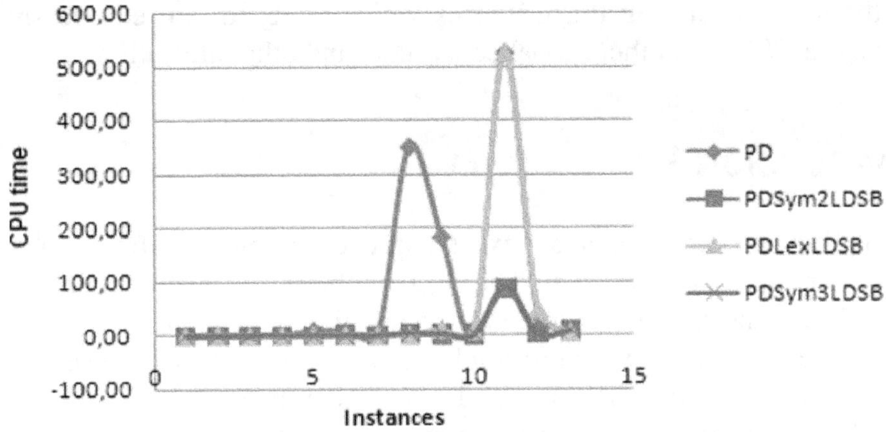

On the other hand, we notice that the realized CPU time on different instances, via application of the hybridization of static and dynamic symmetry breaking techniques, are better than the methods without any symmetry breaking, and largely better than with static symmetry breaking. For example, we have the instance ⟨9,18,8,3⟩ which represents a portfolio with 9 tranches and 18 inner CDOs; the realized CPU time with LDSB is largely better than the Lex technique, since we have 0.156, 0.955 and 0.321 CPU times compared to 2009.371 seconds. The same behavior of the different techniques is seen on the CDO squared portfolio ⟨9,24,8,2⟩ composed of 9 tranches and 24 inner CDOs, where we have 0.086, 1.043 and 0.178 compared to 3269.871 seconds. Additionally, the application of the static symmetry breaking Lex fails to solve some instances while integrating the LDSB method yields good results. For example, the portfolio ⟨15,15,4,1⟩ composed of 15 tranches and 15 inner portfolios represents a real failure when applying the Lex technique, whereas the results given by the integrating of LDSB, 2.173, 0.318 and 4.683 seconds, are very efficient.

Consequently, symmetry breaking with LDSB is very reliable. Including the third type of symmetry (180° rotation) does not slow down the process of the (PD) problem resolution, because it allows a good level of domain filtering. Considering the rotation symmetry improves significantly the CPU times.

Finally, combining static and dynamic symmetry breaking techniques allows having efficient CDO Squared portfolios in a very reasonable time. Furthermore, regarding the instances which were not solved, we should propose a CSP with other global constraints and other algorithms.

CONCLUSION

We introduced in this chapter exact approaches coming from Constraint Programming exact approach. The (PD) problem, as mentioned above, is strongly symmetric, thus taking in consideration the symmetrical nature of the problem should be very profitable. In previous works on the set model, researchers have detected the row and column symmetries. In this chapter, we added and approved a new symmetry which is the 180° rotation symmetry.

We proposed a corresponding CP model, and CPLex model which correspond respectively to the (PD) problem without symmetry breaking and with Lex symmetry breaking. A hybridization of static and dynamic symmetry breaking techniques was given. The resolution of the problem under the Gecode solver allowed the exploitation of CSP techniques and algorithms, which is noticed on the experiments carried out on non-trivial instances of a CDO Squared portfolio.

The best results were yielded through the integration of the LDSB breaking technique. Indeed, the best provided portfolios in reasonable time came from the different realized combinations on static and dynamic techniques. Thus, including dynamic symmetry breaking to solve the problem proved very efficient. In addition, another CSP model could be given to tackle the instances which were not solved with the proposed global constraint.

In the next chapter, we introduce simple and population local approaches to solve the problem of CDO Squared Portfolio Design. We will see the efficiency of the incomplete methods on the problem.

REFERENCES

Ahuja, R. K., Magnanti, T. L., & Orlin, J. B. (1993). *Network flows: theory, algorithms, and applications*. Retrieved from https://books.google.dz/books?id=WnZRAAAAMAAJ

Beldiceanu, N., Carlsson, M., Demassey, S., & Petit, T. (2007). Global constraint catalog: Past, present and future. Constraints, 12(1), 21–62.

Flener, P., Frisch, A., Hnich, B., Jefferson, C., Kiziltan, Z., Miguel, I., ... Walsh, T. (2003). Breaking symmetries in matrix models: A brief overview. *Proceedings of the Tenth Workshop on Automated Reasoning*, 27-28.

Flener, P., Frisch, A. M., Hnich, B., Kiziltan, Z., Miguel, I., Pearson, J., & Walsh, T. (2001). Symmetry in matrix models. *Proceedings of the CP'01 Workshop on Symmetry in Constraints*, 41–48.

Flener, P., Frisch, A. M., Hnich, B., Kiziltan, Z., Miguel, I., Pearson, J., & Walsh, T. (2002). Breaking row and column symmetries in matrix models. Lecture Notes in Computer Science, 2470, 462–476. doi:10.1007/3-540-46135-3_31

Flener, P., Pearson, J., & Reyna, L. G. (2004). Financial portfolio optimization. LNCS, 3258, 277-241.

Flener, P., Pearson, J., Reyna, L. G., & Sivertsson, O. (2007). Design of financial CDO squared transactions using constraint programming. *Constraints*, *12*(2), 179–205. doi:10.100710601-006-9014-4

Flener, P., Pearson, J., Sellmann, M., Hentenryck, P. V., & Agren, M. (2009). Dynamic structural symmetry breaking for constraint satisfaction problems. *Constraints*, *14*(4), 506–538. doi:10.100710601-008-9059-7

Flener, P., Pearson, J., & Reyna, L. G. (2004). Financial portfolio optimization. *LNCS, 3258*, 227–241.

GECODE. (n.d.). Retrieved from https://www.gecode.org/

Hall, M. Jr. (1964). Block designs. In E. F. Beckenbach (Ed.), *Applied Combinatorial Mathematics* (pp. 369–405). New York: Wiley.

Mears, C., de la Banda, M. G., Demoen, B., & Wallace, M. (2014). Lightweight dynamic Symmetry Breaking. *Constraints*, *19*(3), 195–242. doi:10.100710601-013-9154-2

Nadel, B. A. (1989). Constraint satisfaction algorithms. *Computational Intelligence*, *5*(3), 188–224. doi:10.1111/j.1467-8640.1989.tb00328.x

Régin, J. C. (1994). A Filtering Algorithm for Constraints of Difference in CSPs. *Proceedings of the 12th National Conference on Artificial Intelligence*, 362-367.

Reischuk, R. M., Schulte, C., Stuckey, P. J., & Tack, G. (2009). Maintaining state in propagation solvers. In *Fifteenth International Conference on Principles and Practice of Constraint Programming* (Vol. 5732, pp. 692–706). Lisbon, Portugal: Springer-Verlag; doi:10.1007/11564751_71.

Rossi, F., van Beek, P., & Walsh, T. (2006). *Foundations of Artificial Intelligence*. Amsterdam: Elsevier Science.

Schulte, C. (2002). Programming Constraint Services. Lecture Notes in Artificial Intelligence, 2302. doi:10.1007/3-540-45945-6

Schulte, C., & Stuckey, P. J. (2008). Efficient constraint propagation engines. *ACM Transactions on Programming Languages and Systems*, *31*(1), 1–43. doi:10.1145/1452044.1452046

Schulte, C., & Tack, G. (2005). Views and iterators for generic constraint implementations. Principles and Practice of Constraint Programming - {CP} 2005, 11th International Conference, {CP} 2005, Proceedings.

Schulte, C., Tack, G., & Lagerkvist, M. Z. (2019). *Modeling and programming with gecode*. Retrieved May 28, 2019, from https://www.gecode.org/doc-latest/MPG.pdf

Sivertsson, O. (2005). *Construction of Synthetic CDO Squared* (Master's thesis). Computing Science, Department of Information Technology, Uppsala University, Sweden.

Chapter 6
Simple and Population Local Search Approaches for Portfolio Design Problem

ABSTRACT

This chapter introduces a local search optimization technique for solving efficiently a financial portfolio design problem that consists of assigning assets to portfolios, allowing a compromise between maximizing gains, and minimizing losses. This practical problem appears usually in financial engineering, such as in the design of CDO-squared portfolios. This problem has been modeled by Flener et al., who proposed an exact method to solve it. It can be formulated as a quadratic program on the (0,1) domain. It is well known that exact solving approaches on difficult and large instances of quadratic integer programs are known inefficient. That is why the authors have adopted local search methods, namely simple local search and population local search. They propose neighborhood and evaluation functions specialized on this problem. To boost the local search process, they propose also a greedy algorithm to start the search with an optimized initial configuration. Experimental results on non-trivial instances of the problem show the effectiveness of the incomplete approach.

DOI: 10.4018/978-1-7998-1882-3.ch006

INTRODUCTION

The problem tackled in this book was firstly modeled in a set model and solved by CP techniques. Even though the techniques used came from the CP paradigm, the applied approach was based on a series of attempts, which is similar to the behavior of incomplete approaches. Therefore, thinking of approached methods and their application on the problem proved unavoidable.

In this chapter, we propose local search approaches, namely simple and population-based, to tackle a financial portfolio design problem *(PD)* proposed and described in Chapter 3, modeling practical problems in financial engineering such as CDO-squared (Chapter 1). Local search methods have succeeded in tackling combinatorial problems with large instances in many domains (e.g., tsp, scheduling, etc.). When solving combinatorial problems, even if exact methods are complete and guarantee to treat the whole search space, they are usually inefficient on difficult and large instances. Thus, on such problems, the search space should be partially parsed, but intelligently visited, moving from solution to solution optimizing the objective function; this is the main idea of local search methods (João, 2001).

As noticed in Chapter 3, one practical instance of the portfolio design model is the CDO-squared model which is a critical problem in equitable management of clients' portfolios (Gomes and Selman, 2001). We point out that a portfolio is a financial term denoting a collection of investments held by a financial institution or an individual.

In (Flener, Pearson, Reyna & Sivertsson, 2007), the authors proposed a solving approach based on Constraint Programming techniques. They reported that finding the optimal solution is a hard combinatorial problem, and they provide solutions for small instances. However, they proposed a strategy to deconstruct a problem in order to translate large instances into small instances, exploiting some symmetries. Their approach is based on exact methods, but its output has the same nature as local search methods' output.

In fact, due to the combinatorial nature of this problem, applying incomplete methods on the given 0-1 matricial model (Chapter 3) (Lebbah, 2015), should be more efficient. In this chapter, by considering the particular semantic of (PD) constraints, neighborhood and evaluation functions are proposed. An efficient implementation is realized in the INCOP environment (Neveu & Trombettoni, 2003), which has been extended in order to tackle the non-linear constraints, since the 0-1 matricial model is quadratic.

The chapter is organized as follows. In section 2, we address an overview of Local Search aspects and their contribution in solving large instances of complex problems. In section 3, we introduce the adapted algorithms to the (PD) problem. Neighborhood and evaluating functions are also given in this section. In section 4, the greedy algorithm which computes a good initial solution is detailed. In section 5, experiments on several instances[1] are carried out, and a detailed analysis of the results is introduced. Finally, a conclusion and some perspectives are given.

BACKGROUND

Local Search techniques (Teofilo & Gonzalez, 2007) are based on constructive and iterative algorithms. They are created to remedy against the complex methods which require significant fine-tuning. The process of a local search is based generally on starting by an initial solution and improving the current solution by making local changes (in the neighborhood of the current solution), until no progress is possible.

Population-based methods (Luke, 2013) differ from the simple local search, in terms of handling a sample of candidate solutions rather than a single solution. Each solution is involved by tweaking the quality assessment. The behavior of population approach prevents algorithm from falling into the trap of local optima, or being just a parallel hill-climber, since the candidate solutions affect how other candidates will hill-climb in the quality function. The detected good solution in the solutions' sample should cause the rejection of poor solutions or their improvement by being incorporated into good ones.

In the literature, we find numerous local search algorithms, such as Evolutionary Algorithms (SA), Simulated Annealing (SA), and Tabu Search as simple approaches. Additionally, we have Genetic algorithm, Go With the Winners (GWW) and Ant Colony Algorithm as population based algorithms. This kind of algorithms is generally used to tackle substantial problems in a minimum CPU time, and in the case where we need just an approached optimized solution, a good optimized solution, to the problem.

Local search algorithms can be utilized by population-based search techniques in the step of handling a solution within the corresponding population. Thus, a thoughtful hybridization of both techniques should provide better results for the problem in question.

Table 1. Solving the instance PD<15,350,100,λ> and comparison between Flener et al. method and IDWalk local search method.

	Previous approach	IDWalk
Decomposition	06.PD⟨15,60,17,4⟩+PD⟨15,50,10,2⟩	Without
Overlap λ	26	25
Average overlap	26	24.57
Temps CPU (second)	>3600	235.81

Building a CDO Squared portfolio is a complex problem which is modeled in quadratic constraints (Chapter 3), which are mathematically hard to tackle with exact methods. That is why we study in this chapter the behavior of simple and population local search approaches.

In the previous research work given in (Flener, Pearson, Reyna & Sivertsson, 2007), the authors launched a challenge to solve a big CDO Squared portfolio which includes 15 tranches and 350 inner CDOs $PD\langle 15,350,100,\lambda\rangle$ with less than 26 overlaps. In other words, they launched the challenge to build a portfolio which should be more efficient and more optimized.

Effectively, we start by trying the simple local search method IDWalk that requires a simple fine-tuning on the instance $PD\langle 15,350,100,\lambda\rangle$, and the challenge has been raised with providing a better result λ=25, as depicted in Table 1.

This example shows that IDWalk is more efficient than the previous approach with respect to the overlap value and to the runtime [1]. In addition, the previous technique, the portfolio (or the instance) must be split into 7 sub CDO Squared portfolios, to be solved, while the instance is solved by a simple local search algorithm. According to the value of λ and its average, the local search technique yields a more optimized portfolio.

APPLIED LOCAL SEARCH APPROACHES

In this section we adapt the given local search methods in Chapter 2, to be applied on the portfolio design problem. The problem is modeled by a 0-1 matricial model (Model 3.14 in Chapter 3).

Simulated Annealing (SA) Method

As is known, this method, inspired from the metallurgy domain, is characterized by the temperature *T*, which is important in metal cooling (for more details see (Talbi, 2009)). The main steps of this method applied on the (PD) problem are given as follows:

1. Starting with an initial solution, and evaluate where is the objective function.
2. Choosing the variable $Var_{Conflict}$ with *val_conflict* (computed with formula (8)) having the highest absolute value and which is less selected.
3. Flipping $Var_{Conflict}$ value, then computing a new solution S_1 in the neighborhood of S_0. Evaluation of S_1 through $val(S_1)$ (as given in the section …).
   a. if ($val(S_0) \geq val(S_1)$) then S_1 is adopted improving the current solution S_0.
   b. If $val(S_0) < val(S_1)$ then we compute $v = exp^{-\frac{(val(S_1) - val(S_0))}{T}}$. We take a randomized value *r* in [0,1]. If $r \leq v$ then S_0 is replaced by S_1 and *val_conflict* matrix is updated.
4. *T* is decreased slowly at each iteration. If $T < \epsilon$ then the algorithm is stopped and S_0 is declared as an optimal solution else we continue with the step 2.

The given SA algorithm is different from the standard form of SA, since there the transition function is not a random neighbor, whereas in the adapted algorithm we choose the best neighbor through the neighborhood function FLIP given below. Consequently, we lose the Markov chain properties (Darrall et al., 2003) guaranteeing convergence. However, termination is guaranteed by the finiteness of solutions and the strict decreasing of the temperature.

IDWalk Method

IDWalk (Intensification and Diversification Walk) (Neveu et al., 2004) is characterized by two parameters: *MN* which is the maximum neighbors to cover and *SN* (spare neighbor) which is the neighbor to wind. Consider the current solution *CS* and the best solution *BS*. According to (PD) problem, this method is defined in two steps:

- **Intensification:**
    a. Starting with an initial solution S_0, and evaluate $val(S_0)$ where val is the objective function. S_0 is considered as the current solution CS.
    b. The MN neighbors of the current solution are explored.
    c. We choose the best neighbor BN, by flipping the variable $Var_{Conflict}$ (as given in section …),
    d. if BN is better than the current solution, CS is replaced by BN and *val-conflict* is updated.
- **Diversification:**

if BN does not improve CS then we choose the best one in SN first neighbors. In the case of $SN=1$ we choose a randomized neighbor.

IDWalk is a simple and effective metaheuristic requiring only one parameter, which is the maximum number of candidate neighbors. Practically, IDWalk has been more efficient than Tabu-Search.

The simplicity and the effectiveness in using and parameterizing IDWalk makes it a good candidate to be compared to Simulated-Annealing.

GWW Method

Considering the threshold T, the current solution CS and the worst solution WS. According to (PD) problem, this method is defined in the following steps:

1. Starting with a population of n initial particles (solutions) $S = \{S_0, S_1, \ldots S_{N-1}\}$ distributed randomly.
2. The threshold T is fixed to $SW \in S$, such as SW is the solution having the biggest value $val(S_i)$, $i \in 0..n-1$.
3. Applying a specific simple local search method on each $S_i \in S$, as T the evaluation of the best solution.
4. Each $S_i \in S$ is replaced by the best found within the corresponding neighborhood:
    (a) $\forall s \in S$, if $val(s) \geq val(CS)$ then s called dead particles.
    (b) $\forall s \in S$, if $val(s) < val(CS)$ then s called living particles.
    (c) CS is replaced by the best solution in S.
    (d) SW is replaced by the worst solution in S and T by $val(SW)$.
5. If stop condition reached then return CS (the best-found solution), else go to step 3.

Evaluation Function

Conceptually, a (PD) instance is characterized by a feasible space and an objective function which associates a cost value to each solution. The cost function (or the evaluation function) *EVAL* computes the number of the violated constraints in the model, with regard to the configuration *M*:

$$EVAL(M) = \sum_{k\in 1..m} \begin{cases} +1 \text{ if } i^{th} \text{ constraint is violated with } M \\ 0 \; else \end{cases} \quad (6.1)$$

Where *m* is the constraints' number. The function EVAL is also the objective function of the portfolio design problem tackled. Obviously, the optimal solutions match the configurations, which satisfy all the constraints.

Neighborhood Function *FLIP*

Let (PD) be the optimization problem described in chapter 3. Let *M* be a configuration (or solution) of a (PD) instance. The neighborhood function defines the set of neighbor configurations *N(M)* of *M*, by applying some modifications on *M*.

The neighborhood function *FLIP* is used in the local search approaches, applied on the configuration *M*, outputs a new configuration $M' \in N(M)$, which is computed by flipping the *0-1*value of the variable $M_{l,c}$ having the highest conflict value. The selection of the variable $M_{l,c}$ depends on the applied local search method.

In the case of simple local search methods, we spot the two indices (*l*,*c*) of the selected variable $M_{l,c}$ having the most conflicts and being the least changed:

$$(l,c) = \arg\max_{i\in 1..v, j\in 1..b}(abs(val\_conflict_{i,j}) - compt_{i,j})$$

where $compt_{i,j}$ is the counter of the number of times the variable $M_{i,j}$ has been changed. Matrix *val_conflict* contains conflicts evaluation of the individual variable $M_{i,j}$. We associate a conflict value $val\_conflict_{i,j}$ to each variable $M_{i,j}$ as given below:

$$val\_conflict_{i,j} = \sum_{k \in 1..m} \begin{cases} +1 & \text{if } M_{i,j} \in vars(C_k), C_k \text{ has the form "} f_k(M)=0 \text{"} \\ & \text{and } val(f_k(M)) < 0 \\ -1 & \text{if } M_{i,j} \in vars(C_k), C_k \text{ has the form "} f_k(M)=0 \text{"} \\ & \text{and } val(f_k(M)) > 0 \\ -1 & \text{if } M_{i,j} \in vars(C_k), C_k \text{ has the form "} f_k(M) \leq 0 \text{"} \\ & \text{and } val(f_k(M)) > 0 \\ 0 & else \end{cases} \tag{6.7}$$

Where m is the number of constraints in (*PD*) system, $vars(C_k)$ is the set of variables appearing in constraint C_k, $val(f_k(M))$ is the value of f_k function at the configuration M. In other words, when computing $val\_conflict_{i,j}$, we consider +1 (resp. -1), if the left hand side of the constraint C_k should be increased (resp. decreased) in the direction of its satisfaction. Let $M[1..v][1..b]$ be some configuration; we identify $Var_{Conflict}$ as the variable corresponding to the largest absolute conflict. Consequently, the value of this variable is changed: if it has the null value *0*, it is replaced by *1*, else *0*. The matrix M of the configuration is changed by applying the described modification on the variable $Var_{conflict}$.

GREEDY INITIAL SOLUTION

Local search algorithms need an initial configuration to start the search. A random generated configuration is usually used. Precisely, the goal of this greedy algorithm 1, is to return a configuration matrix m with a very few violated constraints, compared with a random generated configuration. *Greedyinit* takes into account the origin of the considered constraint: *ct="row"* for the row constraint, and *ct="overlap"* for the overlap constraint (see definition 1). The first loop of *greedyinit* tries to fill some diagonals to satisfy as well as possible the overlap constraint of the (PD) model. The second loop tries to satisfy the row constraint. In the second loop, to satisfy the maximum of the row constraints, the algorithm tries to fill r cells in the row. At the first iteration, the algorithm jumps λ columns, and $\lambda+1$ in the remaining iterations. While the number of jumps is high, the risk of violating the overlap constraint is decreased. The jump is fixed to $\lambda+1$ to not penalize excessively the row constraint.

Algorithm 1 GreedyInit(PD < v, b, r, λ >)

```
Input: v number of tranches; b number of titles; r number of
titles per tranche; λ number of overlaps;
M matrix v × b initialized to zero.
Ensure: An initial configuration matrix M [v × b] reducing the
number of conflicts {Overlap constraint}
for i∈1..λ + 1 do
   FillDiagonal(i , "Overlap")
end for
  {Row constraint}
    i ← λ + ( λ + 1)
while i≤ b do
    FillDiagonal(i , "Row")
    i  ← i + ( λ + 1)
end while
return M
```

Algorithm *GreedyInit* is based on *FillDiagonal* Algorithm 2 which fills with 1 the diagonal beginning at *(1, i)*. *FillDiagonal* begins by computing the max number of cells (*Max* variable in the algorithm) that can be filled in the diagonal beginning at *(1, i)*. *Max* depends on the matrix dimensions $v \times b$ and the value of *i*. For instance, let be the matrix $M_{<7,7,3,1>}$ illustrated below: the diagonal at *(1,i=1)* has *Max=7* cells to fill; the diagonal at *(1, i=2)* has *Max=6*; and the diagonal at *(1,i=4)* has *Max=4*.

Algorithm 2 FillDiagonal(i, Ct)

```
Input: v number of tranches; b number of titles; Mmatrix v × b;
Ct = "Overlap" or "Row"
Ensure: Filling the diagonal of M [v × b] starting at(1 , i)
Max ← if (b ≥ (min(v , b) + i - 1)) then min(v , b)
       else b - i + 1
for j ∈1 .. Max do
    M[ j][i + j - 1] ← 1
end for
if (Ct = "Overlap") then
    Jump ← i - (b - min(v , b) + 1)
else if (Ct = "Row") then
    Jump ← 0
end if
for j ∈1..v - Max do
    M[Max + j][Jump + j] ← 1
end for
return M
```

The first loop of *filldiagonal* algorithm fills the diagonal beginning at *(1, i)* until reaching the last row or the last column, by using the variable *max*. In the second loop, *filldiagonal* completes the first loop by filling a second diagonal beginning at the next row, precisely *(max+1, jump+1)*, in order to satisfy the overlap and row constraints. The *jump* variable depends on the nature of the considered constraint. Concerning the *row* constraint, since in this case we should consider only the current row, then simply *jump=0* meaning that the diagonal begins at *(max+1,1)*. However, for the overlap constraint, we should avoid increasing overlaps with other rows. Thus *jump* is fixed to *i-(b-min(v,b)+1)* enabling us to avoid overlaps with the first *i* diagonals where we take into account some gap *b-min(v, b)* in the case where $v \geq b$.

Algorithm *GreedyInit* is illustrated in the following table. The first diagonal 1_1 is the standard one which begins at *(1,1)* and finishes at *(7, 7)*. The third diagonal containing 1_3 begins at *(1,4)*, ends at *(4,7)*, but since it does not reach the last line, it continues at the first column of the next line *(5,1)* to finish at the last row at *(7, 3)*. Notice that the application of the algorithm on the instance ⟨7,7,3,1⟩, building a portfolio including 7 tranches and 7 inner CDOS, allows us to obtain directly a configuration with *0* conflicted constraints, illustrated in the table above.

$$M_{<7,7,3,1>} = \begin{array}{|ccccccc|} 1_1 & 1_2 & 0 & 1_3 & 0 & 0 & 0 \\ 0 & 1_1 & 1_2 & 0 & 1_3 & 0 & 0 \\ 0 & 0 & 1_1 & 1_2 & 0 & 1_3 & 0 \\ 0 & 0 & 0 & 1_1 & 1_2 & 0 & 1_3 \\ 1_3 & 0 & 0 & 0 & 1_1 & 1_2 & 0 \\ 0 & 1_3 & 0 & 0 & 0 & 1_1 & 1_2 \\ 1_2 & 0 & 1_3 & 0 & 0 & 0 & 1_1 \end{array}$$

$$M_{<10,8,3,2>} = \begin{array}{|cccccccc|} 1_1 & 1_2 & 1_3 & 0 & 0 & 0 & 0 & 0 \\ 0 & 1_1 & 1_2 & 1_3 & 0 & 0 & 0 & 0 \\ 0 & 0 & 1_1 & 1_2 & 1_3 & 0 & 0 & 0 \\ 0 & 0 & 0 & 1_1 & 1_2 & 1_3 & 0 & 0 \\ 0 & 0 & 0 & 0 & 1_1 & 1_2 & 1_3 & 0 \\ 0 & 0 & 0 & 0 & 0 & 1_1 & 1_2 & 1_3 \\ 0 & 0 & 1_3 & 0 & 0 & 0 & 1_1 & 1_2 \\ 0 & 1_2 & 0 & 1_3 & 0 & 0 & 0 & 1_1 \\ 1_1 & 0 & 1_2 & 0 & 1_3 & 0 & 0 & 0 \\ 0 & 1_1 & 0 & 1_2 & 0 & 1_3 & 0 & 0 \end{array}$$

$$M_{<8,14,7,3>} = \begin{array}{|cccccccccccccc|} 1_1 & 1_2 & 1_3 & 1_4 & 0 & 0 & 0 & 1_5 & 0 & 0 & 0 & 0 & 1_6 & 0 \\ 0 & 1_1 & 1_2 & 1_3 & 1_4 & 0 & 0 & 0 & 1_5 & 0 & 0 & 0 & 0 & 1_6 \\ 1_6 & 0 & 1_1 & 1_2 & 1_3 & 1_4 & 0 & 0 & 0 & 1_5 & 0 & 0 & 0 & 0 \\ 0 & 1_6 & 0 & 1_1 & 1_2 & 1_3 & 1_4 & 0 & 0 & 0 & 1_5 & 0 & 0 & 0 \\ 0 & 0 & 1_6 & 0 & 1_1 & 1_2 & 1_3 & 1_4 & 0 & 0 & 0 & 1_5 & 0 & 0 \\ 0 & 0 & 0 & 1_6 & 0 & 1_1 & 1_2 & 1_3 & 1_4 & 0 & 0 & 0 & 1_5 & 0 \\ 0 & 0 & 0 & 0 & 1_6 & 0 & 1_1 & 1_2 & 1_3 & 1_4 & 0 & 0 & 0 & 1_5 \\ 1_5 & 0 & 0 & 0 & 0 & 1_6 & 0 & 1_1 & 1_2 & 1_3 & 1_4 & 0 & 0 & 0 \end{array}$$

Let be a second instance $PD\langle 10,8,3,2\rangle$, building a portfolio including 10 tranches and 8 inner CDOS, having more rows than columns. After applying Algorithm 1, we obtain the configuration $M_{\langle 10,8,3,2\rangle}$ with *0* conflicts.

Let be now the instance $PD\langle 8,14,7,3\rangle$, a portfolio including 8 tranches and 14 inner CDOS, having more columns than rows. After applying Algorithm 1, we obtain the configuration $M_{<8,14,7,3>}$ with 8 conflicts.

Proposition 1

Algorithm 1 has the worst case complexity O(vr).

Proof:

At most r cells per row will be filled, which cannot be greater than *vr*.

The following proposition states some interesting properties on some cases where the greedy algorithm succeeds in satisfying constraints of the *(PD)* problem.

Proposition 2

If

- $\lambda + 1 = r$
- *or* $(\lambda + 1, r) \wedge 2(\lambda + 1) + (r - (\lambda + 1) - 1)(\lambda + 2) \leq b$

then the row constraints are satisfied.

If one of the above conditions is satisfied, and ($r \leq \lambda + 3$), then all the overlap constraints are verified.

Sketch of the Proof: In the first loop of Algorithm 1, we succeed in affecting $\lambda+1$ with the value 1 to each row. Thus, to satisfy row constraints, the second loop of the same algorithm affects the remaining $r-(\lambda+1)$ with the value 1 to each row. At each iteration, the number of the value 1 is increased in each row of the matrix. In the second loop, if $\lambda+1 \neq$ r then we should have

$2(\lambda+1)+(r-(\lambda+1)-1)(\lambda+2)\leq b$ to satisfy all the row constraints. More precisely, since the second loop increases i with $(\lambda+2)$, then the remaining $(r-(\lambda+1)-1)$ non-filled cells with value 1, should be assigned without exceeding b. This states the first property of the proposition.

After the first loop of Algorithm 1, we get at most λ overlaps. After the first loop, *FillDiagonal* is called at the diagonal $2(\lambda+1)$, and in this way we keep the overlap constraints verified. In the second loop we consider diagonals at positions spaced with $\lambda+2$. At the first diagonal spaced with $\lambda+2$, the overlap constraints remain satisfied. Nevertheless, in the following diagonals, there is a risk of violating the overlap constraints. Consequently, when $r\leq\lambda+1+1+1$ the overlap constraints are sure to be satisfied.

By using the greedy algorithm to compute the initial solution, we expect to have a different behavior compared to using a random solution. Intuitively, with an initial random solution, the algorithm is suitable to reach more solutions than with the greedy solution. However, although with random solution we get more solutions, with the greedy we have fewer, but better solutions. In the experimental results given, the greedy version is usually more efficient than the random one.

RESULTS BASED LOCAL SEARCH FRAMEWORK

This section reports experimental results on various instances of a financial portfolio, with simulated annealing and IDWalk local search methods.

The given experiments are carried on the (PD) problem where λ is fixed. The machine used has the following configuration: Linux-Ubuntu 12.04, Intel CPU E5-2603 and 8 GB/RAM. The experiments are realized in INCOP by integrating the neighborhood and evaluation functions, described previously.

In the first set of experiments, we use a random starting configuration. A configuration is an instantiation of the variables with 0-1 values. In (PD), a configuration is the instantiation of the M matrix, where for all (i, j), $M_{i,j}$ is instantiated to 0 or 1. A second series of experiments is launched with an initial configuration computed with GreedyInit algorithm.

Experimental Protocol

Table 2 describes experimented (PD) instances as well as the number of their constraints and variables.

Table 2. Experimented instances

Instance	⟨v,b,r,λ⟩	Variables number	Constraints number
Inst1	⟨7,7,3,1⟩	49	28
Inst2	⟨10,8,3,1⟩	80	55
Inst3	⟨8,14,7,3⟩	112	36
Inst4	⟨11,11,5,2⟩	121	66
Inst5	⟨16,8,3,1⟩	128	136
Inst6	⟨10,15,6,2⟩	150	55
Inst7	⟨9,18,8,3⟩	162	45
Inst8	⟨9,24,8,2⟩	216	45
Inst9	⟨15,15,4,1⟩	225	120
Inst10	⟨10,25,8,2⟩	250	55
Inst11	⟨10,30,9,2⟩	300	55
Inst12	⟨9,37,12,3⟩	333	45
Inst13	⟨10,37,14,6⟩	270	55
Inst14	⟨10,38,10,2⟩	380	55
Inst15	⟨19,20,9,4⟩	380	190
Inst16	⟨15,350,100,25⟩	5250	1575

For the two methods of simple local search, we adopt the following parameters:

- max number of moves is 10 000; max number of neighbors is 300. These parameters come from many tests and general recommendations given by (Neveu B. and Trombettoni G., 2003; Neveu et al., 2004).
- The unique parameter of Simulated Annealing, the initial temperature, is fixed to 0.4.
- For IDWalk method, the second parameter is the so called Spare-neighbor fixed to 150 (for more details see (Neveu et al. 2004)).

For population method GWW, we have parameterized it with several local searches, namely IDWalk, Tabu and Simulated Annealing.

To ensure the termination of the different applied approaches, a time out is needed. It is fixed, experimentally, to *200* seconds.

In order to evaluate the robustness of all the methods of local search we completed 20 runs on each method. Executable files and documentation are available on https://sites.google.com/site/fzlebbahportfolio/.

For each experimented local search algorithm, we give the following columns:

- *SUCC*: the number of successful calls to the local search over 20 calls,
- *AVG-TIME*: the average time of the 20 calls.

The first comparison is realized with the cited parameters: *SUCC* and *AVG-TIME*. The second is done by considering the quality of the found solution, which consists in computing the average of the obtained overlaps, as shown in formula (6.2). More precisely, we should take into account $v(v-1)/2$overlaps, because the first row has overlaps with the remaining *v-1* rows, the second with *(v-2)* rows, and so on until the last two lines. Overall, $no= (v-1)+(v-2)+\ldots+2+1 =v(v-1)/2$overlaps should be considered.

$$\begin{cases} \lambda - Avg = \dfrac{\sum_{i=1}^{no} \lambda_i}{no} \\ no = \dfrac{(v)(v-1)}{2} \text{number of overlaps} \end{cases} \tag{6.2}$$

- λ-AVG: the average of the computed overlaps over 20 runs
- C-AVG: the average of the computed conflicts over 20 runs

Experimental Results

Simple Local Search

Table 3 establishes the results of simulated annealing and IDWalk methods, with random and computed initial configurations. The number of successful calls to the local search over 20 runs (SUCC) and the average time of the 20 calls (AVG-TIME) are given for each method launched with the two types of initial solution.

Table 4. shows the respective averages of the number of failed constraints (C-AVG) and the overlaps (λ-AVG) through the 20 runs, realized by Simulated Annealing and IDWalk methods, with random and computed initial configurations. The average of overlaps made previously (Flener et al.,2007) is also given within the column PrRes.

Table 3. Experimental results of simulated annealing and IDWalk on the instances given by Flener et al., with random and greedy initial configurations, the successful runs and the average of runtimes.

		RandSol		**InitSol**	
Instance		**SimAn**	**IDW**	**SimAn**	**IDW**
Inst1	SUCC./20 AVG-TIME	20 0.00	17 3.70	20 0.01	20 0.00
Inst2	SUCC./20 AVG-TIME	20 0.00	20 00.00	20 0.00	20 0.00
Inst3	SUCC./20 AVG-TIME	20 1.73	01 14.10	20 4.22	20 20.70
Inst4	SUCC./20 AVG-TIME	20 1.15	00 15.63	20 4.01	20 0.02
Inst5	SUCC./20 AVG-TIME	00 15.52	00 16.17	00 23.75	00 42.23
Inst6	SUCC./20 AVG-TIME	19 5.33	00 23.76	20 7.66	00 49.75
Inst7	SUCC./20 AVG-TIME	8 11.43	00 21.20	18 12.32	20 1.61
Inst8	SUCC./20 AVG-TIME	19 8.38	00 50.17	20 15.21	20 5.47
Inst9	SUCC./20 AVG-TIME	20 5.44	00 119.40	20 14.81	00 199.84
Inst10	SUCC./20 AVG-TIME	10 31.96	00 67.76	14 44.70	20 71.43
Inst11	SUCC./20 AVG-TIME	18 19.36	00 64.75	17 37.66	20 9.66
Inst12	SUCC./20 AVG-TIME	20 10.84	20 64.66	17 36.59	20 7.02
Inst13	SUCC./20 AVG-TIME	20 0.01	20 0.03	20 0.02	20 0.02
Inst14	SUCC./20 AVG-TIME	20 4.14	13 48.90	20 11.33	20 3.22
Inst15	SUCC./20 AVG-TIME	00 25.60	00 28.95	00 44.70	00 83.61
Inst16	SUCC./20 AVG-TIME	02 196.76	01 193.31	00 199.84	00 199.92

Column *RandSol* in Table 4 compares the number of success and the runtime average of Simulated Annealing and IDWalk from a random initial configuration. Simulated annealing succeeds in finding the best solution in many runs for all instances in an efficient time, but IDWalk fails in most of the instances. We have also experimented with Tabu Search (where the lengthof

Table 4. Experimental results of simulated annealing and IDWalk on the instances given by Flener et al., with random and greedy initial configurations. the average number of conflicts and the average number of overlaps.

		RandSol		InitSol		
Instance		SimAn	IDW	SimAn	IDW	PrRes
Inst1	C-AVG λ-AVG	0.00 1.00	0.20 0.99	0.00 1.00	0.00 1.00	1
Inst2	C-AVG λ-AVG	0.00 1.07	0.00 1.08	0.00 1.00	0.00 0.98	2
Inst3	C-AVG λ-AVG	0.00 3.00	2.00 2.80	0.00 3.00	2.00 2.64	3
Inst4	C-AVG λ-AVG	0.00 2.00	3.75 1.75	0.00 2.00	0.00 2.00	2
Inst5	C-AVG λ-AVG	8.00 0.68	8.75 0.63	8.00 0.63	8.00 0.70	1
Inst6	C-AVG λ-AVG	0.05 2.00	2.65 1.83	0.00 2.00	2.00 1.64	2
Inst7	C-AVG λ-AVG	0.60 2.88	3.15 2.76	0.10 2.97	0.00 3.00	3
Inst8	C-AVG λ-AVG	0.05 1.99	50.17 1.92	0.00 2.00	0.00 2.00	2
Inst9	C-AVG λ-AVG	0.00 0.86	1.35 0.83	0.00 0.86	1.00 0.81	1
Inst10	C-AVG λ-AVG	0.50 1.95	2.30 1.88	0.30 1.93	0.00 2.00	2
Inst11	C-AVG λ-AVG	0.10 1.99	3.30 1.92	0.15 1.97	0.00 2.00	2
Inst12	C-AVG λ-AVG	0.00 2.97	2.45 2.89	0.15 2.98	0.00 2.97	3
Inst13	C-AVG λ-AVG	0.00 4.89	0.00 4.88	0.00 4.99	0.00 5.00	6
Inst14	C-AVG λ-AVG	0.00 1.94	0.90 1.94	0.00 1.94	0.00 1.98	2
Inst15	C-AVG λ-AVG	5.40 3.48	7.90 3.37	3.30 3.36	3.00 3.38	4
Inst16	C-AVG λ-AVG	1.25 24.57	1.95 24.55	4.50 24.37	3.30 24.33	26

Tabu list is 20) which succeeds in solving only three instances: ⟨7,7,3,1⟩ with 2/20 successes, ⟨10,8,3,2⟩ with 20/20, ⟨10,37,14,6⟩ with 11/20. In the other words, building optimized CDO Squared portfolios, which include 7 tranches and 7 inners portfolios, or 10 tranches and 8 inner portfolios, or 10 tranches and 37 inner portfolios, represents a total success.

We notice that in the most cases, Simulated Annealing presents a total success on 20 runs. Simulated Annealing remains more efficient than IDWalk in runtime.

- **Random Initial Configuration**
  Column *RandSol* in Table 4 compares the quality of results calculated by formula (9) between Flener et al., Simulated annealing and IDWalk. We notice that the average of the overlaps given beyond the set model is equal to λ. The applied approaches on the 0-1 matricial model are more efficient. In most instances, the number of overlaps of the given solutions is perfectly minimized.
  The average of the violated constraints realized by Simulated Annealing is less than IDWalk. Therefore, Simulated Annealing is more efficient, regarding the rate of violated constraints.
- **Greedy Initial Solution**
  Running IDWalk algorithm on random initial solutions has not been successful. Thus, we have adopted an initial configuration coming from a fast-greedy algorithm *GreedyInit* (Algorithm 1) trying to reduce the number of conflicts.
  In Table 5, we report the behavior of the greedy Algorithm 1 to minimize the number of the conflicted constraints, compared to a randomly generated configuration. We notice that Algorithm 1 computes better initial configurations: all the conflicts are significantly lower than the randomly generated configurations. In some instances, such as ⟨7,7,3,1⟩ and ⟨10,8,3,2⟩, GreedyInit computes initial configurations with *0* conflicts, i.e., the optimized portfolio including 7 tranches and 7 inners portfolios, or 10 tranches and 8 inner portfolios, or 10 tranches and 37 inner portfolios, are computed easily by GreedyInit.

In the randomly generated configuration, we report the interval of number of conflicts. With Algorithm 1, only one configuration can be generated with its number of conflicts given in the third column.

Column *InitSol* in Table 3 compares between Simulated Annealing and IDWalk methods, where the initial configuration is computed with the greedy Algorithm 1. We report the number of successful runs, and the average of runtimes. We notice that running Simulated Annealing and IDWalk with the greedy configuration is efficient. Algorithm 1 allows IDWalk to be more efficient, and competes well with simulated annealing. We observe that in many cases, IDWalk succeeds in all of the 20 runs. We have also experimented with

Table 5. Comparison of the number of conflicted constraints, between the randomly generated initial configuration and the greedy configuration computed with Algorithm 1.

Instance	Random configuration	Greedy configuration
7-7-3-1	10 --25	0
8-14-7-3	11 -- 27	8
9-18-8-3	24 -- 39	17
9-24-8-2	40 -- 45	6
9-37-12-3	43 -- 45	13
10-30-9-2	53 -- 55	8
10-15-6-2	29 -- 54	11
10-8-3-2	11 -- 35	0
10-25-8-2	51 -- 55	9
10-37-14-6	40 -- 54	10
10-38-10-2	52 -- 55	8
10-33-15-6	34 -- 51	10
10-31-22-15	10 -- 11	10
10-38-28-20	10 -- 10	10
11-11-5-2	28 -- 48	13
15-15-4-1	98 – 119	15
16-8-3-1	59-111	23

Tabu Search (where the length of Tabu list is 20) which succeeds in solving only three instances: ⟨7,7,3,1⟩with 20/20 successes, ⟨10,8,3,2⟩ with 20/20, ⟨10,37,14,6⟩ with 20/20. Thus, Tabu search remains inefficient compared with Simulated Annealing and IDWalk. Since the optimized portfolio including 7 tranches and 7 inner portfolios, or 10 tranches and 8 inner portfolios, or 10 tranches and 37 inner portfolios, are already provided by GreedyInit, the initial solution is optimal and the applied local search methods are not launched.

The averages of violated constraints with Simulated Annealing and IDWalk are similar. Therefore, starting with a computed initial solution allows IDWalk to compete with Simulated Annealing, with regard to the rate of violated constraints.

Landscape Analysis

Through Table 4, we can distinguish three types of instances:

Type 1: Very hard instances whose resolution does not give us any success, with a total block on a number of conflicts.

Type 2: Hard instances whose resolution gives us 0 or few successes on 20 runs, but with a slow improvement (decreasing) of conflicts' number.

Type 3: Very easy instances whose resolution gives us an absolute success (20 successes on 20 runs).

Figure 1. Landscape of the instance PD⟨16,8,3,1⟩

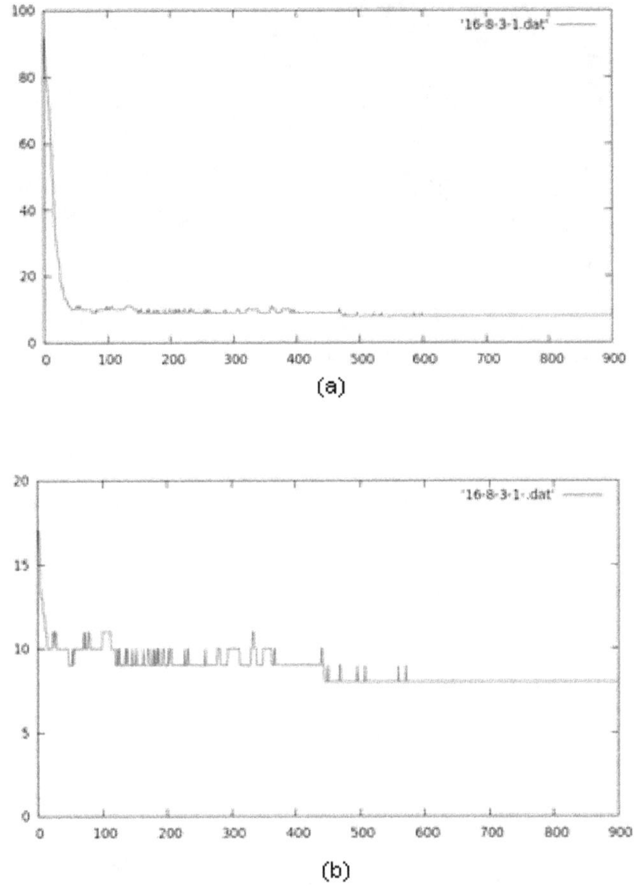

In order to well study the instances and detect the origin of the failure and of the success, we took a sample of each instances' type, namely ⟨16,8,3,1⟩, ⟨19,20,9,4⟩ and ⟨9,37,12,3⟩ which represent respectively the types 1, 2 and 3. This is in order to carry out landscape analysis of each instance.

Instance ⟨16,8,3,1⟩

The CDO Squared portfolio with 16 tranches and 8 inner portfolios, noted ⟨16,8,3,1⟩, can be considered very hard, through the null number of success and the number of conflict that stagnates at 8. The resolution of this instance represents a real block of the method, since we arrive to a number of conflicts without any improvement observed through the realized moves.

Figure 2. Landscape of the instance PD⟨19,20,9,4⟩

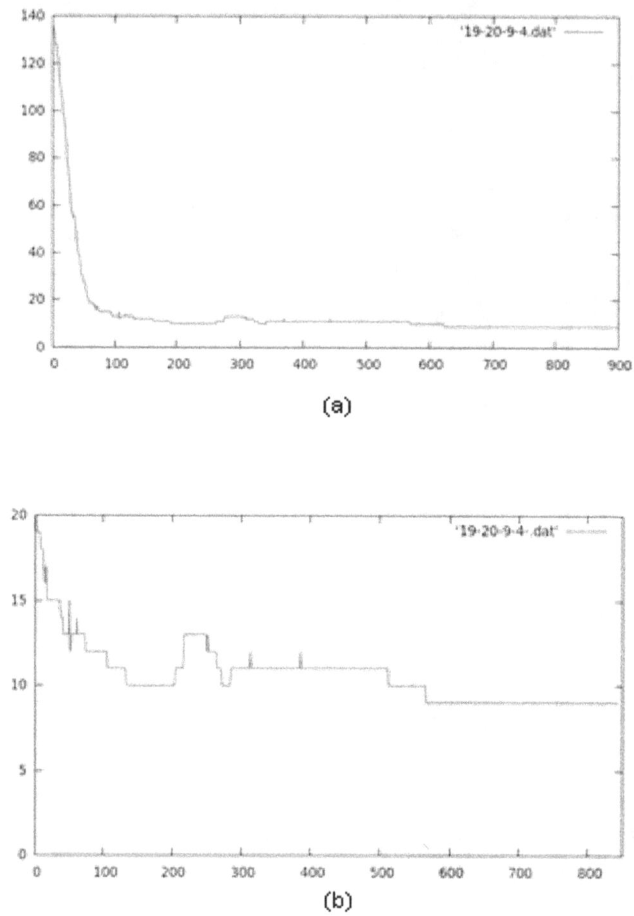

Figure 1 represents a global view of the landscape Figure 1a then we give a closer view to the curve, to analyze the landscape well Figure 1b.

In figure 6.1(a) we notice the quick going down of the curve before reaching 50 moves; the local search approach succeeds in decreasing the number of conflicts (in order to obtain the 0) which was ≥90 at a value ≤20, in less than 50 moves. Just after, the curve becomes very rugged (rugged landscape), a phenomenon that will gradually fade until reaching a neutral landscape. Figure 6.1(b) allows us to analyze the curve well, which is smooth at the beginning, then rugged before becoming neutral reaching number of conflicts 8, a neutral curve that highlights the problem of local minimums.

Figure 3. Landscape of the instance ⟨9,37,12,3⟩

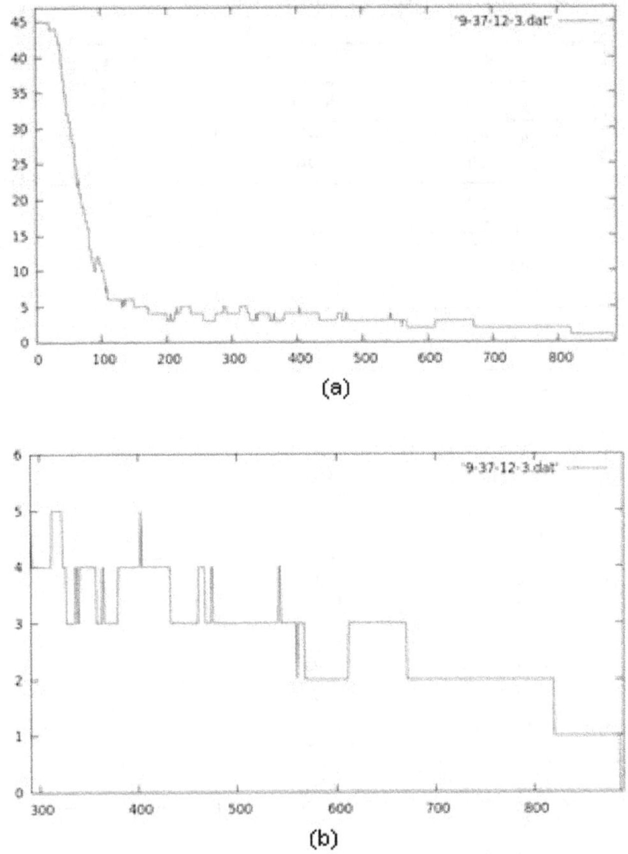

Instance ⟨19,20,9,4⟩

The resolution of the instance ⟨19,20,9,4⟩ (CDO Squared portfolio with 19 tranches and 20 inner portfolios) provides 0 successes, but with a variation of violation degrees between 20 runs. Figure 2 shows firstly the whole landscape (Figure 2a then we give an enlarged view of the neutral part of the landscape in Figure 2b.

We can detect the same phenomenon of the curve decreasing in Figure 1(a), starting with number of conflicts ≥130 towards 20 conflicts in less than 100 moves. We notice via Figure 1(b) a smooth curve, then rugged until becoming neutral; representing a case of the problem of local minimum.

Instance ⟨9,37,12,3⟩

Table 6. Experimental results of GWW combined with simple local search methods, the successful runs and the average of runtimes.

		GWW		
Instance		**GSimAn**	**GIDW**	**GIDWTab**
Inst1	SUCC./20 AVG-TIME	20 1.29	20 0.61	20 28.297
Inst2	SUCC./20 AVG-TIME	20 0.00	20 0.00	20 0.00
Inst3	SUCC./20 AVG-TIME	05 107.56	13 106.84	01 190.53
Inst4	SUCC./20 AVG-TIME	15 165.43	16 90.37	03 183.24
Inst5	SUCC./20 AVG-TIME	00 199.66	00 199.60	00 199.62
Inst6	SUCC./20 AVG-TIME	00 199.65	04 168.71	00 199.63
Inst7	SUCC./20 AVG-TIME	01 189.01	03 094.59	00 199.63
Inst8	SUCC./20 AVG-TIME	01 199.05	09 133.28	00 199.63
Inst9	SUCC./20 AVG-TIME	00 199.65	12 130.95	00 199.64
Inst10	SUCC./20 AVG-TIME	00 199.66	00 199.64	00 199.64
Inst11	SUCC./20 AVG-TIME	00 199.64	02 190.98	00 199.63
Inst12	SUCC./20 AVG-TIME	00 199.65	16 97.10	15 91.35
Inst13	SUCC./20 AVG-TIME	20 0.04	20 0.10	20 0.80
Inst14	SUCC./20 AVG-TIME	00 199.65	20 13.67	20 59.54
Inst15	SUCC./20 AVG-TIME	00 199.64	00 199.64	00 199.63
Inst16	SUCC./20 AVG-TIME	00 199.65	02 184.06	00 199.64

Table 7. Experimental results of GWW combined with simple local search methods, the average of number of conflicts and the average of overlaps

		GWW			
Instance		**GSimAn**	**GIDW**	**GIDWTab**	**PrRes**
Inst1	C-AVG λ-AVG	1.28 1.00	0.00 1.00	0.00 1.00	1
Inst2	C-AVG λ-AVG	0.00 1.06	0.00 1.07	0.00 1.07	2
Inst3	C-AVG λ-AVG	0.80 2.88	0.35 2.99	1.90 2.75	3
Inst4	C-AVG λ-AVG	0.30 1.97	0.20 1.98	1.55 1.82	2
Inst5	C-AVG λ-AVG	8.00 0.69	8.00 0.66	8.05 0.58	1
Inst6	C-AVG λ-AVG	1.45 1.88	0.80 1.94	3.00 1.73	2
Inst7	C-AVG λ-AVG	1.70 2.80	1.25 2.92	2.45 2.77	3
Inst8	C-AVG λ-AVG	1.80 1.81	0.65 1.97	1.95 1.92	2
Inst9	C-AVG λ-AVG	3.15 0.78	0.40 0.82	1.60 0.83	1
Inst10	C-AVG λ-AVG	2.65 1.75	1.00 1.91	2.20 1.85	2
Inst11	C-AVG λ-AVG	3.10 1.72	1.50 1.94	3.30 0.83	2
Inst12	C-AVG λ-AVG	2.15 2.59	0.20 2.95	0.25 2.96	3
Inst13	C-AVG λ-AVG	0.00 4.85	0.00 4.83	0.00 4.93	6
Inst14	C-AVG λ-AVG	2.15 1.69	0.00 1.94	0.00 1.95	2
Inst15	C-AVG λ-AVG	9.70 3.05	5.15 3.50	7.05 3.36	4
Inst16	C-AVG λ-AVG	6.2 20.17	1.65 24.55	10.10 24.36	26

Finally we present the landscape realized by local search approach applied on ⟨9,37,12,3⟩ (portfolio including 9 tranches and 37 inner portfolios), which gives 20 successes on 20 in a reasonable time. Figure 6.3 shows this landscape starting from 45 conflicts until 0 conflicts (all the constraints are satisfied).

We notice in Figure 3(a) a curve that is more or less neutral at the beginning, then a quick convergence from 45 to 5 conflicts in only 100 moves. Figure

Figure 4. Profile of performances of SLS according the number of success

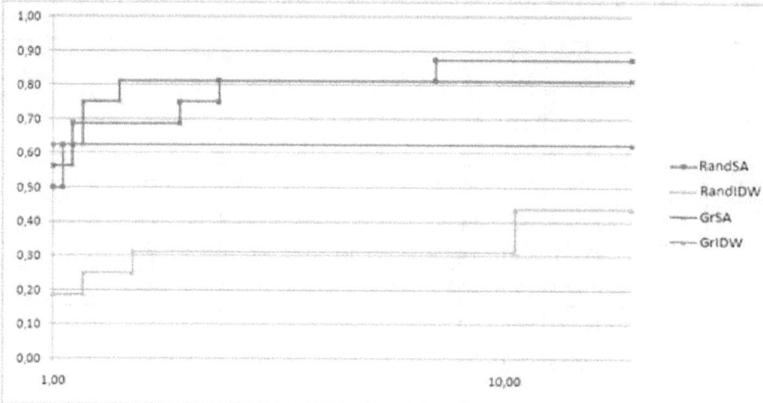

3(b) shows a closer view of the curve after reaching 5 conflicts. We notice a smooth landscape reflecting a good quality of exploration; the method is well adapted to solve the instance.

Finally, we conclude that the method failure on an instance is represented by the neutral parts in the landscape. This phenomenon can be explained by very deep valleys (problem of local minima), which requires the improvement of exploration degree. However, this improvement can decrease the quality of results if the landscape is smooth. A more thoughtful management of the characteristics of each part of the landscape should improve the results. In other words, proposing an exploration procedure adapted to a specific phase in solving the instance.

Population Local Search GWW

In this section, we present the experimental results of GWW combined with Simulated Annealing (column GSimAn), with IDWalk (column GIDW), and with IDWalk combined with Tabu search (column GIDWTab). Table 6 (resp. Table 7) establishes the performances in number of successes and in runtime (resp. in number of violated constraints and in average of overlaps).

Combination of GWW and IDWalk outperforms GWW combined with Simulated Annealing and GWW combined with IDW and Tabu.

In short, the efficiency of the different combinations is still less than the efficiency of simple local search methods.

Figure 5. Profile of performances of SLS according the CPU time

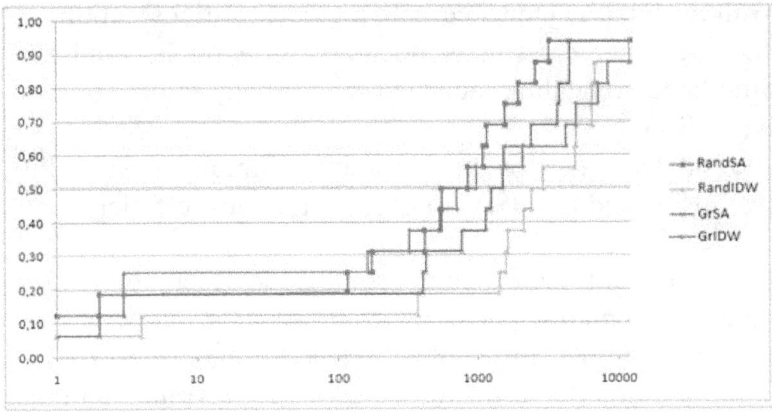

Performance Analysis

To facilitate a high-quality synthesis of the applied methods, we use the performance profiles proposed in (Dolan & Moré, 2002) (see Chapter 2).

In the following figures Figure 4 and Figure 5, we expose an evaluation via the performance percentage of Simple Local Search (SLS) methods, according to the number of success and CPU time. The horizontal axis (the axis of performance reports), we use a logarithmic scale to have a better distinction between the curves in the same figure.

We designate by:

- **RandSA:** Simulated Annealing launched with random generated initial solution.
- **RandIDW:** IDWalk launched with random generated initial solution.
- **GrSA:** Simulated Annealing launched with greedy generated initial solution.
- **GrIDW:** IDWalk launched with greedy generated initial solution.

Figure 4 analyses the realized number of success by each method. This is done by drawing the corresponding performance profiles.

The illustrated curves in Figure 4 can be described in three points:

1. We notice via the curve GrIDW, the realized improvement on the method IDWalk, when it is launched with a greedy initial solution.
2. At the beginning, the best method to consider on the number of success is Simulated Annealing launched with greedy initial solution (see the curve GrSA).
3. At the end, we notice the improvement of Simulated Annealing (see the curves GrSA and RandSA) to become the most efficient.

Figure 5 analyses the CPU time used by each method. This is done by drawing the corresponding performance profiles.

With regard to Figure 2 in Chapter 7, we notice the success of IDWalk with greedy initial solution (GrIDW) against IDWalk with random initial solution (RandIDW). Moreover, GrIDW is the most efficient at the beginning, but at the end, Simulated Annealing becomes the best in its two versions: random initial solution and greedy initial solution, namely GrSA and RandSA.

CONCLUSION

In this chapter, we addressed at the beginning the general principle of local search approaches and their efficiency to solve complex problems. We illustrated via an example the reliability of a simple local search in solving a large instance of the Portfolio Design problem, while the CP approaches fails on the set model.

In this chapter, we adapted to the 0-1 matricial model, some specified local search methods, given in Chapter 2, namely simple and population. With respect to the structure of the (PD) problem, we proposed the neighborhood function and evaluation function, which are heuristics allowing respectively to move from one solution to another in the neighborhood of the current solution, and evaluating the rate of conflict.

We presented many algorithms coming from local and population aspects of incomplete methods. These algorithms which were simply adapted to the (PD), and combined with GWW technique, were launched from a random solution at first and secondly from a greedy solution computed via the algorithm GreedyInit. We have to highlight that GreedyInit algorithm yielded the optimized portfolios in some cases, which is a proof of its efficiency.

In spite of the simplicity of evaluation and neighborhood functions, local search approaches are promising on non-trivial instances of the (PD) problem, especially after having launched the solver from a greedy solution.

However, the experimental results beyond the population-based approach GWW were poor compared to the simple local search approaches, according to the CPU time and the portfolio quality. Indeed, since GWW handles a sample of solutions, the method takes a long time to solve or to build a portfolio. Thus, the parallelization of GWW should improve the CPU time, and thereby the quality of the realized portfolios.

The deep landscape analysis given of the no-solved instances showed the problem of local minimum, which prevents us scanning all the feasible region and to approach the optimum. Consequently, we will present in Chapter 7 Variable Neighborhood Search (VNS), and Skewe VNS (SVNS), to solve the problem in question for the Portfolio Design (PD) problem.

REFERENCES

Ashwani, B. (2007). *Collateral dept obligations.* Tech. rep. Retrieved October, 2007 from http://www.planmanconsulting.com/gsic/doc/collateral-debt-obligations.pdf

Bellare, M., & Rogaway, P. (1995). The complexity of approximating a nonlinear program. *Official Journal of Mathematical Programming. Springer.*, *I*(3), 429–442. doi:10.1007/BF01585569

Crawford, J. M., Ginsberg, M., Lucks, E., & Roy, A. (1996). Symmetry-breaking predicates for the search problems. In *Proceedings of the Fifth International Conference on Principles of Knowledge Representation and Reasoning (KR'96)*, (pp. 148-159). Cambridge, MA: Morgan Kaufmann.

Darrall, Jacobson & Johnson. (2003). The Theory and Practice of Simulated Annealing. In Handbook of Metaheuristics (pp. 287-319). Academic Press.

David, W. (1997). No free lunch theorems for optimization. *IEEE Trans. Evolutionary Computation-Journal*, *1*(1), 67–82. doi:10.1109/4235.585893

Flener, P., Pearson, J., Reyna, L. G., & Sivertsson, O. (2007). Design of financial cdo squared transactions using constraint programming. *Constraints*, *12*(2), 179–205. doi:10.100710601-006-9014-4

Gomes, C. P., & Selman, B. (2001). Algorithm portfolios. *Artificial Intelligence-Journal-Elsevier*, *126*(1-2), 43–62. doi:10.1016/S0004-3702(00)00081-3

Gomes, C. P., & Selman, B. (2001). Algorithm portfolios. *Artificial Intelligence Journal, 126*(1-2), 43-62.

Gonzalez, T. F. (2007). *Handbook of Approximation Algorithms and Metaheuristics*. New York: Chapman & Hall, Taylor & Francis Group. doi:10.1201/9781420010749

João, P. (2001). *Metaheuristics for combinatorial optimisation* (working paper 9/01). Faculdade de Ciências da Universidade de Lisboa and Faculdade de Ciências da Universidade de Porto.

Kraft, H. (2003). Elasticity approach to portfolio optimization. International Journal of Mathematical Methods of Operations Research, 58, 159-182. doi:10.1007001860300296

Lebbah, F. Z., & Lebbah, Y. (2015). A local search approach to solve a financial portfolio design problem. *International Journal of Applied Metaheuristic Computing, 6*(2), 1–17. doi:10.4018/IJAMC.2015040101

Luke, S. (2013). *Essentials of Metaheuristics* (2nd ed.). Lulu. Available at https://cs.gmu.edu/~sean/book/metaheuristics/

Neveu, B., & Trombettoni, G. (2003). Incop: An open library for incomplete combinatorial optimization. In *Principles and Practice of Constraint Programming -9th International Conference*. Springer Berlin Heidelberg.

Neveu, B., Trombettoni, G., & Glover, F. (2004). Idwalk: a candidate list strategy with a simple diversification device. In *Principles and Practice of Constraint Programming, 10th International Conference*. Springer.

Nikolaev & Jacobson. (2011). Using Markov chains to analyze the effectiveness of local search algorithms. Discrete Optimization Journal, 8, 160-173.

Rodriguez, D., Cotta, C., & Fernandez, A. J. (2009). Finding Balanced Incomplete Block Designs with Metaheuristics. In *Evolutionary Computation in combinatorial optimization: 9th European Conference, EvoCOP* (vol. 5482, pp. 156-167). Tübingen, Germany: Springer. 10.1007/978-3-642-01009-5_14

Svenja, H. (2008). Pricing portfolio credit derivatives by means of evolutionary algorithms. In *Collateralized debt obligations: Structure and valuatio* (pp. 7-39). Springer.

Talbi, E.-G. (Ed.). (2009). *Metaheuristics-From Design to Implementation*. New York: Wiley.

Tawarmalani, M., & Sahinidis, N. V. (Eds.). (2002). *Convexification and Global Optimization in Continuous and Mixed-Integer Nonlinear Programming*. Kluwer Academic Publishers Group. doi:10.1007/978-1-4757-3532-1

Wetzel, G., & Zabbata, F. (1998). A constraint programming approach to portfolio selection. In H. Prade (Ed.), *13th European Conference on Artificial Intelligence, Proceedings*. John Wiley and Sons.

ENDNOTE

1 The instances are taken from Flener et al. (2007), since they are given by a specialized financial institution.

Chapter 7
VNS Metaheuristics to Solve a Financial Portfolio Design Problem:
VNS and SVNS Approaches

ABSTRACT

This chapter introduces a VNS-based local search for solving efficiently a financial portfolio design problem described in Chapter 1 and modeled in Chapter 3. The mathematical model tackled is a 0-1 quadratic model. It is well known that exact solving approaches on large instances of this kind of model are costly. The authors have proposed local search approaches to solve the problem, and the efficiency of this type of method has been proved. This chapter shows that the matricial 0-1 model of the problem enables specialized VNS algorithms by taking into account the particular structure of the financial problem considered. First experiments show that VNS with simulated annealing is effective on non-trivial instances of the problem.

INTRODUCTION

In this chapter, we propose VNS based local search approaches to tackle a proposed financial portfolio design problem (*PD*), modelling practical problems in financial engineering (Model 3.14 in Chapter 3). One noticeable and practical instance of this portfolio design model is the CDO Squared

DOI: 10.4018/978-1-7998-1882-3.ch007

portfolio, which is a critical problem in equitable management of clients' portfolios.

The search for the optimal solution, or building the optimized portfolio, is a hard-combinatorial problem, because of the large size of the financial portfolio instances. Indeed, applying exact methods (Chapter 4 and Chapter 5) provided averagely good results, especially Constraint Programming techniques. Thus, moving towards approached techniques is unavoidable to improve the yielded results.

Applying Local Search techniques on the problem proved their effectiveness on non-trivial instances. However as a human being, we want better and better optimized solutions, and the next purpose is to implement VNS approaches on the problem. We focused on VNS because it offers a good level of neighborhood diversification.

In this chapter, we apply two variants of Variable Neighborhood Search, namely based VNS and skewed VNS (SVNS), with Simulated Annealing and IDWalk. The implemented neighborhood functions are the FLIP function described in Chapter 6 and a new one called the Swap function.

The portfolios provided through these approaches prove their efficiency, particularly VNS combined with Simulated Annealing.

This chapter is organized as follows. In section 2, a brief overview of the Variable Neighborhood Search is given, with a small example which highlights the contribution of a VNS approach on the (PD) problem. In section 3, the VNS adapted algorithm to the problem in 0-1 matricial model is given. In section 4, we apply the Skewed VNS algorithm to the (PD) problem in a 0-1 matricial model. In section 5, all the experimental information and results are introduced, in addition to a deep synthesis of the provided results. Finally, we conclude the chapter.

BACKGROUND

According to (Fonseca & Santos, 2014), VNS variants are able to outperform the winner of third ITC solver[1], which applied a Simulated Annealing algorithm. Thus, the efficiency of applying local search methods on the (PD) problem leads to consideration of implementing Variable Neighborhood Search (VNS) techniques.

Table 1. Solution of ⟨10,37,14,6⟩ with the VNS approach

0100100100011100000000001101011100 1001
0110101001100000011000100000011011001
0000000100000000101110100001110011111
0001010111100000010101101000000101001
1100000000011100101000101101010100010
0111010011001000011010001000010000110
1000001001010010000110001110001100011
0000010110110010010010100110110000100
0101001010101001000000110110001100010
1101111001011000000101100000000010010

Table 2. Computed average overlap of IDWalk with a greedy initial solution and VNS-IDWalk-Swap on the computed portfolio ⟨10,37,14,6⟩

	IDWalk-InitSol	SVNS-IDW-Swap
λ-AVG	5.00	4.91
Run-time (seconds)	0.02	0.00

The Variable Neighborhood Search method (VNS), was proposed by Mladenovic´ and Hansen in 1997. It relies on dynamic neighborhood models in exploring the feasible region (solutions space) of a combinatorial optimization problem. It is a recently developed metaheuristic and could be considered as a frame work of building new heuristics. VNS is an approach which allows a good level of neighborhood diversification, since it offers the opportunity to explore distant neighborhoods. Indeed, the realized jumps from a neighborhood to another via the shaking step, allows a good scanning of the solutions space. Thus, the risk of getting stuck in local minima is minimized.

There are different variants of VNS, namely Variable Neighborhood Descent (VND), Reduced VNS (RVNS) and Skewed VNS (SVNS) (Hansen & Mladenovic´, 2003).

To illustrate the relevance of a VNS approach, we consider the instance ⟨10,37,14,6⟩, a CDO Squared portfolio including 10 tranches and 37 inner portfolios. As depicted in Table 7.1, the VNS based approach local search method provides a portfolio with the overlapping average *λ-AVG = 4.91*, which is due to considering all the features of the portfolio problem and the efficiency of the VNS approach.

Table 1 shows two cases of overlaps, as follows:

- pair with italic-bold form represents 3 overlaps,
- pair with bold form represents 6 overlaps.

In the given solution in Table 1, the overlap values belong to the interval [3, 6]. The computed average overlaps given in Table 2 shows that the SVNS approach combined with IDWalk method provides better results than IDWalk with a greedy initial solution. The SVNS approach provides better optimized portfolios in better CPU time. Thus, applying VNS and SVNS approaches on the (PD) problem can be more reliable than a Simple Local Search method.

VNS FOR PORTFOLIO DESIGN PROBLEM

Variable Neighborhood Search (VNS) (Mladenovic´ & Hansen, 1997) is a metaheuristic that manages a local search technique in order to avoid becoming stuck at a local minimum. The main idea of the VNS algorithm is to explore the search space with a systematic change of neighborhood. The success of VNS comes from the fact that a local minimum for one neighborhood structure may not be a local minimum for a different neighborhood structure, enabling improvements toward the global minimum.

The pseudo-code of VNS algorithm for *(PD)* is given in Algorithm 7.1. It starts with selection of an initial configuration matrix.

Algorithm 1 VNSPD(ls, K_{max}, SM)

```
Input: PD⟨v,b,r,λ⟩; K_max VNS parameter; ls local search method,
SM method of generating new point in the neighborhood;
Initialize M randomly
while (not time-out) and (Eval(M)≠0) do
   k←1;
   while (k ≤ K_max) and (Eval(M)≠0) and (not time-out) do
      M'← Shake(SM,M,k);
      M"← LS(M');
      if Eval(M") < Eval(M) then
         M ← M";
         k←1;
      else
         k←k+1;
      end if
   end while
end while
```

```
procedure Shake(SM,M,k)
  M'←M;
  for i in 1..k do
    if SM=Flip then
      (i,j)←RandomSelectIn(1..v,1..b);
      M'_ij ← abs(1 − M'_ij);
    else
      l←RandomSelectIn(1..v);
      v_1←RandomSelectIn(1..b) with M_lv1 = 1;
      v_0←RandomSelectIn(1..b) with M_lv0 = 0;
      M'_lv1 = 0; M'_lv0 = 1;
    endif
  end for
  return M';
end procedure
```

Local search *LS* and *Shake* functions perform the exploration of the search space. Function *Shake* diversifies the solution by flipping *k* variables randomly selected. By this way, increasing *k* enables *VNS* algorithm exploring far from the current solution. The result x' of *Shake* procedure is used as the starting point for the local search *LS*. After exploring local neighbors, the best solution x'' of the local search is compared with x by using the evaluation function *Eval*. We notice that *Eval(x)* consists simply in computing the number of failed constraints in (*PD*) over the configuration x. If x'' is better than x, it is affected to x and the algorithm loops over again with $k=1$. Otherwise, k is incremented and the algorithm continues from the shaking phase with the next neighborhood structure. This inner loop is stopped after all neighborhood structures are exhausted or a solution satisfying all the constraints is found. The outer loop iterates until a maximum CPU time is reached or a solution is found.

SVNS (SKEWED VNS) FOR PORTFOLIO DESIGN PROBLEM

In general, VNS finds the best results compared to the simple local search approaches; particularly the solutions' landscape, which contains many local minima. This is due to the ease of VNS in exploring far neighborhoods to avoid the phenomenon of local minima. Consequently, often adopting far neighborhoods pushes VNS to behave like a multi-start method, and prevents VNS from converging via small local changes to the global minimum.

To address this phenomenon, a new variant of VNS called SVNS (Skewed Variable Neighborhood Search) is proposed. This revised version is given in Algorithm 1 SVNSPD. In this algorithm, we relax the condition of adopting the new solution. Specifically, to intensify the research around the current solution and in the neighborhood structure, we use a new evaluation function (instead of the *Eval* function) which allows a degree of tolerance in the current solution.

Relaxing the adoption condition of the solution with the function *Eval*, uses the linear evaluation function based on the distance: the expression $Eval(M'')$ is replaced by $Eval(M'') - \alpha\rho(M, M'')$ where $\rho(M, M'')$ is distance between *M* and *M"*, and α is a given parameter. Once we have Boolean variables, we adopted the *Hamming* distance. The α parameter is fixed to the default value 1 (Fonseca & Santos, 2014).

Algorithm 2 SVNSPD(ls,K_{max},SM)

```
Input: PD⟨v,b,r,λ⟩; K_max VNS parameter; ls local search method,
SM method of generating new point in the neighborhood;
Initialize M randomly
while (not time-out) and (Eval(M)≠0) do
   k←1;
  while (k ≤ K_max) and (Eval(M)≠0) and (not time-out) do
     M' ← Shake(SM,M,k);
     M" ← LS(M');
     if Eval(M") < Eval(M) then
       M ← M";
       k←1;
    else
      α←1;
      ρ ← card{(i,j)|i ∈ 1..v, j ∈ 1..b, M"_ij ≠ M_ij}
      if Eval(M") − αρ < Eval(M) then
    M ← M";
    k←1;
      else
        k←k+1;
      end if
    end if
  end while
end while
```

BASIS COMPONENTS OF VNS AND SVNS

The applied VNS and SVNS approaches start with complete and non-optimal configuration. The variable neighborhood method repairs the current solution by applying local changes, to decrease the evaluation function.

To apply VNS approaches on the (PD) problem, we have to include a Local Search method, in order to explore the neighborhood of the current solution. The applied local search algorithms within VNS and SVNS are Simulated Annealing and IDWalk.

Evaluation Function

The evaluation function used with VSN and SVNS is similar to that considered in the previous chapter. This cost function (or the evaluation function) called *EVAL* computes the number of the violated constraints in the model, with regard to the configuration *M*:

$$EVAL(M) = \sum_{k \in 1..m} \begin{cases} +1 \text{ if } i^{th} \text{ constraint is violated with } M \\ 0 \ else \end{cases}$$

Where m is the constraints' number. The function EVAL is also the objective function of the portfolio design problem tackled. Obviously, the optimal solutions match the configurations, which satisfy all the constraints.

Neighborhood Functions

FLIP Neighborhood Function

The neighborhood function *FLIP* is used by the local search approaches within VNS and SVNS. It is applied on the configuration *M*, and outputs a new configuration $M' \in N(M)$ (Neighborhood of M), which is computed by flipping the *0-1* value of the randomly chosen variable, in contrast to the *FLIP* function given in the previous chapter, which is applied on the variable having the biggest *val_conflict* value.

SWAP Neighborhood Function

We suppose that the local search starts by an assigning where *r* units placed in each row, so fully satisfying the constraint $\forall i \in 1..v, \sum_{j\in 1..b} M_{ij} = r$. To keep this row constraint constantly satisfied, we adopt the *SWAP* neighborhood function, which swaps between two variables, the first one 0 and the second 1. Specifically, the studied *SWAP* function proceeds in three steps:

1. Select randomly a variable M_{lc_1} among those having the value 1.
2. In the same row of the previous selected variable, chose randomly a second variable M_{lc_2} among those having the value 0.
3. Affect 0 to M_{lc_1} and 1 to M_{lc_2}.

Therefore, the row constraint is constantly satisfied. The local search methods adopting this function have to verify only the overlapping constraint:

$$\forall i \in 1..v, \forall t > i, \sum_{j=1}^{b} M_{ij} M_{tj} \leq \lambda$$

RESULTS BASED VARIABLE NEIGHBORHOOD SEARCH FRAMEWORK

This section reports experimental results on various instances of the *(PD)* problem, with VNS and SVNS methods, each combined with a specific local search method and a specific neighborhood function.

The realized experiments are carried on the (PD) problem where λ is fixed. The machine used has the following configuration: Linux-Ubuntu 12.04, Intel CPU E5-2603 and 8 GB/RAM. The experiments are realized in INCOP after being extended by VNS and SVNS procedures, and integrating the previously described neighborhood and evaluation functions.

The experiments have been performed on the 0-1 matricial model (Model 3.14 in Chapter 3). We use a random starting configuration (We recall that a configuration is an instantiation of the variables with some values. In (PD), a configuration is the instantiation of the *M* matrix, where for all *(i, j)*, $M_{i,j}$ is instantiated to *0* or *1*).

Table 3. Experimented instances

Instance	⟨v,b,r,λ⟩	Variables number	Constraints number
Inst1	⟨7,7,3,1⟩	49	28
Inst2	⟨10,8,3,1⟩	80	55
Inst3	⟨8,14,7,3⟩	112	36
Inst4	⟨11,11,5,2⟩	121	66
Inst5	⟨16,8,3,1⟩	128	136
Inst6	⟨10,15,6,2⟩	150	55
Inst7	⟨9,18,8,3⟩	162	45
Inst8	⟨9,24,8,2⟩	216	45
Inst9	⟨15,15,4,1⟩	225	120
Inst10	⟨10,25,8,2⟩	250	55
Inst11	⟨10,30,9,2⟩	300	55
Inst12	⟨9,37,12,3⟩	333	45
Inst13	⟨10,37,14,6⟩	270	55
Inst14	⟨10,38,10,2⟩	380	55
Inst15	⟨19,20,9,4⟩	380	190
Inst16	⟨15,350,100,25⟩	5250	1575

Experimental Protocol

Table 3 (as Table 3 in Chapter 6) describes experimented (PD) instances as well as the number of their constraints and variables.

We present the experimental results on different variants of VNS on (PD) instances, with algorithms 7.1 and 7.2 (VNSPD and SVNSPD) by using Simulated Annealing (SIM-ANN) and IDWalk algorithm. We experiment using the following VNS strategies:

1. Basic VNS with Simulated Annealing and FLIP neighborhood function: VSF.
2. Basic VNS with Simulated Annealing and SWAP neighborhood function: VSS.
3. Basic VNS with IDWalk and FLIP neighborhood function: VIF.
4. Basic VNS with IDWalk and SWAP neighborhood function: VIS.
5. Skewed VNS with Simulated Annealing and FLIP neighborhood function: SSF.

6. Skewed VNS with Simulated Annealing and SWAP neighborhood function: SSS.
7. Skewed VNS with IDWalk and FLIP neighborhood function: SIF.
8. Skewed VNS with IDWalk and SWAP neighborhood function: SIS

For the two adopted simple local search methods, we have the following parameters:

- Max number of moves is 10 000; max number of neighbors is 300. These parameters come from many tests and general recommendations given by (Neveu B. and Trombettoni G., 2003; Neveu et al., 2004).
- The unique parameter of Simulated Annealing, the initial temperature, is fixed to 0.4.
- For IDWalk method, the second parameter is the so called Spare-neighbor fixed to 150 (for more details see (Neveu et al. 2004)).

The unique parameter of VNS called K_{max} (Mladenovic´ & Hansen,2009) (Chapter2), is fixed to the maximal number of variables $v \times b$.

In our experiments, the time out is fixed to *200* seconds.

To evaluate the robustness of all the methods of different approaches of VNS we performed 20 runs on each method. Executable files and documentation are available on https://sites.google.com/site/fzlebbahportfolio/.

For each experimented local search algorithm, we give the following columns:

- *SUCC*: the number of successful calls to the local search over 20 calls,
- *AVG-TIME*: the average time of the 20 calls.

The first comparison is realized with the cited parameters: *SUCC* and *AVG-TIME.* The second is done by considering the quality of the found solution, which consists in computing the average of the obtained overlaps, as shown in formula (6.2) (Chapter 6).

- λ-AVG: the number of overlaps average computed over 20 runs.
- C-AVG: the average of the computed conflicts over 20 runs.

Table 4. Experimental results of CPU times and number of success

Instance		VNSPD				SVNSPD			
		SIM-ANN		IDW		SIM-ANN		IDW	
		FLIP VSF	SWAP VSS	FLIP VIF	SWAP VIS	FLIP SSF	SWAP SSS	FLIP SIF	SWAP SIS
Inst1	SUCC./20	20	20	20	20	20	20	20	20
	AVG-TIME	0.00	0.00	7.51	0.01	0.01	0.01	10.41	0.01
Inst2	SUCC./20	20	20	20	20	20	20	20	20
	AVG-TIME	0.00	0.00	0.00	0.00	0.00	0.00	0.00	0.00
Inst3	SUCC./20	20	20	03	20	20	20	02	20
	AVG-TIME	2.34	1.51	182.96	0.25	2.66	1.54	189.90	0.12
Inst4	SUCC./20	20	20	03	20	20	20	01	20
	AVG-TIME	1.24	2.27	169.80	0.34	1.35	2.20	196.64	1.10
Inst5	SUCC./20	00	00	00	00	00	00	00	00
	AVG-TIME	199.66	199.77	199.76	199.71	199.83	193.85	199.83	199.83
Inst6	SUCC./20	20	20	19	20	20	20	00	20
	AVG-TIME	5.29	1.70	5.57	4.89	10.33	6.27	199.84	3.04
Inst7	SUCC./20	17	20	00	20	20	20	00	20
	AVG-TIME	50.18	9.35	199.72	5.52	47.70	10.66	199.84	6.40
Inst8	SUCC./20	20	20	01	20	20	20	00	20
	AVG-TIME	7.78	10.96	199.05	7.64	12.69	14.97	199.84	6.46
Inst9	SUCC./20	20	20	04	20	20	20	20	20
	AVG-TIME	5.55	8.87	163.85	1.69	0.00	0.00	0.00	0.00
Inst10	SUCC./20	17	20	00	18	20	15	00	18
	AVG-TIME	62.50	47.49	199.75	72.75	93.55	111.11	199.82	67.78
Inst11	SUCC./20	20	10	18	08	20	05	00	06
	AVG-TIME	20.19	143.43	20.05	162.07	62.79	167.38	199.80	151.28
Inst12	SUCC./20	20	20	20	20	20	20	01	20
	AVG-TIME	10.77	9.39	11.10	1.73	17.67	9.48	199.59	1.91
Inst13	SUCC./20	20	20	20	20	20	20	20	20
	AVG-TIME	0.01	0.01	0.07	0.00	0.02	0.01	0.11	0.01
Inst14	SUCC./20	20	20	12	20	20	20	08	20
	AVG-TIME	4.99	5.92	84.60	0.21	8.27	5.93	126.07	0.21
Inst15	SUCC./20	00	00	00	00	00	00	00	00
	AVG-TIME	199.70	199.73	199.72	199.80	199.81	199.81	199.65	199.65
Inst16	SUCC./20	13	00	01	00	01	00	00	00
	AVG-TIME	193.08	199.77	195.95	199.75	199.18	199.81	199.63	199.77

Experimental Results

Table 4 reports the performances of VNS and SVNS algorithms, considering the two neighborhood functions FLIP and SWAP. The number of successful calls to the variable local search over 20 runs (SUCC) and the average time of the 20 calls (AVG-TIME) are given for each method.

Table 4 shows that VNS and SVNS combined with Simulated Annealing provides the best combinations. The instances Inst5, Inst15 and Inst16, which represent respectively a portfolio with 16 tranches and 8 inner portfolios, a portfolio with 19 tranches and 20 inner portfolios and a portfolio with 15 tranches and 350 inner portfolios, represent the most difficult instances. Applying VNS with Simulated Annealing and the FLIP function is the only method that succeeded in solving Inst16 in 13 runs. We can also notice that SVNS combined with Simulated Annealing and SWAP function is the strongest, since it succeeds in all the runs, except the three instances Inst5, Inst15 and Inst16. Consequently, we conclude that VNS method combined with Simulated Annealing and FLIP function is the most efficient combination. VNS + Simulated Annealing + FLIP function is the most efficient combination in building optimized CDO Squared portfolios.

Table 5 reports the respective averages of the number of failed constraints (C-AVG) and the overlaps (λ-AVG) over the 20 runs, realized by each variable local search. The average of overlaps made by the CP applied on the set model (Flener et al.,2007) is in the last column PrRs.

We notice that the computed λ-AVG in (Flener et al., 2007), is constantly equal to λ, since they use the equality in the second type of the constraints (i.e., $M_{ij}M_{ij}=\lambda$ in (PD) model). In most instances, the overlap average of VNS approaches with Simulated Annealing is strictly less than λ. This shows that the VNS approach performs clearly in solving the original (PD) problem. ⟨16,8,3,1⟩ (portfolio including 16 tranches and 8 inner portfolios) and ⟨19,20,9,4⟩ (portfolio including 19 tranches and 20 inner portfolios) are the only unsolved instances, but the number of the constraints not satisfied is low (resp. 7.95 and 4.65) compared to the number of constraints (resp. 136 and 190). In addition, we notice that in the failed runs providing approached solutions, the number of overlaps is strictly greater than λ but still very close to λ. In Inst5 having 136 constraints, all the combinations succeeded in reaching only eight failed constraints, and the average overlap is very close to λ=1.

Table 5. Experimental results of C-AVG and λ-AVG

Instance		VNSPD				SVNSPD				PrRs
		SIM-ANN		IDW		SIM-ANN		IDW		
		FLIP VSF	**SWAP VSS**	**FLIP VIF**	**SWAP VIS**	**FLIP SSF**	**SWAP SSS**	**FLIP SIF**	**SWAP SIS**	
Inst1	C-AVG	0.00	0.00	0.00	0.00	0.00	0.00	0.00	0.00	
	λ-AVG	1.00	1.00	1.00	1.00	1.00	1.00	1.00	1.00	1
Inst2	C-AVG	0.00	0.00	0.00	0.00	0.00	0.00	0.00	0.00	
	λ-AVG	1.08	1.08	1.09	1.08	1.07	1.08	1.09	1.09	2
Inst3	C-AVG	0.00	0.00	1.30	0.00	0.00	0.00	1.20	0.00	
	λ-AVG	3.00	3.00	2.82	3.00	3.00	3.00	2.97	3.00	3
Inst4	C-AVG	0.00	0.00	2.25	0.00	0.00	0.00	2.50	0.00	
	λ-AVG	2.00	2.00	1.75	2.00	2.00	2.00	1.81	2.00	2
Inst5	C-AVG	7.95	8.00	8.60	8.00	8.00	8.00	8.50	8.00	
	λ-AVG	0.68	1.00	0.67	1.00	0.72	1.04	0.70	1.04	1
Inst6	C-AVG	0.00	0.00	0.05	0.00	0.00	0.00	2.45	0.00	
	λ-AVG	2.00	2.00	1.84	2.00	2.00	2.00	1.92	2.00	2
Inst7	C-AVG	0.15	0.00	2.20	0.00	0.00	0.00	2.30	0.00	
	λ-AVG	2.95	3.00	2.80	3.00	3.00	3.00	2.87	3.00	3
Inst8	C-AVG	0.00	0.00	1.80	0.00	0.00	0.00	2.30	0.00	
	λ-AVG	2.00	2.00	1.91	2.00	2.00	2.00	2.00	2.00	2
Inst9	C-AVG	0.00	0.00	1.05	0.00	0.00	0.00	0.00	0.00	
	λ-AVG	0.75	0.68	0.76	0.76	0.07	0.68	0.07	0.73	1
Inst10	C-AVG	0.15	0.00	2.10	0.10	0.00	0.30	2.90	0.10	
	λ-AVG	1.97	2.00	1.92	2.00	1.99	2.00	1.95	2.00	2
Inst11	C-AVG	0.00	0.50	0.10	0.60	0.00	0.75	3.15	0.70	
	λ-AVG	2.00	2.00	1.94	2.00	2.00	2.00	2.00	2.00	2
Inst12	C-AVG	0.00	0.00	0.00	0.00	0.00	0.00	3.00	0.00	
	λ-AVG	2.97	2.97	2.87	2.96	2.97	2.97	2.93	2.96	3
Inst13	C-AVG	0.00	0.00	0.00	0.00	0.00	0.00	0.00	0.00	
	λ-AVG	4.87	4.90	4.91	4.88	4.80	4.90	4.87	4.66	6
Inst14	C-AVG	0.00	0.00	0.80	0.00	0.00	0.00	1.05	0.00	
	λ-AVG	1.94	1.93	1.88	1.93	1.93	1.94	1.94	1.93	2
Inst15	C-AVG	4.90	2.85	7.25	2.85	4.6	3.15	7.65	3.10	
	λ-AVG	3.50	3.82	3.40	3.84	3.50	3.84	3.42	4.83	4
Inst16	C-AVG	1.55	4.35	1.75	2.85	1.70	4.35	3.70	2.85	
	λ-AVG	24.59	24.89	24.53	24.83	24.52	25.00	24.37	24.79	26

Performance Analysis

To facilitate a high-quality synthesis of the applied methods, we use the performance profiles proposed in (Dolan & Moré, 2002) (Chapter 2).

Figure 1. Profile of performances of VNS/SVNS according to the number of success

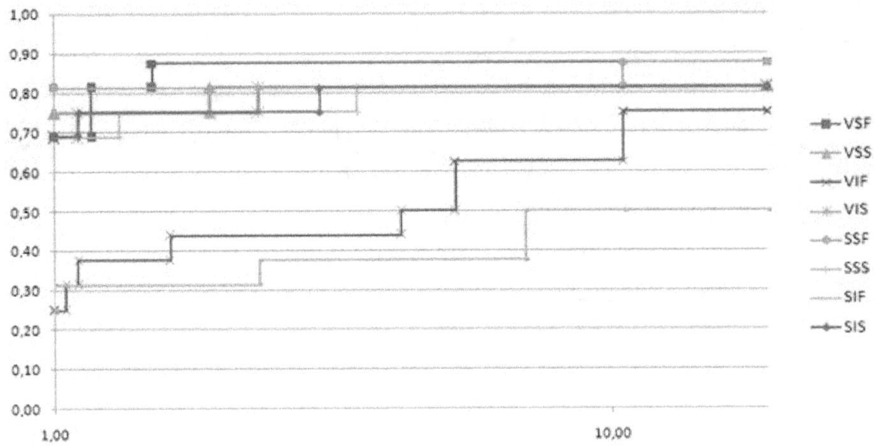

Figure 1 and Figure 2 show respectively the implemented Variable Neighborhood Approaches according to the evolution of the number of success and CPU time.

We designate by:

VSF: VNS method combined with Simulated Annealing and launched with FLIP neighborhood function.

VSS: VNS method combined with Simulated Annealing and launched with SWAP neighborhood function.

VIF: VNS method combined with IDWalk and launched with FLIP neighborhood function.

VIS: VNS method combined with IDWalk and launched with SWAP neighborhood function.

SSF: SVNS method combined with Simulated Annealing and launched with FLIP neighborhood function.

SSS: SVNS method combined with Simulated Annealing and launched with SWAP neighborhood function.

SIF: SVNS method combined with IDWalk and launched with FLIP neighborhood function.

SIS: SVNS method combined with IDWalk and launched with SWAP neighborhood function.

Figure 1 analyzes the realized number of success by each method. This is done by drawing the corresponding performance profiles.

Figure 2. Profile of performances of VNS/SVNS according to the CPU time

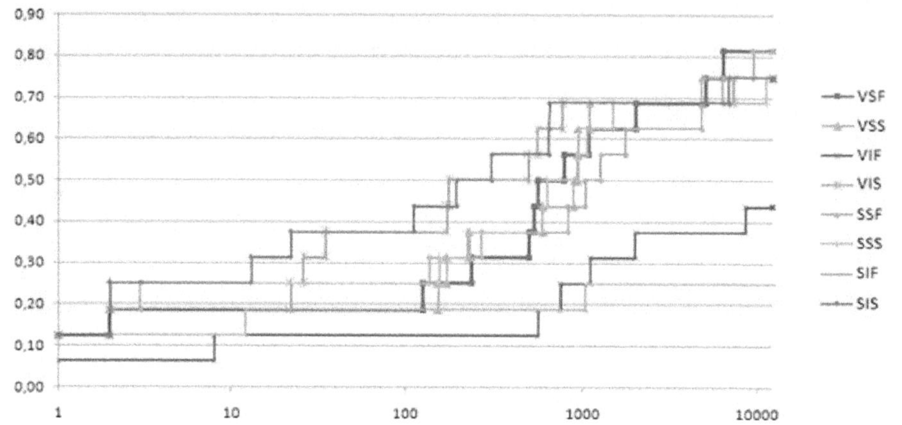

The illustrated curves in Figure 1 can be described in three points:

1. SSF method and others start with the best performances.
2. We notice an improvement of SSF so it becomes as efficient as VSF. At the end, VSF and SSF methods are the best in number of success.
3. At the end, we notice the improvement of SSF to become as powerful as VSF.

Figure 2 analyses the realized CPU time by each method. This is done by drawing the corresponding performance profiles.

With regard to Figure 2, we notice the success of the SIS method at the beginning, to become the best in CPU time, although VSF becomes more powerful at the end (VSF is faster than SIS).

FUTURE RESEARCH DIRECTIONS

We have so far applied a panoply of exact and approximated methods. We have to highlight that approximate approaches, especially VNS, were more efficient. To have a global analysis, including Flener et al. results, we will present in the next chapter a deep analysis of the approximate methods and of the exact methods.

CONCLUSION

In this chapter, we tackled the financial problem Variable Neighborhood Search (VNS) approaches. The strong point of VNS is the high level of diversification that is realized through the shaking step. The purpose of this chapter is to implement these approached methods combined with the most efficient local search methods on the (PD) problem according to Chapter 6, namely Simulated Annealing and IDWalk. Appropriate neighborhood functions were introduced and implemented in this chapter.

VNS and SVNS approaches were applied on non-trivial instances of the well-known CDO-squared portfolio design problem. The neighborhood diversiðcation aspect of the approaches consists in ñipping *k* variables randomly chosen, which allows the resolution process to attempt the optimized portfolio. Increasing *k* enables VNS and SVNS to explore new, larger neighborhoods. In spite of the simplicity of the VNS approach with simulated annealing, their results as given are really promising. In other words, VNS and SVNS combined with Simulated Annealing gave the most important results beyond the optimizing criteria of the financial portfolio.

Parallelizing Variable Neighborhood Search by launching Local Search within different neighborhoods should minimize the CPU-time and thereby allow more time to explore more neighborhoods.

In the next chapter we give a general analysis of all the implemented approaches, exact and approached techniques, over the instances of Portfolio Design problem.

REFERENCES

De Souza, C. M., & Martins, P. (2008). Skewed VNS enclosing second order algorithm for the degree constrained minimum spanning tree problem. *European Journal of Operational Research*, *191*(3), 677–690. doi:10.1016/j.ejor.2006.12.061

Dolan, E. D., & Moré, J. J. (2002). Benchmarking optimization software with performance profiles. *Mathematical Programming*, *91*(2), 201–213. doi:10.1007101070100263

Fonseca, G., & Santos, H. (2014). Variable Neighborhood Search based algorithms for high school timetabling. *Computers & Operations Research*, *52*, 203–208. doi:10.1016/j.cor.2013.11.012

Hansen, P., & Mladenovic´, N. (2003). A Tutorial on Variable Neighborhood Search. GERAD and Mathematical Institute, SANU.

Hansen, P., & Mladenovic, N. (2009). Variable neighborhood search methods. In *Encyclopedia of optimization, second edition*, (3975-3989). Academic Press.

Kirkpatrick, S., Jr., & Vecchi, M. P. (1983a). Optimization by simulated annealing. *Science*, *220*, 671-680.

Mladenovic´, N., & Hansen, P. (1997). Variable neighborhood search. *Computers & OR*, *24*(11), 1097–1100. doi:10.1016/S0305-0548(97)00031-2

Neveu, B., & Trombettoni, G. (2003). Incop: An open library for incomplete combinatorial optimization. In *Principles and Practice of Constraint Programming -9th International Conference* (pp. 909–913). Kinsale, Ireland: Springer.

Neveu, B., Trombettoni, G., & Glover, F. (2004). Id walk: A candidate list strategy with a simple diversification device. LNCS, 3258, 432-437. doi:10.1007/978-3-540-30201-8_32

ENDNOTE

1 ITC is International Timetabling Competition.

Chapter 8
Global Results Synthesis:
Comparison

ABSTRACT

This chapter provides a global synthesis of the realized results by applying exact and approximate approaches on the portfolio design (PD) problem. The authors introduce an experimental analysis of best approaches based on linear programming and constraint programming techniques, according to the CPU time. Next, a global experiment synthesis of the best approximate approaches based on Simulated Annealing, IDWalk, Tabu Search, GWW, and VNS is realized according to the number of success and the CPU time. First results show that constraint programming with breaking all the detected symmetries is the best as an exact approach, VNS combined with simulated annealing is effective on non-trivial instances of the problem, and simulated annealing is the most effective as a simple local search.

INTRODUCTION

Through the previous chapters of this book, we introduced and applied various approaches coming from two classes of optimization techniques, namely complete and incomplete methods. Each type of method is applied and analyzed separately. The Linear Programming approaches are discussed in Chapter 4, Constraint Programming approaches in Chapter 5, Local Search approaches in Chapter 6 and finally the VNS approaches which are studied in Chapter 7. Finally, a general analysis of all the applied techniques is needed, in order

DOI: 10.4018/978-1-7998-1882-3.ch008

to filter the applied methods according to their effectiveness in computing the desired optimized CDO Squared portfolio.

Thus, in this chapter, we provide a global synthesis of exact and approximate methods applied on a financial portfolio design problem (PD) modeled in a 0-1 quadratic model (Model 3.14 in Chapter 3). We analyze the results reached with exact approaches, namely Linear Programming and Constraint Programming. The best solutions given are provided by the LP approach without symmetry breaking and implemented under the SCIP solver, and the CP approach with breaking all the detected symmetries, by combining static and dynamic techniques of symmetry breaking.

We offer a general synthesis of the experimental results of the applied approximate methods, respectively Simple and Population based Local Search, and Variable Neighborhood Search. The best results achieved were provided by Simulated Annealing launched with the FLIP neighborhood function (Chapter 6), Skewed Variable Neighborhood Search combined with IDWalk and launched with the SWAP neighborhood function, and Variable Neighborhood Search combined with Simulated Annealing and launched with the FLIP neighborhood function.

A global synthesis of exact and approximate approaches is given separately, due to the major differences between the two. In exact approaches, the quality of solutions is proved and the CPU time is conditioned by the size of the instance. But approximate approaches provide acceptable solutions in a reasonable CPU time.

The chapter is organized as follows. In Section 2, the best realized experimental results with exact approaches are given along with a global synthesis of the corresponding methods. In section 3, we introduce the results of the implemented approximate methods. We present a summary table and performance profiles, to lead to a clear and global synthesis. Finally, we conclude the chapter.

SYNTHESIS ON EXACT APPROACHES

Experimental results of Linear Programming (LP) and Constraint Programming (CP) applied on the (PD) problem are given respectively in Chapter 4 and Chapter 5.

In Chapter 4, we introduced two Linear Programs: Model (4.1) that is earned through a linearization procedure, and Model (4.4) that is expanded by the constraints expressing lexicographical symmetry breaking. We noticed that the both LPs (4.1) and (4.4) are very close in CPU time until the instance Inst6 $\langle 10,15,6,2 \rangle$, where the curve PD-Lex diverges, which expresses the slowness of symmetry breaking under SCIP.

In Chapter 5, CP models are given via Model (5.1) without symmetry breaking and via Model (5.2) with considering column and row lexicographical symmetry constraints (Flener, Frisch, Hnich, Kiziltan, Miguel, Pearson & Walsh, 2001; Flener, Frisch, Hnich, Kiziltan, Miguel, Pearson & Walsh, 2002; Flener, Frisch, Hnich, Jefferson, Kiziltan, Miguel, Pearson & Walsh, 2003). Dynamic symmetry breaking (Benhamou, 1994; Gent & Smith, 1999; Benhamou & Saïdi, 2007; Mears, de la Banda, Demoen & Wallace, 2014) and different combinations of symmetry breaking techniques are also applied.

To summarize the results reached through applied exact approaches, we propose in this chapter a global synthesis of the most reliable methods coming from LP and from CP, and the obtained results in (Flener et al., 2007).

In Table 1, we introduce in columns 2 and 3 the realized CPU time in seconds, through the implemented approaches in SCIP (Achterberg, 2005; Achterberg, 2009; Achterberg, Berthold, Heinz, Koch & Wolter, 2008a; Achterberg, Berthold, Koch & Wolter, 2008b) and under GECODE (Schulte, 2002; Schulte & Tack, 2005; Schulte & Stuckey, 2008;Schulte, Tack & Lagerkvist, 2019), namely:

- PD-SCIP: PL (Model (4.4) in Chapter 4) without breaking symmetry launched in the SCIP solver.
- PD-Sym3LDSB: CP (Model (5.1) in Chapter 5) with static row and column breaking symmetry, and dynamic 180° rotation breaking symmetry, launched under the GECODE solver.

In the 4th column labeled PrRes we introduce the realized CPU times in (Flener, Pearson, Reyna & Sivertsson, 2007).

The bold results represent the best achieved CPU times for each tackled instance. We notice that applying CP techniques on the 0-1 matricial model is better than on the set model.

Figure 1 shows the curves -PD- and -PDSym3LDSB-, which designate respectively the resolution without symmetry breaking under the SCIP solver and the resolution with breaking the three symmetries (row, column and 180° rotation symmetries) under the GECODE solver. These two curves introduce the realized CPU times on the solved instances in less than an hour.

Table 1. Best experimental results by exact approaches

Instance	PD-SCIP	PD-Sym3LDSB	PrRes
Inst1	1.67	**0.00**	**0.00**$_{(PD)}$
Inst2	>3600	**0.00**	-
Inst3	33.53	**0.03**	-$_{(PD)}$|0.00$_{(BIBD)}$
Inst4	47.50	0.03	**0.01**$_{(PD)}$
Inst5	>3600	>3600	**0.00**$_{(PD)}$
Inst6	178.92	**0.15**	0.52$_{(PD)}$
Inst7	96.22	**0.32**	0.01$_{(BIBD)}$|0.76$_{(PD)}$
Inst8	304.33	**0.18**	0.01$_{(BIBD)}$|0.25$_{(PD)}$
Inst9	>3600	**4.68**	28.62$_{(PD)}$
Inst10	1860.47	3.00	**0.02**$_{(PD)}$
Inst11	2658.31	**2.173**	0.01$_{(BIBD)}$|373$_{(PD)}$
Inst12	1260.36	>3600	**3.05**$_{(PD)}$
Inst13	588.80	90.35	**0.16**$_{(PD)}$
Inst14	6204.09	2.25	**0.62**$_{(PD)}$
Inst15	>3600	**9.22**	0.16$_{(BIBD)}$|>3600$_{(PD)}$
Inst16	>3600	>3600	>3600

Figure 1. Comparison of the best realized CPU times under GECODE and SCIP, according to the variables number

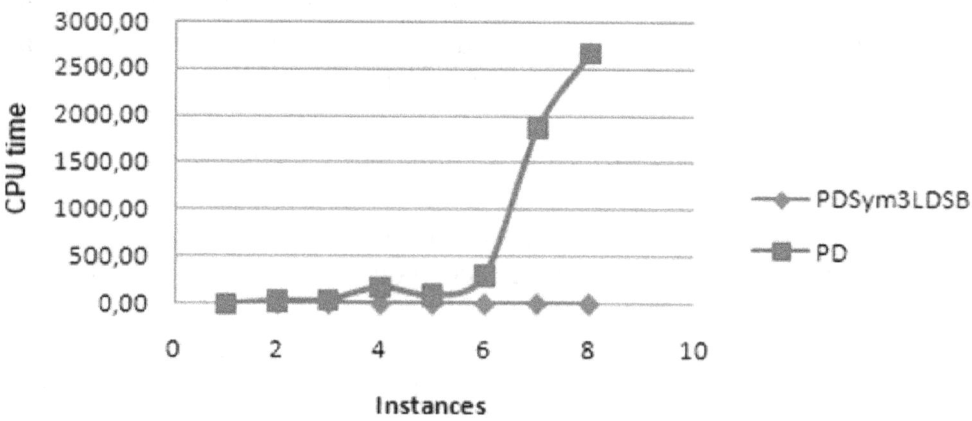

We notice the divergence of the -PD- curve from the instance Inst6 (Instance $\langle 10,15,6,2 \rangle$), a CDO Squared including 15 tranches and 350 inner portfolios, and the stability of the curve -PDSym3LDSB- with reasonable realized CPU times.

SYNTHESIS OF APPROXIMATE APPROACHES

Experimental results of Simple and Population based Local Search (SLS and PLS) and Variable Neighborhood Search (VNS) applied approaches on the (PD) problem are given respectively in Chapter 7 and Chapter 8. In chapter 2, we introduced different approaches: Simulated Annealing, IDWalk, Tabu search and GWW. We adopted the proposed matricial (Model (3.14) in Chapter 3), as we introduced an evaluation function *EVAL*, a neighborhood function *FLIP* and a greedy algorithm *GreedyInit* to compute the initial solution. According to the number of success and CPU time, Simulated Annealing was the best in its two versions: random initial solution and greedy initial solution, namely GrSA and RandSA.

In Chapter 7, VNS and SVNS approaches were proposed and adapted on the (PD) matricial model. We introduced in the chapter a new neighborhood function called SWAP. According to the number of success and CPU time, Skewed VNS combined with IDW and launched with the SWAP neighborhood function, and VNS method combined with Simulated Annealing and launched with the FLIP neighborhood function, were the best.

To summarize the results reached through applied approximate approaches, we present in this section a global synthesis of the best methods.

In Table 2, we introduce in columns 2, 3, 4 and 5 the realized CPU times in seconds, through the respective implemented approaches, namely:

GrSA: Simulated Annealing launched with greedy generated initial solution.
RandSA: Simulated Annealing launched with random generated initial solution.
SIS: SVNS method combined with IDWalk and launched with the SWAP neighborhood function.
VSF: VNS method combined with Simulated Annealing and launched with the FLIP neighborhood function.

Table 2. The best experimental results by approximate approaches, the successful runs and the average of runtimes.

Instance		GrSA	RandSA	SIS	VSF	GIDW
Inst1	SUCC./20 AVG-TIME	20 0.01	20 0.00	20 0.01	20 0.00	20 0.61
Inst2	SUCC./20 AVG-TIME	20 0.00	20 0.00	20 0.00	20 0.00	20 0.00
Inst3	SUCC./20 AVG-TIME	20 4.22	20 1.73	20 0.12	20 2.34	13 106.84
Inst4	SUCC./20 AVG-TIME	20 4.01	20 1.15	20 1.10	20 1.24	16 90.37
Inst5	SUCC./20 AVG-TIME	00 23.75	00 15.52	00 199.83	00 199.66	00 199.60
Inst6	SUCC./20 AVG-TIME	20 7.66	19 5.33	20 3.04	20 5.29	04 168.71
Inst7	SUCC./20 AVG-TIME	18 12.32	8 11.43	20 6.40	17 50.18	03 094.59
Inst8	SUCC./20 AVG-TIME	20 15.21	19 8.38	20 6.46	20 7.78	09 133.28
Inst9	SUCC./20 AVG-TIME	20 14.81	20 5.44	20 0.00	20 5.55	12 130.95
Inst10	SUCC./20 AVG-TIME	14 44.70	10 31.96	18 67.78	17 62.50	00 199.64
Inst11	SUCC./20 AVG-TIME	17 37.66	18 19.36	06 151.28	20 20.19	02 190.98
Inst12	SUCC./20 AVG-TIME	17 36.59	20 10.84	20 1.91	20 10.77	16 97.10
Inst13	SUCC./20 AVG-TIME	20 0.02	20 0.01	20 0.01	20 0.01	20 0.10
Inst14	SUCC./20 AVG-TIME	20 11.33	20 4.14	20 0.21	20 4.99	20 13.67
Inst15	SUCC./20 AVG-TIME	00 44.70	00 25.60	00 199.65	00 199.70	00 199.64
Inst16	SUCC./20 AVG-TIME	00 199.84	02 196.76	00 199.77	13 193.08	02 184.06

In the sixth column we introduce the realized results by the hybrid method GWW+IDWalk, the best applied population based Local Search on (PD) problem.

To provide a deep synthesis of the applied approximate approaches, we took both best categories: SLS (Simple Local Search) and VNS (in both versions: basic and skewed), in addition of the hybrid method GWW+IDWalk (denoted

Global Results Synthesis

Figure 2. Performance profiles of the efficient methods according to the number of success

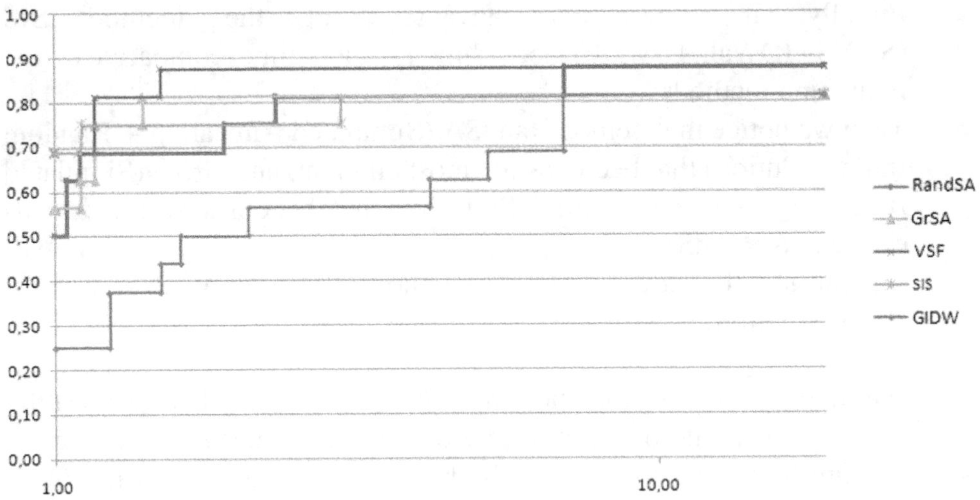

Figure 3. Performance profiles of the efficient methods according to the CPU time

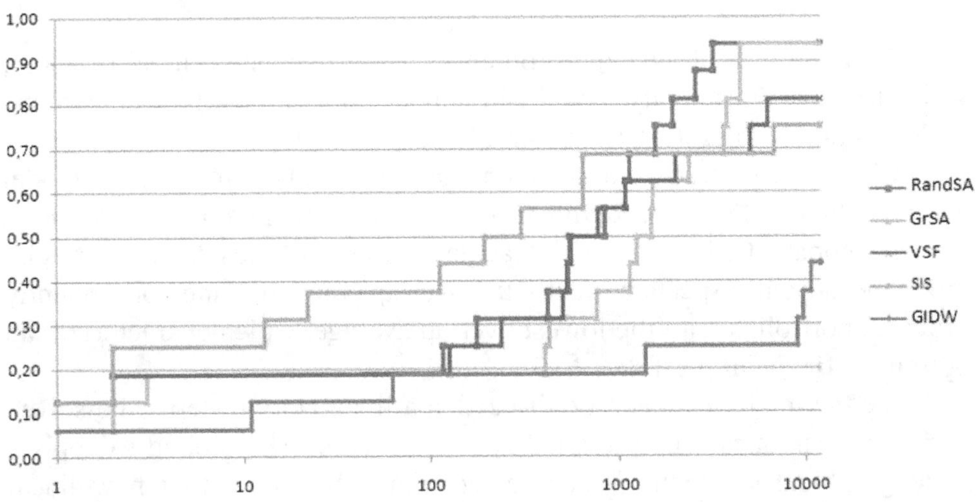

GIDW). In figures 2 and 3, we join the curves which illustrate respectively the performance profiles in number of success and in CPU time.

According to the number of success, Figure 2 highlights the VSF method compared to the remaining methods. We can perceive the efficiency of the population method GWW combined with IDWalk.

Figure 3 can be described in three points:

- Initially, it shows the advantage of the method SIS (SVNS+IDWalk+SWAP) according to CPU time compared to the remaining methods.
- Then we notice the method RandSA (Simulated Annealing + Random Initial Solution) that becomes the most efficient, and GrSA (Simulated Annealing + Gready Initial Solution) that becomes at the end as efficient as RandSA.
- We can see the slowness of the method GIDW (IDWalk + Greedy Initial Solution).

From both figures, we conclude that VSF (VNS+ Simulated Annealing + FLIP) method is the most appropriate one according to the number of success. On the other hand, the methods SIS (SVNS + IDWalk+SWAP), RandSA and GrSA are the best according to the CPU time.

CONCLUSION

CDO Squared portfolio design problem is a complex and critical problem, which needs a high-quality model taking in consideration all the constraints in details and highlighting all the problematic aspects.

In Chapter 3, we described two mathematical models, namely the set model given in (Flener, Pearson, Reyna & Sivertsson, 2007) and the 0-1 matricial model (Lebbah,2014a). The model tackled in this book was the 0-1 matricial model because it respects perfectly the overlap constraint and consequently provides portfolios with the lowest overlap average, which characterizes an optimized financial portfolio.

Since the model is quadratic, it needed a linearization step to be solved with LP techniques. The provided Linear Program is exploited to apply a lexicographical symmetry breaking technique, by integrating new linear constraints. Thus, the problem is modeled into two PLs, which were solved under the SCIP solver.

The problem can be seen as a Constraint Satisfaction Problem, since the lowest value of the optimized overlap is computed in advance. To tackle the problem by CP techniques, we introduced the corresponding CSP without consideration of the symmetries, and a CSP which includes lexicographic ordering constraints. Both CSPs were solved under the GECODE solver.

The results indicated the exact approaches were not very effective on the (PD) problem. Thus, a panoply of approximate approaches was adapted and applied, in addition to the integrating of the appropriate evaluation and neighborhood functions.

According to the realized synthesis on the applied exact methods on the 0-1 model, we deduce that Constraint Programming techniques are more efficient than the Linear Programming techniques as an exact approach.

Including a greedy algorithm allows Local Search approaches to improve the obtained results in terms of the CPU time and the rate of success, except Tabu search that remains unsuccessful. Simulated Annealing and IDWalk are the most effective approaches.

Applying the Variable Neighborhood Search approaches, namely VNS and SVNS with FLIP and SWAP proposed neighborhood functions, combined with simple Local Search methods, improved the quality of the portfolios generated, which depends upon the overlapping rate.

Regarding GWW combined with IDWalk, it remains less efficient, compared to the remaining applied approaches.

Overall, we conclude that:

- According to the CPU time, applying the CP techniques with static and dynamic symmetry breaking is very competitive as an exact method compared to the results given in the previous scientific works.
- According to the quality of the built CDO Squared portfolios, Simulated Annealing launched with the both proposed neighborhood functions, and VNS combined with Simulated Annealing, provide better results compared to the exact method.

In order to improve the results given through Linear Programming and Constraint Programming techniques, we should apply appropriate algorithms, which take in consideration the 0-1 domain of the variables and the nature of the constraint.

Using parallelization techniques, such as MPI (Message Passing Interface) and OMP (Open Multi Processing) within Population based Local Search and Variable Neighborhood Search approaches, should be more profitable in terms of decreasing the CPU time.

Modeling and solving the (PD) problem with Graph Theory techniques remains an interesting lead to be explored.

REFERENCES

Flener, P., Frisch, A. M., Hnich, B., Kiziltan, Z., Miguel, I., Pearson, J., & Walsh, T. (2001). Symmetry in matrix models. *Proceedings of the CP'01. Workshop on Symmetry in Constraints*, 41-48.

Flener, P., Frisch, A. M., Hnich, B., Kiziltan, Z., Miguel, I., Pearson, J., & Walsh, T. (2002). Breaking row and column symmetries in matrix models. Lecture Notes in Computer Science, 462–476. doi:10.1007/3-540-46135-3_31

Flener, P., Pearson, J., Reyna, L. G., & Sivertsson, O. (2007). Design of financial cdo squared transactions using constraint programming. *Constraints*, *12*(2), 179–205. doi:10.100710601-006-9014-4

Flener, P., Frisch, A., Hnich, B., Jefferson, C., Kiziltan, Z., Miguel, I., ... Walsh, T. (2003). Breaking symmetries in matrix models: A brief overview. *Proceedings of the Tenth Workshop on Automated Reasoning*, 27-28.

Benhamou, B., & Saïdi, M. R. (2007). Local symmetry breaking during search in CSPs. Principles and Practice of Constraint Programming - CP 2007, 13th International Conference, CP 2007 Proceedings, 195-209.

Benhamou, B. (1994). Study of symmetry in constraint satisfaction problems. *Proceedings of, CP-94*, 246–254.

Achterberg, T. (2005). SCIP-A framework to integrate constraint and mixed integer programming. Technical Report, ZIB. *Takustr*, *7*, 14195.

Achterberg, T. (2009). SCIP: Solving Constraint Integer Programs. *Math. Program. Comput.*, *1*(1), 1-41.

Achterberg, T., Berthold, T., Heinz, S., Koch, T., & Wolter, K. (2008a). Constraint Integer Programming: Techniques and applications. Technical Report 08-43, ZIB. *Takustr, 7*, 14195.

Achterberg, T., Berthold, T., Koch, T., & Wolter, K. (2008b). Constraint integer programming: A new approach to integrate CP and MIP. *Integration of AI and OR Techniques in Constraint Programming for Combinatorial Optimization Problems, 5th International Conference, CPAIOR 2008*, 5015, 6-20. 10.1007/978-3-540-68155-7_4

Gent, I. P., & Smith, B. (1999). Symmetry breaking during search in constraint programming. *Proceedings ECAI'2000*, 599-603.

Lebbah, F. Z., & Lebbah, Y. (2015a). A local search approach to solve a financial portfolio design problem. *International Journal of Applied Metaheuristic Computing*, *6*(2), 1–17. doi:10.4018/IJAMC.2015040101

Lebbah, F. Z. & Lebbah, Y. (2015b). VNS approach for solving a financial portfolio design problem. *Electronic Notes in Discrete Mathematics, 47*, 125-132.

Mears, C., de la Banda, M. G., Demoen, B., & Wallace, M. (2014). Lightweight dynamic symmetry breaking. *Constraints*, *19*(3), 195–242. doi:10.100710601-013-9154-2

Schulte, C. (2002). Programming Constraint Services. Lecture Notes in Artificial Intelligence, 2302. doi:10.1007/3-540-45945-6

Schulte, C., & Stuckey, P. J. (2008). Efficient constraint propagation engines. *ACM Transactions on Programming Languages and Systems*, *31*(1), 1–43. doi:10.1145/1452044.1452046

Schulte, C., & Tack, G. (2005). Views and iterators for generic constraint implementations. *Proceedings of Principles and Practice of Constraint Programming. 11th International Conference*, 1-5. 10.1007/11564751_71

Schulte, C., Tack, G., & Lagerkvist, M. Z. (2019). *Modeling and programming with GECODE.* Retrieved May 28, 2019, from https://www.gecode.org/doc-latest/MPG.pdf

Glossary

BIBD: Balanced Incomplete Block Design

CDO: Collateralized Debt Obligation

CDO^2: Collateralized Debt Obligation Squared

CP: Constraint Programming/Constraint Program

CP_{PD}: Corresponding CP model of (PD) problem without considering any symmetry

CP_{PDLEX}: Corresponding CP model of (PD) problem with breaking row and column symmetries by using Lex method

CSP: Constraint Satisfaction Problem

EVAL: Evaluation function which computes the number of the violated constraints

FLIP: Neighborhood function, which flips a selected variable

GECODE: GEneric COnstraint DEvelopment environment

GreedyInit: A greedy algorithm which computes a good initial configuration

GrIDW: IDWalk launched with greedy generated initial solution

GrSA: SA launched with greedy generated initial solution

GWW: Go With the Winners

IDWalk: Identification Diversification Walk

ILP: Integer Linear Programming/ nteger Linear program

INCOP: Incomplete Combinatorial OPtimization

LDSB: Lightweight Dynamic Symmetry Breaking

Lex: Static symmetry breaking by ordering the rows (or the columns) in Lexicographical order

LP: Linear Programming/Linear Program

LS: Local Search

MIP: Mixed-Integer Programming/Mixed-Integer Program

OPD: Optimization Portfolio Design problem

PD: Portfolio Design problem

PDLexLDSB: Method to solve CP_{PD} with breaking row symmetry by using Lex, and column symmetry by using LDSB

PD_{Lin}: Linear version of (PD) problem

PD_{LinLex}: Linear version of (PD) problem with static symmetry Breaking

PDSym2LDSB: Method to solve CP_{PD} with breaking row and column symmetries by using LDSB

PDSym3LDSB: Method to solve CP_{PD} with breaking all symmetries by using LDSB

RandIDW: IDWalk launched with random generated initial solution.

RandSA: Simulated Annealing launched with random generated initial solution.

SA: Simulated Annealing

SBDD: Symmetry Breaking by Dominance Detection

SCIP: Solving Constraint Integer Programs

SIF: SVNS method combined with IDWalk and launched with FLIP neighborhood function

SIS: SVNS method combined with IDWalk and launched with SWAP neighborhood function

SLS: Simple Local Search

SSF: SVNS method combined with SA and launched with FLIP neighborhood function

SSS: SVNS method combined with SA and launched with SWAP neighborhood function

SVNS: Skewed Variable Neighborhood Search

SWAP: Neighborhood function, which swaps between two variables

VIF: VNS method combined with IDWalk and launched with FLIP neighborhood function

VIS: VNS method combined with IDWalk and launched with SWAP neighborhood function

VNS: Variable Neighborhood Search

VSF: VNS method combined with SA and launched with FLIP neighborhood function

VSS: VNS method combined with SA and launched with SWAP neighborhood function

Related Readings

To continue IGI Global's long-standing tradition of advancing innovation through emerging research, please find below a compiled list of recommended IGI Global book chapters and journal articles in the areas of entrepreneurship, microenterprise, and microfinance. These related readings will provide additional information and guidance to further enrich your knowledge and assist you with your own research.

Ahamad, S. S., Sastry, V. N., & Udgata, S. K. (2018). Formal Verification of Secure Payment Framework in MANET for Disaster Areas. In M. Khosrow-Pour, D.B.A. (Ed.), Entrepreneurship, Collaboration, and Innovation in the Modern Business Era (pp. 68-101). Hershey, PA: IGI Global. doi:10.4018/978-1-5225-5014-3.ch004

Al-Marri, M., & Al-Hasan, S. (2018). The Effectiveness of Financing the Marketing of Small and Medium-Sized Enterprises in Qatar and the Gulf Co-Operation Council (GCC) Countries: With a Special Focus on Advertising. In A. Woldie & B. Thomas (Eds.), *Financial Entrepreneurship for Economic Growth in Emerging Nations* (pp. 129–147). Hershey, PA: IGI Global. doi:10.4018/978-1-5225-2700-8.ch007

Almeida, R. M., Abreu, R., & Perez-Lopez, J. A. (2018). Nascent Entrepreneurship and Sustainability on the Beverage Sector. In A. Carrizo Moreira, J. Guilherme Leitão Dantas, & F. Manuel Valente (Eds.), *Nascent Entrepreneurship and Successful New Venture Creation* (pp. 215–238). Hershey, PA: IGI Global. doi:10.4018/978-1-5225-2936-1.ch010

Aninze, F., El-Gohary, H., & Hussain, J. (2018). The Role of Microfinance to Empower Women: The Case of Developing Countries. *International Journal of Customer Relationship Marketing and Management, 9*(1), 54–78. doi:10.4018/IJCRMM.2018010104

Ayopo, B. A., Isola, L. A., Niyan, T. J., & Bosede, A. V. (2018). Microfinance and Entrepreneurship in Nigeria: A Macro Analysis. In R. Das (Ed.), *Microfinance and Its Impact on Entrepreneurial Development, Sustainability, and Inclusive Growth* (pp. 65–84). Hershey, PA: IGI Global. doi:10.4018/978-1-5225-5213-0.ch004

Bandera, C., Bartolacci, M. R., & Passerini, K. (2016). Knowledge Management and Entrepreneurship: A Contradictory Recipe. *International Journal of Knowledge Management, 12*(3), 1–14. doi:10.4018/IJKM.2016070101

Baporikar, N. (2016). Entrepreneurship Culture of SMEs in India's Tourism Sector. *International Journal of Strategic Information Technology and Applications, 7*(2), 14–27. doi:10.4018/IJSITA.2016040102

Baryshev, A. A. (2017). Entrepreneurial Action as Metaphorical Process and its Metaphorics. *International Journal of Actor-Network Theory and Technological Innovation, 9*(1), 24–39. doi:10.4018/IJANTTI.2017010103

Bastida, R., & Mas-Machuca, M. (2019). Relationship Between Mission Drift and Financial Strategies in Social Enterprises. In C. Maher (Ed.), *Handbook of Research on Value Creation for Small and Micro Social Enterprises* (pp. 151–167). Hershey, PA: IGI Global. doi:10.4018/978-1-5225-6298-6.ch008

Bernardino, S., Santos, J. F., & Ribeiro, J. C. (2018). Social Entrepreneurship and Entrepreneurial Ecosystems: An Empirical Examination. In L. Carvalho (Ed.), *Handbook of Research on Entrepreneurial Ecosystems and Social Dynamics in a Globalized World* (pp. 181–210). Hershey, PA: IGI Global. doi:10.4018/978-1-5225-3525-6.ch008

Carvalho, J. M. (2018). Social Innovation, Entrepreneurship, and Sustainability. In L. Carvalho (Ed.), *Handbook of Research on Entrepreneurial Ecosystems and Social Dynamics in a Globalized World* (pp. 147–180). Hershey, PA: IGI Global. doi:10.4018/978-1-5225-3525-6.ch007

Carvalho, L. C., Vázquez, D. G., & Gil, M. T. (2018). Local Municipalities' Involvement in Promoting Entrepreneurship: An Analysis of Web Page Orientation to the Entrepreneurs in Portuguese Municipalities. In L. Carvalho (Ed.), *Handbook of Research on Entrepreneurial Ecosystems and Social Dynamics in a Globalized World* (pp. 1–19). Hershey, PA: IGI Global. doi:10.4018/978-1-5225-3525-6.ch001

Çetin, I., & Keser, H. Y. (2018). Women Entrepreneurship in MENA and Europe: Empowerment Through Microfinance. In R. Das (Ed.), *Microfinance and Its Impact on Entrepreneurial Development, Sustainability, and Inclusive Growth* (pp. 30–51). Hershey, PA: IGI Global. doi:10.4018/978-1-5225-5213-0.ch002

Chakraborty, S. (2018). Effect and Effectiveness of Microfinance in the Presence of Political Environment: A Study of Microfinance Institutions of West Bengal, India. In R. Das (Ed.), *Microfinance and Its Impact on Entrepreneurial Development, Sustainability, and Inclusive Growth* (pp. 296–307). Hershey, PA: IGI Global. doi:10.4018/978-1-5225-5213-0.ch016

Che, Y., & Zhang, B. (2019). Contextual Determinants of E-Entrepreneurship: Opportunities and Challenges. *International Journal on Semantic Web and Information Systems, 15*(3), 1–15. doi:10.4018/IJSWIS.2019070101

Cheek, R., Sale, M., & Wolverton, C. C. (2018). UX (User Experience)-Driven Website Design Utilizing Analytic Hierarchy Process (AHP) Multi-Attribute Decision Modeling. In M. Khosrow-Pour, D.B.A. (Ed.), Entrepreneurship, Collaboration, and Innovation in the Modern Business Era (pp. 121-135). Hershey, PA: IGI Global. doi:10.4018/978-1-5225-5014-3.ch006

Cîrstea, A. C. (2017). Entrepreneurship Development in Northeast Region of Romania. *International Journal of Sustainable Economies Management, 6*(3), 1–9. doi:10.4018/IJSEM.2017070101

Dalkir, K. (2018). Connecting and Sharing Tacit Knowledge: Do Social Media Help or Hinder? In M. Khosrow-Pour, D.B.A. (Ed.), Entrepreneurship, Collaboration, and Innovation in the Modern Business Era (pp. 178-193). Hershey, PA: IGI Global. doi:10.4018/978-1-5225-5014-3.ch009

Daniel, A. D., & Reis de Castro, V. (2018). Entrepreneurship Education: How to Measure the Impact on Nascent Entrepreneurs. In A. Carrizo Moreira, J. Guilherme Leitão Dantas, & F. Manuel Valente (Eds.), *Nascent Entrepreneurship and Successful New Venture Creation* (pp. 85–110). Hershey, PA: IGI Global. doi:10.4018/978-1-5225-2936-1.ch004

Dantas, J. G., Moreira, A. C., & Valente, F. M. (2018). National Culture, Societal Values, and Type of Economy: Are They Relevant to Explain Entrepreneurial Activity? In L. Carvalho (Ed.), *Handbook of Research on Entrepreneurial Ecosystems and Social Dynamics in a Globalized World* (pp. 75–103). Hershey, PA: IGI Global. doi:10.4018/978-1-5225-3525-6.ch004

Dantas, J. G., & Valente, F. M. (2018). Entrepreneurship, Non-Cognitive Skills, and Education. In A. Carrizo Moreira, J. Guilherme Leitão Dantas, & F. Manuel Valente (Eds.), *Nascent Entrepreneurship and Successful New Venture Creation* (pp. 29–57). Hershey, PA: IGI Global. doi:10.4018/978-1-5225-2936-1.ch002

Das, S. K., & Chatterjee, T. (2018). Impact of Microfinance on Consumption of Tribal Groups: A Study With a focus to Bankura Districts of West Bengal. In R. Das (Ed.), *Microfinance and Its Impact on Entrepreneurial Development, Sustainability, and Inclusive Growth* (pp. 308–321). Hershey, PA: IGI Global. doi:10.4018/978-1-5225-5213-0.ch017

de Vries, I. (2019). Exploring the Personal Drive Behind Small Social-Venture Set-Ups in the Netherlands: Encounters With Local Help and Hindrance. In C. Maher (Ed.), *Handbook of Research on Value Creation for Small and Micro Social Enterprises* (pp. 75–94). Hershey, PA: IGI Global. doi:10.4018/978-1-5225-6298-6.ch004

del Mar Miralles-Quiros, M., Miralles-Quiros, J. L., & Daza-Izquierdo, J. (2018). The Role of High-Tech Entrepreneurship on Regional Development. In A. Carrizo Moreira, J. Guilherme Leitão Dantas, & F. Manuel Valente (Eds.), *Nascent Entrepreneurship and Successful New Venture Creation* (pp. 259–271). Hershey, PA: IGI Global. doi:10.4018/978-1-5225-2936-1.ch012

Dinçer, H., Hacıoğlu, Ü., & Yüksel, S. (2018). Evaluating the Effects of Economic Imbalances on Gold Price in Turkey With MARS Method and Discussions on Microfinance. In R. Das (Ed.), *Microfinance and Its Impact on Entrepreneurial Development, Sustainability, and Inclusive Growth* (pp. 115–137). Hershey, PA: IGI Global. doi:10.4018/978-1-5225-5213-0.ch007

Doyle, G. J. (2019). Socializing Economic Development in Ireland: Social Enterprise – An Untapped Resource. In C. Maher (Ed.), *Handbook of Research on Value Creation for Small and Micro Social Enterprises* (pp. 168–187). Hershey, PA: IGI Global. doi:10.4018/978-1-5225-6298-6.ch009

Egbuta, I. C., & Gilbert, L. L. (2018). Problems Financing Small Business Enterprises in the Current Economic, Business, and Organizational Environment in Nigeria: With Recommendations for Future Support Initiatives. In A. Woldie & B. Thomas (Eds.), *Financial Entrepreneurship for Economic Growth in Emerging Nations* (pp. 111–128). Hershey, PA: IGI Global. doi:10.4018/978-1-5225-2700-8.ch006

Epepe, U. D. (2019). Small Social Enterprises and Online Advertising: Overview of Constraints in Some Selected Cities in Nigeria. In C. Maher (Ed.), *Handbook of Research on Value Creation for Small and Micro Social Enterprises* (pp. 229–253). Hershey, PA: IGI Global. doi:10.4018/978-1-5225-6298-6.ch012

Erçek, M., & Sarıtemur, M. (2018). The Dynamics of Entrepreneurial Networks: A Qualitative Assessment of University Incubator's Role in the Early Stages of Hi-Tech Startups. In A. Carrizo Moreira, J. Guilherme Leitão Dantas, & F. Manuel Valente (Eds.), *Nascent Entrepreneurship and Successful New Venture Creation* (pp. 239–258). Hershey, PA: IGI Global. doi:10.4018/978-1-5225-2936-1.ch011

Eryılmaz, M. (2019). A Discussion on the Relationship Between Information and Communication Technologies (ICT) and Entrepreneurship. *International Journal of E-Entrepreneurship and Innovation, 9*(1), 13–22. doi:10.4018/IJEEI.2019010102

Eryılmaz, M. E., & Bektaş, O. (2018). An Examination of the Relationship Between Vision Content and Amount of Innovation in SMEs: Findings From Turkey. In L. Carvalho (Ed.), *Handbook of Research on Entrepreneurial Ecosystems and Social Dynamics in a Globalized World* (pp. 20–44). Hershey, PA: IGI Global. doi:10.4018/978-1-5225-3525-6.ch002

Farinha, L., Ferreira, J. J., Nunes, S., & Ratten, V. (2017). Conditions Supporting Entrepreneurship and Sustainable Growth. *International Journal of Social Ecology and Sustainable Development, 8*(3), 67–86. doi:10.4018/IJSESD.2017070105

França, A., Vilares, A., Frankenbach, S., Vereb, V., & Moreira, A. C. (2018). The Challenging Dynamics of Nascent Entrepreneurship. In A. Carrizo Moreira, J. Guilherme Leitão Dantas, & F. Manuel Valente (Eds.), *Nascent Entrepreneurship and Successful New Venture Creation* (pp. 1–28). Hershey, PA: IGI Global. doi:10.4018/978-1-5225-2936-1.ch001

Ganguly, S. (2018). Micro-Finance and Poverty in India: A State-Level Analysis of Impact Assessment. In A. Woldie & B. Thomas (Eds.), *Financial Entrepreneurship for Economic Growth in Emerging Nations* (pp. 194–216). Hershey, PA: IGI Global. doi:10.4018/978-1-5225-2700-8.ch010

Giacosa, E. (2018). The Increasing of the Regional Development Thanks to the Luxury Business Innovation. In L. Carvalho (Ed.), *Handbook of Research on Entrepreneurial Ecosystems and Social Dynamics in a Globalized World* (pp. 260–273). Hershey, PA: IGI Global. doi:10.4018/978-1-5225-3525-6.ch011

Giacosa, E., & Giovando, G. (2018). Italian Tourism Sector as an Example of Entrepreneurship and Growth for Companies. In L. Carvalho (Ed.), *Handbook of Research on Entrepreneurial Ecosystems and Social Dynamics in a Globalized World* (pp. 313–331). Hershey, PA: IGI Global. doi:10.4018/978-1-5225-3525-6.ch014

Han, L., Xiang, X., & Yang, X. (2018). Emerging Economies and Financing of SMEs. In A. Woldie & B. Thomas (Eds.), *Financial Entrepreneurship for Economic Growth in Emerging Nations* (pp. 22–45). Hershey, PA: IGI Global. doi:10.4018/978-1-5225-2700-8.ch002

Hannibal, M., & Rasmussen, E. S. (2018). Digital Entrepreneurship: A Longitudinal Case Study in a Traditional Firm. In M. Khosrow-Pour, D.B.A. (Ed.), Entrepreneurship, Collaboration, and Innovation in the Modern Business Era (pp. 1-21). Hershey, PA: IGI Global. doi:10.4018/978-1-5225-5014-3.ch001

Hossain, S. F. (2019). Social Networking and Its Role in Media Entrepreneurship: Evaluating the Use of Mobile Phones in the Context of Online Shopping – A Review. *Journal of Media Management and Entrepreneurship*, *1*(1), 73–86. doi:10.4018/JMME.2019010105

Huamaní, G. A., Fernández-López, S., Gómez, I. N., Rey-Ares, L., Rodríguez-Gulías, M. J., & Rodeiro-Pazos, D. (2018). The Role Models as Determinants of New Technology-Based Firms: An Exploratory Study. In A. Carrizo Moreira, J. Guilherme Leitão Dantas, & F. Manuel Valente (Eds.), *Nascent Entrepreneurship and Successful New Venture Creation* (pp. 272–288). Hershey, PA: IGI Global. doi:10.4018/978-1-5225-2936-1.ch013

Hussein, S. A., & Mswaka, W. (2018). Entrepreneurial Motives of Egyptian Entrepreneurs: Empirical Evidence From Egypt. *International Journal of Customer Relationship Marketing and Management*, *9*(1), 1–18. doi:10.4018/IJCRMM.2018010101

Jana, S. K., Karmakar, A. K., & Sarkar, K. (2018). Efficiency Analysis of Microfinance Institutions (MFIs) in India Using DEA. In R. Das (Ed.), *Microfinance and Its Impact on Entrepreneurial Development, Sustainability, and Inclusive Growth* (pp. 218–230). Hershey, PA: IGI Global. doi:10.4018/978-1-5225-5213-0.ch012

Jankelowitz, L., & Myres, K. (2019). Micro Social Enterprises in Developing Countries: The South African Experience. In C. Maher (Ed.), *Handbook of Research on Value Creation for Small and Micro Social Enterprises* (pp. 1–25). Hershey, PA: IGI Global. doi:10.4018/978-1-5225-6298-6.ch001

Kakembo, S. H., & Ahmad, A. U. (2019). Employing Islamic Microfinance in Addressing Poverty Challenges in Brunei: A Mudarabah Approach. *International Journal of Corporate Finance and Accounting*, *6*(1), 49–61. doi:10.4018/IJCFA.2019010104

Ktoridou, D., Epaminonda, E., & Karayiannis, A. (2018). Multidisciplinary Group Case-Based Learning Environment: An Education Paradigm to Cultivate Entrepreneurial Thinking. In M. Khosrow-Pour, D.B.A. (Ed.), Entrepreneurship, Collaboration, and Innovation in the Modern Business Era (pp. 262-277). Hershey, PA: IGI Global. doi:10.4018/978-1-5225-5014-3.ch013

Kulothungan, G. D., Oham, C., & Jirel, P. (2019). Managing Uncertainty in Small and Micro Social Enterprises: A Cynefin-Bricolage Framework. In C. Maher (Ed.), *Handbook of Research on Value Creation for Small and Micro Social Enterprises* (pp. 327–348). Hershey, PA: IGI Global. doi:10.4018/978-1-5225-6298-6.ch017

Kumar, A., Sikdar, P., & Alam, M. M. (2018). E-Retail Adoption in Emerging Markets: A Perspective on Predictive Constructs. In M. Khosrow-Pour, D.B.A. (Ed.), Entrepreneurship, Collaboration, and Innovation in the Modern Business Era (pp. 40-67). Hershey, PA: IGI Global. doi:10.4018/978-1-5225-5014-3.ch003

Lado-Sestayo, R., & Vivel-Bua, M. (2018). Women and Entrepreneurship: An Analysis of the Determinants in the Tourism Sector. In A. Carrizo Moreira, J. Guilherme Leitão Dantas, & F. Manuel Valente (Eds.), *Nascent Entrepreneurship and Successful New Venture Creation* (pp. 203–214). Hershey, PA: IGI Global. doi:10.4018/978-1-5225-2936-1.ch009

Lee, J. J., & Imanaka, J. L. (2018). Theorizing Virtuality in Enterprise Social Systems. In M. Khosrow-Pour, D.B.A. (Ed.), Entrepreneurship, Collaboration, and Innovation in the Modern Business Era (pp. 102-120). Hershey, PA: IGI Global. doi:10.4018/978-1-5225-5014-3.ch005

Lewis, A., Thomas, B. C., & Sanders, G. M. (2018). Attracting the Right Employees?: The Effects of Social Media as an Innovative E-Entrepreneurship Recruitment Method for Enterprises. In M. Khosrow-Pour, D.B.A. (Ed.), Entrepreneurship, Collaboration, and Innovation in the Modern Business Era (pp. 194-220). Hershey, PA: IGI Global. doi:10.4018/978-1-5225-5014-3.ch010

Lima, M. J., & Carvalho, L. C. (2018). Collaboration: The Path to SME Performance Increase – A Case Study in a Portuguese Wine Region. In L. Carvalho (Ed.), *Handbook of Research on Entrepreneurial Ecosystems and Social Dynamics in a Globalized World* (pp. 243–259). Hershey, PA: IGI Global. doi:10.4018/978-1-5225-3525-6.ch010

Liu, C. (2019). Financing Social Enterprises: A Systematic Approach. In C. Maher (Ed.), *Handbook of Research on Value Creation for Small and Micro Social Enterprises* (pp. 126–150). Hershey, PA: IGI Global. doi:10.4018/978-1-5225-6298-6.ch007

López-Cózar-Navarro, C., & Priede-Bergamini, T. (2018). Nascent Social Entrepreneurship: Economic, Legal, and Financial Framework. In A. Carrizo Moreira, J. Guilherme Leitão Dantas, & F. Manuel Valente (Eds.), *Nascent Entrepreneurship and Successful New Venture Creation* (pp. 132–152). Hershey, PA: IGI Global. doi:10.4018/978-1-5225-2936-1.ch006

Luke, B. (2019). A Review of Third Sector Reporting Frameworks: Communicating Value Created in Small and Micro Social Enterprises. In C. Maher (Ed.), *Handbook of Research on Value Creation for Small and Micro Social Enterprises* (pp. 26–45). Hershey, PA: IGI Global. doi:10.4018/978-1-5225-6298-6.ch002

Maher, C. (2018). Public Policy: Implications for Small Third Sector Social Enterprises in UK Regions. In L. Carvalho (Ed.), *Handbook of Research on Entrepreneurial Ecosystems and Social Dynamics in a Globalized World* (pp. 126–146). Hershey, PA: IGI Global. doi:10.4018/978-1-5225-3525-6.ch006

Maher, C. (2019). Social Value and Public Services Procurement. In C. Maher (Ed.), *Handbook of Research on Value Creation for Small and Micro Social Enterprises* (pp. 293–310). Hershey, PA: IGI Global. doi:10.4018/978-1-5225-6298-6.ch015

Maher, S. M. (2019). The Development of National Health Service Social Enterprises in England. In C. Maher (Ed.), *Handbook of Research on Value Creation for Small and Micro Social Enterprises* (pp. 95–108). Hershey, PA: IGI Global. doi:10.4018/978-1-5225-6298-6.ch005

Majumder, A., & Bhattacharyya, R. (2018). An Introspective Study on the Governance Practices of Major Microfinance Institutions (MFIs) in India. In R. Das (Ed.), *Microfinance and Its Impact on Entrepreneurial Development, Sustainability, and Inclusive Growth* (pp. 275–295). Hershey, PA: IGI Global. doi:10.4018/978-1-5225-5213-0.ch015

Malhotra, M. (2018). Role of Microfinance in Financial Inclusion in India. In R. Das (Ed.), *Microfinance and Its Impact on Entrepreneurial Development, Sustainability, and Inclusive Growth* (pp. 322–343). Hershey, PA: IGI Global. doi:10.4018/978-1-5225-5213-0.ch018

Mani, M. (2018). Entrepreneurship Education in Engineering Curriculum: Some Insights Into Students' Viewpoints. In M. Khosrow-Pour, D.B.A. (Ed.), Entrepreneurship, Collaboration, and Innovation in the Modern Business Era (pp. 243-261). Hershey, PA: IGI Global. doi:10.4018/978-1-5225-5014-3.ch012

Manzoor, A. (2017). Womenpreneurs in Mena Region. *International Journal of E-Entrepreneurship and Innovation*, *7*(1), 16–28. doi:10.4018/IJEEI.2017010102

Manzoor, A. (2018). High-Growth Entrepreneurship in the MENA Region. *International Journal of ICT Research in Africa and the Middle East*, *7*(1), 54–65. doi:10.4018/IJICTRAME.2018010104

Manzoor, A. (2018). Role of Microfinance Institutions in Development of India. In R. Das (Ed.), *Microfinance and Its Impact on Entrepreneurial Development, Sustainability, and Inclusive Growth* (pp. 138–155). Hershey, PA: IGI Global. doi:10.4018/978-1-5225-5213-0.ch008

Martín, I., Ramos, M., & Herrero, L. A. (2018). Intrapreneurship in Business Innovation: The Importance of Intellectual Capital Protection – Capitalize on the Commitment of Its Human Capital. In A. Carrizo Moreira, J. Guilherme Leitão Dantas, & F. Manuel Valente (Eds.), *Nascent Entrepreneurship and Successful New Venture Creation* (pp. 153–174). Hershey, PA: IGI Global. doi:10.4018/978-1-5225-2936-1.ch007

Martínez-Azúa, B. C., Mesías, F. J., & Elghannam, A. (2018). Perceptions of Extremaduran Firms Towards Innovation: Manufacturing vs. KIBS Comparative Study. In L. Carvalho (Ed.), *Handbook of Research on Entrepreneurial Ecosystems and Social Dynamics in a Globalized World* (pp. 290–312). Hershey, PA: IGI Global. doi:10.4018/978-1-5225-3525-6.ch013

Mazumdar, D., Bisai, S., & Bhattacharjee, M. (2018). Performance of SHGs in the Backward Districts of West Bengal: An Analysis. In R. Das (Ed.), *Microfinance and Its Impact on Entrepreneurial Development, Sustainability, and Inclusive Growth* (pp. 231–256). Hershey, PA: IGI Global. doi:10.4018/978-1-5225-5213-0.ch013

Moreira, A. C., & Freitas da Silva, P. M. (2018). Internationalization in Business-to-Business Markets: The Importance of New Product Development. In L. Carvalho (Ed.), *Handbook of Research on Entrepreneurial Ecosystems and Social Dynamics in a Globalized World* (pp. 460–487). Hershey, PA: IGI Global. doi:10.4018/978-1-5225-3525-6.ch020

Mukherjee, A., & Das, R. C. (2018). Impact of Microfinance on Investment Decision and Consumption Smoothing: A Theoretical Approach. In R. Das (Ed.), *Microfinance and Its Impact on Entrepreneurial Development, Sustainability, and Inclusive Growth* (pp. 52–64). Hershey, PA: IGI Global. doi:10.4018/978-1-5225-5213-0.ch003

Mukhopadhyay, P., Sinha, M., Chaudhury, A. R., & Sengupta, P. P. (2018). Microfinance, Micro-Entrepreneurial Activities Through Self-Help Groups, and Socio-Economic Empowerment of Women: A Study of Burdwan District of West Bengal, India. In R. Das (Ed.), *Microfinance and Its Impact on Entrepreneurial Development, Sustainability, and Inclusive Growth* (pp. 85–102). Hershey, PA: IGI Global. doi:10.4018/978-1-5225-5213-0.ch005

Murphy, L. J., Abdulai, A., Anwar, K., Abdullah, A., & Thomas, B. C. (2018). Financial Entrepreneurship in Three Emerging Economies: A Comparative Study of Ghana, Pakistan, and Yemen. In A. Woldie & B. Thomas (Eds.), *Financial Entrepreneurship for Economic Growth in Emerging Nations* (pp. 1–21). Hershey, PA: IGI Global. doi:10.4018/978-1-5225-2700-8.ch001

Natário, M. M. (2018). Evaluating the Determinants of Nascent Entrepreneurship Among Countries. In A. Carrizo Moreira, J. Guilherme Leitão Dantas, & F. Manuel Valente (Eds.), *Nascent Entrepreneurship and Successful New Venture Creation* (pp. 326–342). Hershey, PA: IGI Global. doi:10.4018/978-1-5225-2936-1.ch016

Ndinguri, E., Machtmes, K., Machtmes, R. J., & Hill, J. I. (2018). Entrepreneurs and Technology: Use and Access of Technology for Idea Generation. In M. Khosrow-Pour, D.B.A. (Ed.), Entrepreneurship, Collaboration, and Innovation in the Modern Business Era (pp. 22-39). Hershey, PA: IGI Global. doi:10.4018/978-1-5225-5014-3.ch002

Nisha, N., Iqbal, M., & Rifat, A. (2018). Service Quality and Knowledge as Determinants of Mobile Health Services: Empirical Investigation and Further Considerations. In M. Khosrow-Pour, D.B.A. (Ed.), Entrepreneurship, Collaboration, and Innovation in the Modern Business Era (pp. 151-177). Hershey, PA: IGI Global. doi:10.4018/978-1-5225-5014-3.ch008

O'Reilly, K. A., Kelley, B. M., & Lancendorfer, K. M. (2018). Leveraging Virtual Communities to Enhance Brand Equity: A Case Study. In M. Khosrow-Pour, D.B.A. (Ed.), Entrepreneurship, Collaboration, and Innovation in the Modern Business Era (pp. 136-150). Hershey, PA: IGI Global. doi:10.4018/978-1-5225-5014-3.ch007

Oham, C. (2019). Faith-Based Social Enterprise and Value Creation in Communities. In C. Maher (Ed.), *Handbook of Research on Value Creation for Small and Micro Social Enterprises* (pp. 109–125). Hershey, PA: IGI Global. doi:10.4018/978-1-5225-6298-6.ch006

Oncioiu, I., Duca, I., Postole, M. A., & Ciobanasu, M. (2018). A Comparative Study of Financing Innovation Capacity for Romanian SMEs in a Global Economy. In A. Woldie & B. Thomas (Eds.), *Financial Entrepreneurship for Economic Growth in Emerging Nations* (pp. 69–84). Hershey, PA: IGI Global. doi:10.4018/978-1-5225-2700-8.ch004

Patra, S. (2018). Determinants of Participation and Impact of Microfinance: An Econometric Analysis. In R. Das (Ed.), *Microfinance and Its Impact on Entrepreneurial Development, Sustainability, and Inclusive Growth* (pp. 156–184). Hershey, PA: IGI Global. doi:10.4018/978-1-5225-5213-0.ch009

Pego, A., & Bernardo, M. D. (2018). Decision Making in Rural Tourism Management: The Case of Algarve. In L. Carvalho (Ed.), *Handbook of Research on Entrepreneurial Ecosystems and Social Dynamics in a Globalized World* (pp. 274–289). Hershey, PA: IGI Global. doi:10.4018/978-1-5225-3525-6.ch012

Piccarozzi, M., Silvestri, C., & Stefanoni, A. (2018). Positive Effects of the Innovative Start-Up on University Spin-Offs: A Recent Italian Legislation. In A. Carrizo Moreira, J. Guilherme Leitão Dantas, & F. Manuel Valente (Eds.), *Nascent Entrepreneurship and Successful New Venture Creation* (pp. 289–307). Hershey, PA: IGI Global. doi:10.4018/978-1-5225-2936-1.ch014

Pjero (Beqiraj), E., & Kordha, E. (2019). Social Enterprises and Fundraising Challenge: Crowd Funding as an Innovative Solution for Developing Countries – Best Practices in Albania. In C. Maher (Ed.), Handbook of Research on Value Creation for Small and Micro Social Enterprises (pp. 271-292). Hershey, PA: IGI Global. doi:10.4018/978-1-5225-6298-6.ch014

Potts, M., & Puia, G. M. (2018). The Divergence of Entrepreneurial Landscapes in the European Union. In M. Khosrow-Pour, D.B.A. (Ed.), Entrepreneurship, Collaboration, and Innovation in the Modern Business Era (pp. 291-307). Hershey, PA: IGI Global. doi:10.4018/978-1-5225-5014-3.ch015

Preto, M. T., & Farlens, T. (2018). Creativity, Entrepreneurship, and Labor Dynamics: The Role of Creative Workers in Portugal. In L. Carvalho (Ed.), *Handbook of Research on Entrepreneurial Ecosystems and Social Dynamics in a Globalized World* (pp. 488–502). Hershey, PA: IGI Global. doi:10.4018/978-1-5225-3525-6.ch021

Raghunath, K. M., Patro, C. S., & Sirisha, K. (2019). Paraphernalias of Entrepreneurship – A Contemplating Outlook. *International Journal of E-Entrepreneurship and Innovation*, *9*(1), 47–62. doi:10.4018/IJEEI.2019010105

Ratten, V., & Dana, L. (2017). Sustainable Entrepreneurship, Family Farms and the Dairy Industry. *International Journal of Social Ecology and Sustainable Development*, *8*(3), 114–129. doi:10.4018/IJSESD.2017070108

Razzaque, S. (2018). Effects of Peer Monitoring and Contract Choice on Repayment Rates Under Group Liability Lending: A Laboratory Microfinance Experiment From Australia. *International Journal of Applied Behavioral Economics*, *7*(3), 1–33. doi:10.4018/IJABE.2018070101

Rego, M. D., Lucas, M. R., Vieira, C., & Vieira, I. (2018). Entrepreneurial Ecosystems in Low-Density Regions: Business Incubation Practices in Alentejo. In L. Carvalho (Ed.), *Handbook of Research on Entrepreneurial Ecosystems and Social Dynamics in a Globalized World* (pp. 45–74). Hershey, PA: IGI Global. doi:10.4018/978-1-5225-3525-6.ch003

Rohlfer, S. (2018). The Ambiguous Role of Trade Unions in Startup Formation. In A. Carrizo Moreira, J. Guilherme Leitão Dantas, & F. Manuel Valente (Eds.), *Nascent Entrepreneurship and Successful New Venture Creation* (pp. 308–325). Hershey, PA: IGI Global. doi:10.4018/978-1-5225-2936-1.ch015

Rua, O. L., & Correia, M. J. (2018). Analysing Innovation in Healthcare Organizations: An Empirical Study From Portugal. In L. Carvalho (Ed.), *Handbook of Research on Entrepreneurial Ecosystems and Social Dynamics in a Globalized World* (pp. 212–242). Hershey, PA: IGI Global. doi:10.4018/978-1-5225-3525-6.ch009

Rwamigabo, E. R. (2019). Challenges and Opportunities of Micro or Small Social Enterprises in Rwanda. In C. Maher (Ed.), *Handbook of Research on Value Creation for Small and Micro Social Enterprises* (pp. 254–270). Hershey, PA: IGI Global. doi:10.4018/978-1-5225-6298-6.ch013

Sahu, K. K. (2018). Sustainability of Microfinance Institutions in India. In R. Das (Ed.), *Microfinance and Its Impact on Entrepreneurial Development, Sustainability, and Inclusive Growth* (pp. 257–274). Hershey, PA: IGI Global. doi:10.4018/978-1-5225-5213-0.ch014

Saiz-Alvarez, J. M., Colvin-Díez, J., & Cuñado, J. H. (2017). Digital Entrepreneurial Charity, Solidarity, and Social Change. *International Journal of E-Entrepreneurship and Innovation*, *7*(1), 29–48. doi:10.4018/IJEEI.2017010103

Sana, A. K., & Biswas, B. (2018). Risk Management Practices in Indian Microfinance Sector: A Study of Some Selected Institutions in West Bengal. In R. Das (Ed.), *Microfinance and Its Impact on Entrepreneurial Development, Sustainability, and Inclusive Growth* (pp. 1–29). Hershey, PA: IGI Global. doi:10.4018/978-1-5225-5213-0.ch001

Sánchez-García, J. C., & Hernández-Sánchez, B. R. (2018). Nascent Entrepreneurs, Psychological Characteristics, and Sociocultural Background: Psycho-Sociocultural Background of Nascent Entrepreneurs. In A. Carrizo Moreira, J. Guilherme Leitão Dantas, & F. Manuel Valente (Eds.), *Nascent Entrepreneurship and Successful New Venture Creation* (pp. 111–131). Hershey, PA: IGI Global. doi:10.4018/978-1-5225-2936-1.ch005

Sánchez-García, J. C., Rodriguez-Gómez, E., Hernández-Sánchez, B. R., & Pérez-Díaz, J. M. (2018). Entrepreneurship Education as a Key Antecedent to Boost Nascent Entrepreneurs. In A. Carrizo Moreira, J. Guilherme Leitão Dantas, & F. Manuel Valente (Eds.), *Nascent Entrepreneurship and Successful New Venture Creation* (pp. 58–84). Hershey, PA: IGI Global. doi:10.4018/978-1-5225-2936-1.ch003

Siakas, K. V., Georgiadou, E., & Siakas, D. (2018). Knowledge Sharing in Distributed Teams: Influence of National and Organizational Culture. In M. Khosrow-Pour, D.B.A. (Ed.), Entrepreneurship, Collaboration, and Innovation in the Modern Business Era (pp. 221-242). Hershey, PA: IGI Global. doi:10.4018/978-1-5225-5014-3.ch011

Sinha, M., Mukhopadhyay, P., Chaudhury, A. R., & Sengupta, P. P. (2018). Capturing the Performances of Self-Help Groups Across Indian States: A Dynamic Quantitative Exploration. In R. Das (Ed.), *Microfinance and Its Impact on Entrepreneurial Development, Sustainability, and Inclusive Growth* (pp. 207–217). Hershey, PA: IGI Global. doi:10.4018/978-1-5225-5213-0.ch011

Snoussi, W., & Béjaoui, A. (2018). The Influence of Specific Criteria of Emerging Markets on SME Financing in MENA Markets. In A. Woldie & B. Thomas (Eds.), *Financial Entrepreneurship for Economic Growth in Emerging Nations* (pp. 46–68). Hershey, PA: IGI Global. doi:10.4018/978-1-5225-2700-8.ch003

Sousa, M. A., Palacios, T. B., & Martínez-Azúa, B. C. (2018). Factors Affecting Internationalization Degree of Higher Education Institutions in Portugal and Spain. In L. Carvalho (Ed.), *Handbook of Research on Entrepreneurial Ecosystems and Social Dynamics in a Globalized World* (pp. 348–377). Hershey, PA: IGI Global. doi:10.4018/978-1-5225-3525-6.ch016

Tambunan, T. T. (2018). MSMEs and Access to Financing in a Developing Economy: The Indonesian Experience. In A. Woldie & B. Thomas (Eds.), *Financial Entrepreneurship for Economic Growth in Emerging Nations* (pp. 148–172). Hershey, PA: IGI Global. doi:10.4018/978-1-5225-2700-8.ch008

Teixeira, N., Pardal, P. N., & Rafael, B. G. (2018). Internationalization, Financial Performance, and Organizational Challenges: A Success Case in Portugal. In L. Carvalho (Ed.), *Handbook of Research on Entrepreneurial Ecosystems and Social Dynamics in a Globalized World* (pp. 379–423). Hershey, PA: IGI Global. doi:10.4018/978-1-5225-3525-6.ch017

Tomaževič, N., & Cantele, S. (2019). Social Entrepreneurship and Social Enterprises in Slovenia: Strengths and Weaknesses From an Analysis of the Institutional Framework. In C. Maher (Ed.), *Handbook of Research on Value Creation for Small and Micro Social Enterprises* (pp. 207–228). Hershey, PA: IGI Global. doi:10.4018/978-1-5225-6298-6.ch011

Vargas-Hernández, J. G., & Bhattacharjee, K. (2018). Microfinance and Rural Entrepreneurship in Mexico: A Budget Study for PROMUSAG. In R. Das (Ed.), *Microfinance and Its Impact on Entrepreneurial Development, Sustainability, and Inclusive Growth* (pp. 103–114). Hershey, PA: IGI Global. doi:10.4018/978-1-5225-5213-0.ch006

Vargas-Hernández, J. G., & Ortiz, C. L. (2018). Impacts of Microfinance Strategic Management and Social Capital on Women Entrepreneurship in Rural Mexico. In R. Das (Ed.), *Microfinance and Its Impact on Entrepreneurial Development, Sustainability, and Inclusive Growth* (pp. 185–205). Hershey, PA: IGI Global. doi:10.4018/978-1-5225-5213-0.ch010

Vargas-Hernández, J. G., & Ortiz, C. L. (2019). Social Capital as a Factor of Success in Mexican Cooperatives: Case – Cooperativa "Las Chiquihuitecas" Producer of Grana Cochinilla. In C. Maher (Ed.), *Handbook of Research on Value Creation for Small and Micro Social Enterprises* (pp. 311–326). Hershey, PA: IGI Global. doi:10.4018/978-1-5225-6298-6.ch016

Vázquez, D. G. (2018). Improvement in Higher Education: The Role of Chairs in University Social Responsibility. In L. Carvalho (Ed.), *Handbook of Research on Entrepreneurial Ecosystems and Social Dynamics in a Globalized World* (pp. 333–347). Hershey, PA: IGI Global. doi:10.4018/978-1-5225-3525-6.ch015

Vecco, M., & Srakar, A. (2018). Nascent Cultural and Creative Entrepreneurship: Between Entrepreneurial Economics and Institutional Entrepreneurship. In A. Carrizo Moreira, J. Guilherme Leitão Dantas, & F. Manuel Valente (Eds.), *Nascent Entrepreneurship and Successful New Venture Creation* (pp. 175–202). Hershey, PA: IGI Global. doi:10.4018/978-1-5225-2936-1.ch008

Wale-Oshinowo, B. A., Uba, C. D., Adeyeye, M. M., & Omobowale, A. O. (2019). Understanding Social Entrepreneurship in the African Context: An Exploratory Review of Evidence From Nigeria. In C. Maher (Ed.), *Handbook of Research on Value Creation for Small and Micro Social Enterprises* (pp. 188–206). Hershey, PA: IGI Global. doi:10.4018/978-1-5225-6298-6.ch010

Watson, E. S., & Roberts, P. (2019). Applying a Cross-Cultural Health Systems Strengthening Diagnostic Tool: The Experiences of a Small Social Enterprise Delivering Health Care Services in England. In C. Maher (Ed.), *Handbook of Research on Value Creation for Small and Micro Social Enterprises* (pp. 46–74). Hershey, PA: IGI Global. doi:10.4018/978-1-5225-6298-6.ch003

Woldie, A., Hagshenas, H., & Thomas, B. C. (2018). The Qualitative Relationship Between Banks and SMEs in Wales. In A. Woldie & B. Thomas (Eds.), *Financial Entrepreneurship for Economic Growth in Emerging Nations* (pp. 86–110). Hershey, PA: IGI Global. doi:10.4018/978-1-5225-2700-8.ch005

Woldie, A., & Ubrurhe, U. (2018). Small and Medium Enterprises' Challenges of Accessing Microfinance in Nigeria. In A. Woldie & B. Thomas (Eds.), *Financial Entrepreneurship for Economic Growth in Emerging Nations* (pp. 229–253). Hershey, PA: IGI Global. doi:10.4018/978-1-5225-2700-8.ch012

Yang, J. G. (2018). The Advantages and Disadvantages of Internet Commerce in China. In M. Khosrow-Pour, D.B.A. (Ed.), Entrepreneurship, Collaboration, and Innovation in the Modern Business Era (pp. 278-290). Hershey, PA: IGI Global. doi:10.4018/978-1-5225-5014-3.ch014

Yıldırım, İ. (2018). Access to Finance: Developing Microinsurance Market in Turkey. In A. Woldie & B. Thomas (Eds.), *Financial Entrepreneurship for Economic Growth in Emerging Nations* (pp. 217–228). Hershey, PA: IGI Global. doi:10.4018/978-1-5225-2700-8.ch011

About the Author

Fatima Zohra Lebbah has defended her PhD thesis in science in 2015, Université d'Oran 1 Ahmed Ben Bella - Département d'Informatique in Algeria. Currently she is a Lecturer at Ecole Supérieure en Génie Electrique et Energétique (ESG2E), in Algeria and a member-researcher of Ecole Supérieure en Informatique de Sidi Bel-Abbès - Laboratoire de Recherche en Informatique de Sidi Bel-Abbes (LabRI-SBA) - Equipe de Computational Intelligence and Soft COmputing (CISCO), in Algeria. She is interested in the Combinatorial Optimization problems: modeling and solving techniques.

Index

www.ingramcontent.com/pod-product-compliance
Lightning Source LLC
LaVergne TN
LVHW061534290926
849162LV00004B/785